Female
Hierarchies

Female
Hierarchies

Edited by
Lionel Tiger
Heather T. Fowler
With a new introduction by Lionel Tiger

Transaction Publishers
New Brunswick (U.S.A.) and London (U.K.)

Second printing 2009
New material this edition © 2007 by Transaction Publishers, New Brunswick,
N.J. 08903. Originally Published in 1978 by Beresford Book Service.

Library of Congress Catalog Number: 2007015808
ISBN: 978-1-4128-0642-8
Printed in the United States of America

Library of Congress Cataloging-in-Publication Data

Female hierarchies / [edited by] Lionel Tiger and Heather T. Fowler.
        p. cm.
    Originally published: Chicago : Beresford Book Service, c1978. With a
    new introd. by Lionel Tiger.
      ISBN 978-1-4128-0642-8 (pbk.)
      1. Women—Social conditions. 2. Sex role. 3. Sex differences. I. Tiger,
    Lionel, 1937- II. Fowler, Heather T. (Heather Trexler)

HQ1154.F43 2007
305.401—dc22   2007015808

Contents

Contents

Acknowledgments

The papers herein were presented in preliminary form at a symposium sponsored by the Harry Frank Guggenheim Foundation held in New York in 1974. Needless to say, the symposium could not have been held without the firm and generous support of the Chairman, Mr. Peter Lawson Johnson; President, Dr. Mason W. Gross; and Directors of the Harry Frank Guggenheim Foundation. Individually and as a group the above named persons have consistently sought responsibly to expand understanding of the basic nature of human social structure and its implications for social policy. We are also happy to express appreciation for the congenial overview maintained by the Executive Director of the Foundation, Mr. George Fountaine, and for the effective administration of financial and other systems by Mr. J. W. Koenigsberger and Mr. Paul Perrin. Mrs. Karyl Roosevelt managed with equal grace and magnanimity both to cajole from contributors successive versions of their papers and to supervise passage of manuscripts through a minefield of detail—all this despite the geographical, attitudinal, and disciplinary dispersal of the participants.

Throughout the gestation, planning, execution, and reporting of the symposium, Robin Fox maintained a constructively critical eye on all the proceedings and augmented them fully. We would like to acknowledge the more or less informal contributions of a number of others to this scholarly endeavor: Ian Bowers, Nancy Harvey, Alex Morin, Tim Perper, Helen Safa, Robert Trivers, and Virginia Tiger.

We want, of course, to say that the persons mentioned in this small narrative, individually or as a group, are responsible only for those materials which they themselves contributed or which have been attributed to them directly.

L.T.
H.F.

Symposium Participants

Dr. Mason W. Gross, President, Harry Frank Guggenheim Foundation

Dr. Robin Fox, Research Director, Harry Frank Guggenheim Foundation

Dr. Lionel Tiger, Research Director, Harry Frank Guggenheim Foundation

Mr. Ian Bowers, Research Associate, Harry Frank Guggenheim Foundation

Dr. Virginia Abernethy, Professor of Psychiatry, Director, Division of Human Behavior, Department of Psychiatry, School of Medicine, Vanderbilt University

Dr. Ernst Caspari, Professor of Genetics, Department of Biology, University of Rochester

Dr. Michael Chance, Department of Ethnology, Uffculme Clinic, University of Birmingham

Dr. Erving Goffman, Benjamin Franklin Professor of Anthropology and Sociology, University of Pennsylvania, Philadelphia

Miss Nemone Lethbridge, Barrister and Journalist, London

Dr. William O'Neill, Professor of History, Rutgers University

Dr. Sherry Ortner, Department of Anthropology, University of Michigan

Dr. Joseph Shepher, Department of Sociology, University of Haifa, Mt. Carmel, Haifa

Dr. Evelyne Sullerot, Department of Sociology, University of Paris

Dr. Sandra Wallman, Social Science Research Council, Research Unit on Ethnic Relations, University of Bristol, London

Dr. Adrienne Zihlman, Department of Anthropology, University of California, Santa Cruz

Contributors

VIRGINIA ABERNETHY is Associate Professor of Psychiatry (Anthropology) and Director, Division of Human Behavior in the Department of Psychiatry, Vanderbilt Medical School. She received her doctorate in 1970 from the Social Relations Department, Harvard University, remained in Boston for postdoctoral training, and served on the faculty at Harvard Medical School until going to Vanderbilt. Publications include numerous articles and a book, *Population Pressure and Cultural Adjustment,* to be published in 1978. Her current areas of interest and research are medical education, prostitution, drug and alcohol use, and child abuse legislation.

ERNST W. CASPARI is a geneticist and Professor Emeritus of Biology and at the Center for Evolution and Paleobiology, University of Rochester. He has also taught at the University of Istanbul, Lafayette College, and Wesleyan University. Research areas include developmental and behavior genetics as well as evolution, his special interest being the evolution of humans. He is a Fellow in the American Academy of Arts and Sciences and presently serves as an editor for *Advances in Genetics* and on the editorial boards for *Behavior Genetics* and *Behavioral Science.*

M.R.A. CHANCE is Reader in Ethology, University of Birmingham. He is Head of the Sub-Department of Ethology, Department of Psychiatry, and also of the Ethology Laboratory at Uffculme Clinic and All Saints' Hospital, Birmingham. He is Honorary Research Associate at the Department of Anthropology, University College, London, and a Fellow of the Royal Anthropological Society and the Institute of Biology. In 1966 and 1969 he was Research Advisor to the Department of Anthropology, University of California, Berkeley, and he has also taught at

Rutgers University and the University of California, Irvine. In 1977 he served as President of the Anthropology Section of the British Association for the Advancement of Science meeting in Birmingham.

HEATHER T. FOWLER received her bachelor's degree in sociology from the Pennsylvania State University in 1960. She has a master's degree, also in sociology, from the University of Missouri at Kansas City. While at Missouri, she investigated the correlation between testosterone levels and dominance rank in small, all-female groups. This interest in female social organization continues to be expressed in her work at Rutgers University, where she is a candidate for a doctorate in anthropology. For her current research, she has undertaken an exploration of the role of female choice in human breeding system strategy.

ERVING GOFFMAN is Benjamin Franklin Professor of Anthropology and Sociology at the University of Pennsylvania. He is a graduate of the University of Chicago and taught previously at the University of California, Berkeley. He does ethnography in contemporary society and focuses on the naturalistic study of face-to-face interaction. Among his many publications are: *Asylums: Essays on the Social Situation of Mental Patients and Other Inmates* (1961, Aldine); *Presentation of Self in Everyday Life* (1959, Doubleday); and *Relations in Public* (1972, Harper and Row).

WILLIAM L. O'NEILL is a faculty member of the history department at Rutgers University in New Jersey. He received his bachelor's degree from the University of Michigan and his doctorate from the University of California at Berkeley. His doctoral dissertation examined divorce in the United States between 1889 and 1919 and led to his book *Divorce in the Progressive Era* (Yale University Press, 1967). He is author of *Everyone Was Brave: The Rise and Fall of Feminism in America* (Quadrangle Books, 1969), an institutional history of the half dozen women's organizations that contributed to the final victory of feminism in 1920, when the vote was won; another publication is *Coming*

Apart: An Informal History of America in the 1960s (Quadrangle Books, 1971).

JOSEPH SHEPHER is Associate Professor at the University of Haifa, Israel. He was born in Budapest and, after World War II, left Hungary for Israel, where he joined Kibbutz Kfar Hachoresh. He received his bachelor's and master's degrees from the Hebrew University, Jerusalem, where he studied history, economics, and sociology. Later he obtained his doctorate in anthropology from Rutgers University. He has taught at the Tel Aviv University and at Rutgers; major areas of research and publication are the sociology and anthropology of the kibbutz.

NANCY TANNER is Associate Professor in Anthropology at the University of California, Santa Cruz. She has done four years of anthropological fieldwork among the matrilineal Islamic Minangkabau of West Sumatra, Indonesia. Her research in this area has produced such publications as: "Disputing and the Genesis of Legal Principles: Examples from Minangkabau" and "Speech and Society among the Indonesian Elite: A Case Study of a Multilingual Community." In recent years she has become interested in comparative studies and has written on women's roles from cross-cultural and evolutionary perspectives. Articles include: "Matrifocality in Indonesia, Africa and among Black Americans," "Women in Evolution: Innovation and Selection in Human Origins," and "The Evolution of Human Communication: What Can Primates Tell Us?" (the latter two are co-authored by Adrienne Zihlman).

LIONEL TIGER is Professor of Anthropology in the Graduate School at Rutgers University and Research Director of the Harry Frank Guggenheim Foundation. He has taught at the University of Ghana, the University of British Columbia, and at Livingston College of Rutgers University. His publications include *Men in Groups* (1969); *The Imperial Animal* (1971), with Robin Fox; and *Women in the Kibbutz* (1975), with Joseph Shepher.

SANDRA WALLMAN received her doctorate in 1965 from the London School of Economics, University of London, where she studied social anthropology. She has done fieldwork in western and Southern Africa and in the European Alps. Her main research interests include problems of economic development and nondevelopment, the perception and management of resources, and the anthropology of work. She is presently employed by the British Social Science Research Council, Research Unit in Ethnic Relations, to head a program of research on the marking, maintenance, and movement of "ethnic" boundaries in inner London. Her publications include numerous scholarly articles and the volumes *Take Out Hunger* (1969) and *Perceptions of Development* (1977).

ADRIENNE ZIHLMAN is Associate Professor and Chairman of Anthropology and Fellow of Oakes College at the University of California, Santa Cruz. She obtained her doctorate at the University of California, Berkeley and has done research on the origin and evolution of human locomotion. Her general research interests focus on the anatomical bases of behavior and have involved field work in Africa and research in museums and laboratories around the world. Besides her work on human and primate locomotor systems, she has carried out research on the evolution of human behavior. This research focuses on the social behavioral correlates of male-female anatomical differences, especially those in bones and teeth. Recently she has undertaken research on pygmy chimpanzees, a rare species of limited distribution in central Africa, in order to reconstruct in some detail the anatomical and behavioral changes involved in the "leap" from ape to human. She has lectured and published extensively on primate and human evolution, and on the role of women in evolution.

Introduction to the Transaction Edition

The papers in this volume resulted from at least two concerns. The first was that whereas there was voluminous scholarship and commentary about the dominance relations among males—we can even call it political science—there was far less known and written about the hierarchies among females. One reason for this surely was the general emphasis in studying politics on formal constitutional and governmental structures. In these, male participants were overwhelmingly preponderant and that's whom scholars studied. The relative absence of females in the political science profession, at least until the late 1970's, was another obvious and inhibiting feature of a sharply skewed academic environment.

But there was a second and more parsimonious issue which revolved around Darwin's theories of natural and sexual selection. These were of course at the core of his remarkably influential work and yet it seemed clear to me that there had been drastically inadequate scholarly attention to what females did in this process. They were 50 percent participants in the intricate dance of sexual selection which yielded natural selection. Yet their absolute half-share in this process was substantially less avidly described and analyzed. Surely one reason for this was that the hierarchical interactions among males (virtually throughout the primates) were sharply more dramatic and visible than among females if only because they were larger and interestingly colorful. Large behaviors such as violence, fatality, and mayhem appeared to be male specialties. And it is also clear, in retrospect, that the often-fierce and encompassing hierarchical struggles among women were with undue generality and imprecision subsumed into the categories of kinship and family relationship. Hence they were much "softer" and of less priority in the choice of subjects about which to learn. Even the fact that, by mid-twentieth century, human females were half of most voting populations seemed to fail to generate appropriate quantity and qualities of scholarship.

So the field of female hierarchies seemed wholly ready to be tilled. In a prescient and fortuitous insight into the basic causes of human inequality and aggression, the American industrialist and publisher Harry Frank Guggenheim bequeathed substantial sums of money to a foundation committed to studying just such matters. Guggenheim's parsimonious perception was that these social pathologies, or at least sources of inequality and aggression, derived broadly from the nature of human nature and not only from local and episodic circumstances.

The latter were surely important. But the former—the human nature factor—was haplessly understudied and even actively abjured and opposed as an appropriate subject matter by many well-positioned social scientists. A significant index of conventional thinking in the area was the formal institutional divide between social and natural sciences. An odd and unnecessary apartheid prevailed.

Nonetheless, a burgeoning inventory of biological data ranging from DNA genomics to explorations of brain to studies of other primates in the wild promised new fields to explore. Because we had recently published *The Imperial Animal*[1] Robin Fox and I were asked by Mason Gross, the recently-retired president of Rutgers University and the new president of the H. F. Guggenheim Foundation, to assist him in establishing and executing an appropriate program.

In the process of doing so, it became clear that tackling the subject of female hierarchies promised a decent return on scholarly and financial investment. I had myself published *Men In Groups* in 1969[2] and had boldly announced that I planned to write a companion volume on females in groups.

However, two things became quickly evident. The first was there was no comparably rich database. There were far fewer detailed ethnographies of what women did and thought, even in the intimate familial sphere, and drastically fewer expositions of women's actions in the public ones such as war, politics, and processing resources and managing wealth.

The second was that, other things being equal, it seemed possible that the work was likely best done by a female or females who had perhaps more likelihood of ethnographic and conceptual entrée to the communities of women. Many of these in many parts of the world were totally restricted to men by formal law or harsh custom and often both. And while many feminists claimed there were no serious differences between men and women, at the same time they proposed that men were not capable of understanding what women thought, needed, and did without extensive renovation and retraining. And what were the rules and metric for that?

In addition, because of the surprising amount of academic and public attention paid to *Men In Groups* not all of it friendly, it seemed prudent if not unduly timid to withdraw somewhat from skirmishes about gender. It is scarcely eccentric or self-serving to remark that the period of the mid-sixties through to when this book was first published in 1978 was marked by a relentlessly assertive and sometimes excoriating critique of social science regarded as sexist and male-chauvinist. I became a particular target of this because in *Men In Groups*, I asserted firmly that there were influential (but not necessarily coercive) sex differences which were generically linked to biology. They were "natural" and rooted in reproductive reality and not principally the result of such symptomatic factors as television sit-com stereotypes and craven magazines to say nothing of more profound religious and moral presuppositions.

There were, I announced, obvious differences between male and female participation in socioeconomic systems. But these were not principally (though of course some certainly was) the consequence of male eagerness to oppress and discommode women—a reflection in the sexual realm of Richard Hofstader's *The Paranoid Style in American Politics*. Many of these women after all were the mothers of men, their wives, co-workers, fellow-citizens, friends, and daughters looking to make their way in the world.

My inadvertent timing yielded an often-abrasive response—three bomb threats when I lectured in Canada and an earnest promise of a knee-capping at the New School for Social Research in New York City when I participated in a graduate seminar on social theory, Marxism, and biology. When I attended the annual meeting of the American Anthropological Association people in elevators would turn silent when they read my name tag. There was mayhem and a near-riot when I appeared on the first of David Frost's television shows in America and he later remarked to a friend that that appearance was the most heated he had encountered during his work in the U.S.[3]

All this irrelevant folderol had an impact on this volume. In the grand old and unimaginative dialectic tradition, I bent over backwards to invite contributors to the symposium and then volume who anti-shared my central point of view and who could reflect the politicized temper of the times.

Throughout, I was assisted by my student collaborator, Heather Remoff, who had found her way to work with our department at Rutgers. Rather astonishingly, and with totally intrepid originality, she had convinced the University of Minnesota department supervising her master's social science dissertation to secure blood assays for testosterone in women who occupied different hierarchical positions in their groups. This was completely pioneering work with genuinely new results (yes, there was a relationship) and it was my enormous pleasure to supervise her doctoral thesis which was a study of how and why women chose their mates. Once again she was parsimonious and clear-minded: she interviewed sixty-six women from Central New Jersey in great and permissive detail and her absorbing, valuable, and often unexpected results were appropriately published in a book called Sexual Choice.[4]

Time has made this reissued book which was—let's gulp and sigh and say it—a publishing failure when it first appeared into a plausibly more effective contribution with aid from the marination of time. It should surely benefit from the impact of rather tectonic shifts in social science in emphasis from what males do alone in groups to what females do alone in groups to what both sexes do apart and together. And there has been a recent but pointed ongoing investigation of the relations between females. This has not been focused wholly on well-meant impulses of bright sexual futures but also on the aggression and acrimony which women can produce as skillfully as men.[5] As well as men, women seek and negotiate for status and priority in realms ranging from exclusive shoes to corporate corner offices to showpiece happy families.

The forms and outcomes of the female style may differ from the male one. But the process, preoccupation, and emotional animation are as chronically preoccupying for women as for men even if the symptoms and techniques may appear to be more personal and detailed. But the more women enter the public male-female realm of hierarchical formation as they are currently doing, the clearer it will become that while sisterhood may be powerful, power remains an element of sisterhood.

The book failed in the simple and conventional sense because it was published rather minimally without an interested and welcoming constituency in the academic world. In fact, this world was hostile to the whole enterprise which was in practice its premier if not only audience. Everyone states that there are too many books published, except for their authors or editors. Just as nature abhors a vacuum, authors are bewildered by inattention to the tapestry over which they have hovered for a disproportionate skein of time. But this happens, and happens and happens.

However, all concerned and perhaps, dear reader, we're fortunate that it was published at all. This was mainly because of the intellectual verve of Alex Morin the leader of Aldine Publishing the company and a uniquely remarkable innovator in uniting anthropological and evolutionary material in his publishing program. I vaguely recall but don't want to know the cold facts about the book's publication.

Perhaps the book found the public forum because the Harry Frank Guggenheim Foundation sponsored the conference at which the papers were presented. This was a welcome and also modest, if essential, subvention for a more permanent record of what happened during a few days at the Stanhope Hotel in New York. Happily, this was our hardship posting for the event. If the wealth of foundations is used for undeniably serious conferences and the publication of books, what could be unfragrant about that?

In any event, it was published, if only to modest effect. Nonetheless, the University of California primatologist Sarah Hrdy remarked the book was the first relatively parsimoniously treatment of the subject and I'm confident she is correct in that commentary as she has been in her considerable body of work overall. It's a rewarding pleasure that the volume is once more available to the now-expanded community of persons committed to understanding female behavior and its impact on the formative processes of our and other species.

The Aldine publishing program was more important than its producers and consumers may have thought at the time. It lasts.

Lionel Tiger

Notes

1. Lionel Tiger and Robin Fox, *The Imperial Animal*, Holt, Rinehart and Winston, NY, 1971; 3rd edition with new Introduction by the authors, Transaction Publishers, New Brunswick and London, 1994.

2.   Lionel Tiger, *Men in Groups*, Random House, NY, 1969, 3rd edition, Transaction Publishers, New Brunswick and London, 1996.
3.   Just for the self-referential record an account of all this ruckus is in "My Life in the Human Nature Wars," *The Wilson Quarterly*, Winter 1996.
4.   Heather Remoff, *Sexual Choice*, Dutton, NY, 1984.
5.   The iconic work in this area is Phyllis Chesler, *Woman's Inhumanity to Woman*, 2003.

Introduction

LIONEL TIGER

It is now commonly acknowledged that disproportionate attention has been paid to males in human and other social systems. The activities and perceptions of females have been either ignored or treated as secondary in importance and interest. This fact has been most obvious in empirical research, in ethnographies, and in studies of politics, which have focused essentially on male leadership and economic behavior. This is no less true at the theoretical level. The basic structures used to explain social behavior in sociological, biological, and even in biosociological theoretical work overwhelmingly emphasize the significance and shape of male behavior. Overall, the concern has been with the implications for stratification, sexual selection, and natural selection of what males do among themselves and how they relate to females. For example, in a recent, very sophisticated analysis of aggressive interaction, D.D. Thiessen (1976) at the outset defines his topic in such a way that females are virtually excluded from any formal or significant participation.

Does this mean that females do not conduct aggressive encounters with each other? Or that females have no impact on mate selection and hence on the future of the genotype? Or that the main negotiation of females is with males and not among themselves during this selective process? Do the usually larger size and frequently more elaborate behavioral displays

1

of the males betray the fact that the burden of selective functioning falls on the males and not on the females?

Of course, it is improbable that the answer to these questions is "yes" and that there is little or nothing happening in all-female groups that affects not only how their communities operate but, more importantly in the long run, the genotype of their species. In that case, for those many species in which gregarious social behavior is *sine qua non* for successful reproduction, what are the principles of selection that operate through females? What are the forms of female social grouping that either support, modify, inhibit, or stimulate sexual and hence natural selection?

One of the purposes of the scientific program currently underway at the Harry Frank Guggenheim Foundation is to uncover facets of the process of hierarchical formation in human and other communities in order to better understand, and hopefully ameliorate, the causes and consequences of human inequality. During the establishment and conduct of this program, it became clear very early that an important area of the natural and social sciences that required exploration was precisely this matter of female participation in the genotypical system. Broadly speaking, it remains true that the concept of hierarchy as an explanatory device for many aspects of human and other social systems is durable and helpful. The theory of Darwin and his successors about the relationship between social systems and the unequal reproduction of one's genes sturdily persists. The most important features of natural selection continue to be explained by the differential flow of genes into the genotype as mediated by both changing ecological circumstances and social arrangements.

Accordingly, it was decided to hold a symposium of people from a variety of disciplines to approach the question of female hierarchies. The purpose of the symposium was either to advance understanding of this topic or to indicate, on theoretical grounds, that the concept does not adequately apply to female social systems. It was thought that, as a result of the symposium's focus on females *per se*, fundamentally different understandings of natural selection might emerge, or at very least, that the traditional emphasis on males would be balanced with a comparable one on female behavior.

Needless to say, we were aware that the concept of hierarchy as a construct for explaining features of both human and non-human behavior was under criticism. For example, Hausfater (1975), on the basis of his primate case study, has argued that dominant males have no greater number of copulations with ovulating females than nondominant males. At the same time, Duvall, Bernstein, and Gordon (1976), in a similar study over a longer time span, found that although dominant males do not produce more offspring than other males in any one year, they do live significantly longer. Such genetic reinforcement would certainly have an impact on the individual differences involved in sorting out hierarchical orders (see also Deag 1977).

We hope it will be clear from the papers in this volume that efforts were made to solicit participation and papers from people representing a variety of views on this subject. We hoped that several papers would forcefully challenge the basic concept of hierarchy and fundamentally question many conventional assumptions about the sources of gender-linked behavioral differences. To a considerable extent, this position reflects what one participant (Erving Goffman, personal communication) saw as leaning over backwards to avoid prejudicing the discussion in a biosociological direction.

Nevertheless, I am bound to note that the amount of disarticulation between the papers is troublesome. This may result as much from the subject matter as from the small size of the meeting, which worked to keep the discussion to relatively few areas of concern. For the disarticulation, the senior editor must accept responsibility; a light hand which leaves too faint an impression is no more helpful than a heavy one which unduly forces its form on its surroundings. For example, there should have been at the symposium an explicit representation of both a physiological-endocrinological viewpoint and a comparative psychological one, to draw attention to possible systematic sexual differences located in material reality; the relationship between somatic factors and social behavior is at least definable and often more measurable than relationships between two sets of purely social behaviors (Tiger 1975).

However, the scholarly contribution of each paper is clear, even if the totality provides a less clearly synthetic result than editors aspire to. In her paper, Sandra Wallman manipulates an extended cold shower of epistomological caveats to the technical procedures in research on the broad subject of sex-linked behavior. First, she carefully delineates the differences between sex class, gender, and sex roles. As she makes plain, however, the differences sort better on paper than they do in field situations. Using examples from her own research experiences, she indicates how "our particular epistemology of sex prevents an understanding of the social systems of ourselves and others by masking variations in the significance of being female." And she demonstrates that "this significance . . . varies with technology, setting, class, context, task, rank, race, age, profession, kinship, wealth, and economics . . . with any or all of the other dimensions of a situation of which it can only form a part." Having clarified the epistemological problem and having emphasized the complementarity of the levels of differentiation, Wallman notes that we are still concerned about identifying and accounting for any systematic differences between the behaviors of women and men. She is clearly skeptical that there are looming answers to basic questions about the effect of the genotype on gender-linked behaviors.

Erving Goffman's skepticism is very deeply rooted indeed. In his "Gender Display" he intends to show that it is both unnecessary and invalid to pursue explanations of social-sexual behavior by way of genetics. It is his contention that how men and women comport themselves is a function of convention, social structure, and ideas about social structure that people sustain. The paper he presented at the symposium was illustrated by slides, principally of advertising materials, in which males and females express the stereotyped notions of gender role of the communities producing and using the advertising material.

Goffman carefully outlines the manner in which hierarchical differences between males and females are portrayed in these symbolic artifacts. Females are usually shown in ways Goffman suggests are subordinate and which he takes as a forthright index of various deeply rooted inequities between the sexes.

Goffman's proposition is unarguable. It is a common observation that by the (principally male) concerns of Euro-American society, females suffer disadvantages of various kinds, which are presumably bound to be reflected in so communal a phenomenon as advertising. But he doesn't approach the pre-epistemological question of why the human creature is as concerned as he says it is with this intensity of hierarchical behavior. Nor does he ask why there is such a well-developed skill and sense of society which his own explanation reveals. Is this one of the behaviors which, according to David Hamburg's question, humans find "easy to learn" and which is perhaps influential in evolutionary success? (Hamburg 1963). Furthermore, the very ambition and scope of Goffman's analysis expose him to a theoretical hazard he would wish to avoid: the more successfully his proposition may be applied cross-culturally, the more likely it is to reflect general, and hence perhaps genotypically linked, characteristics of the species.

Goffman also does not deal with an intriguing aspect of the overall issue about human sex differences: are there differences in the ways males and females act hierarchically? It would be useful to employ his lens as carefully on the relations between females as he does on those between males and females. As it stands, the unduly male-focused nature of Goffman's argument leaves open some general questions about gender display within the female group. At the same time, it usefully illuminates the semantics of male and female encounter.

Other contributors to the volume see the possibility of a more significant synthesis than Goffman does between the conventional cultural and the conventional biological. Their effort seems to be directed not at demonstrating a particular behavior as "only natural" but at sorting out those features that approach the natural—that is, behavior reflecting basic biological substrata— from those that are more or less randomly distributed in the species and thus unlikely to be related to any genotypical regularity.

Goffman's implication that such efforts at natural explanation are reductionist has much historical precedent to support it. Yet in actuality, the process of seeking biological data to support sociological explanations for behavior is precisely the opposite of reductionism. This approach means that an entirely new range of complex materials must be added to an already vast array of items to be identified and analyzed in any explanation. For example, Caspari's paper, "The Biological Basis of Female Hierarchies," offers a cautious and probing outline of the biological mechanisms operating towards physical and behavioral differentiation of males and females in a variety of species. We need to know, he implies, whether it is possible, given our information about biological and genetic mechanisms, that males and females are predisposed to form organizationally different hierarchical systems. In this effort Caspari reviews materials on the nature of sexual dimorphism and the workings of sex-linked and sex-controlled genes. He develops a fascinating demonstration of how the differential action of a gene varies with the sex of the carrier and, in turn, allows for genetic behavioral differentiation in some species. Whether the human is such a species remains an open question. Caspari indicates the difficulty of deciding when and if sex differences in humans are due to genetic conditions, to societal influences based on historically produced gender roles, or to some interaction between the two. Whatever the result of this query, Caspari plainly feels that the answer is neither a certainty nor an impossibility, and he directs his detailed comparative perspective to this open area of thought.

Other contributors to this volume also fall within these boundaries in their assertions. That is, they certainly either make or entertain the suggestion that males and females organize themselves differently: 1) that the predisposition to form hierarchies such as they are now known may be more uniquely male than female as a trait; and 2) that when females do organize their behavior along hierarchical lines, these forms may be more or less distinct from male ones. This suggestion has not escaped a heated response on many occasions because, for clearly appreciable historical reasons, the suggestion that one sex differs from the other is held to imply an inferior/superior relationship.

For example, Rosaldo and Lamphere (1974) point out, not without empirical justification, that men everywhere possess more formal prestige than women, that their activities are always recognized as predominantly important, and that cultural systems give pre-eminent authority and value to the activities of men, at least in the arena of public activity. Is this an artifact of economic systems or of religious heritage? Is it part of the reproductive requirement of communities before modern medicine, an unnatural pattern, an enormous and gross bagatelle of history, or is it an accurately perceived regularity of what may be a behaviorally dimorphic species?

Answering this complex question necessarily involves attention to the activities of women as much as it demands a skeptical inspection of the activities of men. Indeed, to reject *a priori* the investigation of differences between male and female hierarchical or other social patterns may reflect a belief that such differences, should they be established, would prove female organizational inferiority. In turn, this same belief betrays a male-centeredness about social patterns: if females conduct themselves differently, then this difference must be to their disadvantage. Of course, this position is a silly one; nonetheless, it may have some influence on those writers on gender who preclude the possible existence of genetically linked sex differences. On the other hand, some feminist writers advocate that females do, or at least should, organize themselves explicitly differently than males. In fact, considerable attention has been paid in many feminist groups to preventing hierarchical structures from forming, to the extent of conducting meetings with circular seating arrangements so that no dramatic focus could emerge to affect the distribution of influence itself. Theirs is a prudent precaution, as readers of Michael Chance's article on the structure of attention will discover. (I am grateful to Gloria Levitas for first drawing my attention to this phenomenon.)

It is presumably acceptable to examine the biological assumption that if female social organization differs from that of males, then it has been selectively favored because of its efficiency or effectiveness in the ecosocial situations in which human groups have found themselves through time. Virginia Abernethy seeks to do just this. In a terse but provocative paper, she analyzes food gathering and mothering as behaviors performed primarily by females over much of evolutionary time, as suggested by the historical and prehistorical record. She concludes that these are activities in which the formation of complex and elaborate hierarchies would offer little functional advantage. Therefore, she suspects that the human female is not hierarchical as far as the public forum is concerned. Her proposition is that the quickness with which *difference* is identified as *discrimination* may in fact represent an overevaluation of the male mode and an underestimation of the functional value of the form of social ordering to which all-female groups tend.

Thus, women in groups may possess more flexibility than men in groups. (Of course we are always concerned here with individuals falling within normative patterns.) When the environment is changing rapidly so that new information must be processed and acted upon quickly, a lattice (female) structure is more effective in solving societal problems than a hierarchical (male) one. Hierarchical levels may be bypassed or ignored because greater interpersonal trust and skills require it. In this context the formal pyramidal structure is unduly cumbersome and impersonal. The implication of Abernethy's argument is that undue devotion to hierarchical notions of a conventional, formal male kind may interfere with efficient operation of social groups confronting rapid social, economic, or other changes. While this position may in part contain a somewhat idealized view of the nonhierarchical pattern and an unduly rigid sense of the traditional hierarchical one, it gains support from some recent experience of organizations as they try to come to terms with the sexual variable in their patterns of work (Hennig and Jardim 1977).

Some of the mechanisms that may underlie this possible greater flexibility in female social organization emerge from M.R.A. Chance's perspective on sex differences in the structure of attention. Chance's concern for a number of years with primate patterns of rank order and affiliation may also apply in part to human behavior. The concept of attention structure revolves around Chance's observation that dominance in primate communities relates not predominantly to the control of resources or violence but, more importantly, to the amount of deference, by visual attention, paid to the leading animals by subordinate ones. In effect, attention structure becomes a control structure as far as work, alarm, direction of group movement, etc. are concerned and thus an unusually subtle, if sometimes elusive, measure of social differentiation in the community.

In his essay, Chance describes two basic modalities of social process that he observes in primate communities—the hedonic and the agonistic. He also concludes that humans have a relatively large latitude of choice in deciding which mode of behavior they wish to use to respond to their environmental conditions. However, he proposes that the choice made, for any individual, is constrained by the ontogeny of that individual and more importantly by its sex. He claims flatly that males are more likely than females to encounter and thus experience environmental conditions that favor the development of agonistic modes of behavior. This must of necessity affect concepts of gender role. In the agonistic mode, an individual's behavior is relatively rigid, since it must perforce focus constantly on the disposition of more or less powerful individuals. The main characteristic of the hedonic mode of expression of attention is flexibility. Chance estimates that the individual's freedom to avoid a hedonic mode depends on the type of social relations within the group in which he or she was raised. This is not an improbable conclusion. For example, he describes how in macaque societies male infants are separated from their mothers much sooner than female infants are—a pattern not uncommon to the human species as well. Sex differences in human initiation practices become interesting in this context (see Cohen 1964; Young 1962; Tiger 1969). When the young macaque males are rejected by their mothers, they are forced to assume the "looking at" mode of response associated with agonistic behavior, principally "looking at" the dominating males. Females, on the other hand, are free to assume the "looking around" hedonic mode. Chance feels that in these primate groups "rank order for males is born out of maternal rejection, threat, and avoidance," a curiously poignant, if complex point to prove, but certainly an important one. Rank order, on the other hand, for females "is acquired from kinship, the rank of their consorts, and the maintenance of an even state of arousal, usually at a low level." The result, at least among adult macaques in the particular colony in Basel, Switzerland, studied by Chance, is that an "agonistic relationship is evident in the attention paid to the males" while "hedonic attention is paid to the females."

Such research with nonhuman primates clearly raises all the vexatious issues about cross-specific translation that any such studies stimulate. Nevertheless it does, if only on almost aesthetic grounds, offer a rich portrait of what might be sex-linked differences in human ontogeny with possible consequences for formal social structure. There are some indications that some human sex differences exist in the manner in which attention is paid to dominant figures (see Chance and Larsen 1976; Raphael 1975). But whether or not this particular pattern actually operates among humans in a structurally formidable way remains to be seen. Making cross-specific or cross-temporal connections in order to seek insight into our behavioral heritage as humans is very fruitful for the production of scientific controversies.

Much of the work in this area is necessarily speculative. Lively and legitimate controversy—indeed, a small industry of disputation—rests on the fragile, though increasingly sturdy, base of a relatively small number of data about human prehistory and the connections with our primate relations. For example, the article in this volume by Adrienne Zihlman and Nancy Tanner challenges in a direct way the "man the hunter" model and proposes instead that we consider a model that focuses on gathering as a hominid adaptation. They conclude that the principal reason for the divergence of the hominid line from the other primates was its improved skill at gathering, not hunting. They regard this improvement in feeding patterns as a qualitatively effective shift that stimulated the invention of tools. They point to what is well-known archeologically: tools associated with gathering, because their composition was probably organic, are lost to the fossil record while those associated with hunting, more likely to be stone, leave behind a record perceptible to modern scientists. This fact could lead to a built-in bias in any model if one were to base speculations on archeological data alone. Zihlman and Tanner go beyond this to raise the significant issue of which, if any, model of primate behavior is appropriate to speculating about evolving humankind. Their observation, which has been proposed elsewhere, is that the choice of a particular primate model often brings about both the inclusion of certain data and the rejection of others and also biases analyses in a direction constant with the model chosen.

This in general is a vexing and complex issue [for recent discussion of the relevance of animal models to the specific case of aggressive behavior, see Eaton (1976), Larsen (1976), and Michael and Crook (1973)]. Whatever problems models may present, the absence of a model is itself a model. Any sort of picture in the mind affects the assessment of data, though plainly it should be a point of departure rather than a stimulus to particular conclusions. Furthermore, it is obviously the case that the nonhuman primates we study are *not* our direct ancestors; they are our primate contemporaries. While they may reveal a variety of adaptations to various econatures, climatic, and other physical circumstances and socioeconomic patterns, they, of course, do not enable us to speak with any certainty about what actually happened to *Homo sapiens*. As Fox (1972:305) has noted, "The relevance of the primate data lies not so much in the models of our early social organization that it provides, as in the information it gives us on the primate biogram into our own very peculiar path of behavioral evolution and it may be the fact that we were *not* doing the things which seem so adaptive for baboons in their various ecological niches that got us where we are."

This is not a light caution. The behaviors humans do not display (which are similar to those of other primates) may be more important than the ones we see. This leaves us, however, with the temptation to use one or another contemporary primate's behavior as a model for our own ancestral pattern. Drawing on biochemical evidence and indications of behavioral continuity, Zihlman and Tanner argue firmly for a consideration of the chimpanzees as providing the primate model most relevant to the human. Departing from some other earlier interpretations in this field, they reject the baboon as a prototype, noting that the rigid social organization and male hierarchy of this species would impede rather than enhance the development of the elaborate forms of social organization apparent in some contemporary hunting-gathering peoples.

In any event, the romanticized picture of affluent hunters and gatherers, e.g., Sahlins (1972) and Lee (1968) may be in itself the result of extrapolation from a rather special and atypical set of data. For example, the San Bushmen are often seen as prototypically peaceful and egalitarian people who live in circumstances of fair material abundance in which females provide 60 to 80 percent of the food the group consumes. Much of this appearance depends on the existence of very productive Mongongo nut trees, and on the relatively poor faunal population of the part of the Kalahari desert occupied by the San. Not only that, but the basis for a fundamental re-evaluation if not outright rejection of the affluence hypothesis has been recently provided by Williams:

> Cultural elaboration of these themes also brings into question the superabundant-food hypothesis . . . the real clincher . . . was there from the beginning. The information does not appear in the book (*Kalahari Hunter-Gatherers,* Lee and DeVore, eds., 1976) and has not, to my knowledge been published elsewhere, but Lee noted in his Ph.D. dissertation of 1965 that two-thirds of the San population in the Dobe region had been removed from there in a resettlement program only two to three years prior to his field work. That there were superabundant gathered foods after two-thirds of the population had been removed is not surprising, nor is the superabundance relevant to general hypotheses concerning hunter-gatherer adaptations (1977:762).

It develops that the matter is not as clearcut as Williams would urge, and that his implication of inadequately reported evidence is at least overstated; see the letter of reply by Lee, *et al.* (1977) on the issue. Within the narrow limits of the reply, perhaps one may accept that systematic depopulation was not responsible for the relatively abundant diet available to the Bushmen. However the question remains salient about the extent to which there was *de facto* removal of some significant competition for resources as a result of various population movements in the area. Furthermore, there is a serious question about the health status of the Bushmen involved. While prior to the publications in question the female contribution to food getting had certainly been underestimated, this does not mean that the diet Bushmen actually enjoyed was nutritionally desirable then or is now, however important the female contribution. It appears that the hypothesis of Bushman affluence remains in serious doubt and along with it the extrapolations related to it, such as those of Zihlman and Tanner. The implication of this heretofore undigested information for the considerable body of writing about hunters and gatherers is likely to be considerable. I believe it is also directly relevant to an assessment of the validity of the new model of hominid evolution sketched here by Zihlman and Tanner.

They suggest that one important reason for the choice of the baboon over, for instance, the chimpanzee model as a guide for speculation about human society was the very visible existence of the hierarchy of dominant males. In a sense, the resonance between the baboon system and the biased male-centered perceptions of the human system caused a mistaken connection to be made between the two patterns. Yet the choice of the baboon model is less bizarre if one first poses the question: "What are we trying to explain by our use of a baboon or any other model?" Perhaps the principal phenomenon to explain is the rapid evolution of the human brain, if only because it is the behavior dependent on the existence of this organ, which usually is seen as distinguishing *Homo sapiens* from the other primates. For the purpose of this understanding, the baboon model has fewer problems than virtues (Fox 1972, 1978). The breeding system model proposed by Zihlman and Tanner provides a number of provocative and considerable notions about differential parental investment and female choice. But it may describe a breeding system finally too random to account for the extraordinarily rapid expansion of the human brain and its associated intelligence and socioeconomic skill.

Furthermore, the picture they sketch of chimpanzee society,

which they regard as more appropriate to their own human model, is not consistent with the story of less benign and hedonistic chimpanzee society told by Wrangham (1975). Also, the relationship they regard as irrelevant between dominant assertive males and breeding success with females who select these males is contradicted by data which describe a genetically verifiable link between high status and genetic success in at least two other primate species (Stephenson 1974; Deag 1977). Although some writers (Hausfater 1975) do not perceive a strong relationship between male hierarchical structure and reproductive successes, a certain amount of variance appears to be explicable by a theory relating the process of selection to hierarchy among males. Zihlman and Tanner note that females reject aggressive males as sexual partners. The authors do not extend their point to attack the notion that in male hierarchies greater sexual access is afforded to top ranking individuals than to low ranking ones. However, their argument seems to include an implication that makes one uneasy; it may result from the equation of aggressive behavior with dominant behavior as perceived by females responding to possible mates. To say females prefer nonaggressive males is not to say that they prefer nondominant ones. As Chance has noted in his contribution to this volume and as Chance and Larsen (1976) have indicated, the assertion of dominance need not depend on aggressive behavior but could rely on more subtle and pacific processes of interpersonal visual relationship. There is no reason to believe that this might not also constitute a device for rank ordering males in their access to females. Structures of attention among females may also constitute effective features of these selective systems. However, in at least one species, aggression and dominance are clearly linked; in the Japanese macaque, an unusual and considerable amount of physical aggression against the female by the male appears to be an essential stage in the copulation process (G. Gray Eaton, personal communication).

Even for the chimpanzee it remains unclear precisely what stimuli, if any, are used by females to determine possible mates. While it is presumably likely that bellicose and vicious males are unfavorably judged as possible partners, some characteristics of assertive behavior not accompanied by bodily viciousness may be regarded as "attractive" by chimpanzee females.

A theme that runs through many of the discussions relating female social organization to biology is the focus on a kin selection model of process and evolution to explain female interactions. For example, Zihlman and Tanner speculate that the gathering process and subsequent sharing is kin-based—an argument well supported by possibly preadaptive versions in the gathering behavior of primates. Furthermore, Abernethy suggests an intriguing, if as yet unresearched hypothesis: in assessing the social networks of women she proposes that a positive correlation might exist between the tightness of the network as revealed particularly by cooperation in childcare and the degree of relatedness through blood kinship.

If this concern with the theme of kin selection is intriguing in articles with a forthright emphasis on breeding system theory, it is even more arresting when it appears almost inadvertently in an essay whose main emphasis is historical. William L. O'Neill's major concern is to trace the historical input to their community of women in various political movements. He notes that although women very likely have always been politically active as individuals, their influence usually has been indirect. Their impact has been through the various males in their social networks. For example, as a form of negative action, a group of young women of North Carolina during the American Revolution agreed not to marry any male who failed to serve in the army. Furthermore, riots based on the scarcity of food had a certain sanction as a form of female protest. Although O'Neill does not directly draw the connection, it is fascinating that women apparently were permitted to cause political upheaval as long as it was related to their function of protecting and feeding their offspring. During the French Revolution, women were punished by law only for seizing property other than bread and for injuring someone. Of course they did not pristinely or automatically limit their activity to seizing bread. After the "Reveillon Riots," two of the four individuals sentenced to death were women, and when one of them was found to be pregnant, she was given a reprieve. In this macabre manner she was granted the special, if precarious, status and immunity given to women and mothers.

As food supplies grew ever more scarce during the turmoil of revolution, the concept that females were the gentler sex was sorely tested by the realities of female behavior. O'Neill offers numerous examples of the ferocity of women: at one point the women of Masannay demanded the extermination of people over sixty in order to conserve food for their own offspring; with the rise in infant mortality, miscarriages, and still-births, women turned against the Revolution in growing numbers.

O'Neill's discussion is not limited to revolutionary movements. While he places emphasis on the French Revolution as the beginning of organized participation of women in political activities, the history of women's suffrage offers an additional opportunity to examine the manner in which women organize. Unfortunately, little information is available, particularly if one wants to consider female activities from the viewpoint of hierarchy or another structural behavior pattern. Such behavior often implies articulated and self-conscious organization, rare in revolutionary times and perhaps even more among women whose social training and possibly even personal and economic circumstances would mitigate against such formalized structures. This absence of clarified and formalized structures may be an analogue of the archeological problem that artifacts used by males are more likely to persist in the archeological record than those used by females. O'Neill's feeling or hunch is that females function much as men do in hierarchical situations though he acknowledges that there are few data to draw from to support such a thesis.

The final paper in the volume by Shepher and Tiger does suggest that male and female hierarchies are structurally different. However, the authors also note that it is difficult to examine in detail, if only because few conditions in modern society "exist that make the emergence of female hierarchies feasible." That is, apart from a few kinds of organization that are largely female managed, such as nunneries and houses of prostitution, there are relatively few organizations that have persisted as long as many male organizations; hence, any principles about different modes of procedure, if these exist, are difficult to extract. However, examples of all-female groups drawn from the Israeli kibbutz movement do suggest several possible differences from all-male groups. The Shepher and Tiger paper, its authors stress, is clearly tentative about its conclusions. Nevertheless, some of their observations coincide with the findings of other contributors to the volume. For example, Abernethy noted that females were able to move in and out of hierarchical structures, depending on the nature of the task to be performed; Shepher and Tiger note that the interaction between the eleven females of a particular family group displays all the characteristics of a female hierarchy when such interaction is task-oriented, but not when tasks are absent. This ability to shift from a nonhierarchical to a hierarchical structure when circumstances demand is illustrated in two other extraordinary situations, one involving an unpleasant incident on an all-female trip and the other which occurred in the kibbutzim during the Yom Kippur war.

A summary statement in the paper is that "female hierarchies are problematic structures that have problems of discipline, reluctance to accept authority, and rather strained relations among the workers." This is in reference to working groups of females in the kibbutz. At the same time we are reminded that emergency situations, such as the ones just cited, are the exception. This observation suggests that it is probably important to appreciate variations in perception attributable to the sex class of the observer. For example, a female may not find the reluctance of women to accept authority as "problematic" if they are able to accept such authority when situations demand it. Instead, amusement might be the proper response to undue devotion to hierarchical structures that principally serve little apparent purpose other than perpetuate themselves.

The essence of the problem addressed in this volume is whether or not females approach females differently than males and if they do, how, and what social structures such relations yield in the larger system. Are these female systems the same as male ones? If they are, much biological literature points to the acceptability of using the concept of hierarchy as at least one point of departure for this investigation of social structure. Or, do females differ from males so much in their patterns of relationship that the concept of hierarchy is less useful or even dysfunctional as a tool for the analysis of human social behavior or even that of the other primates?

Whatever the answers to these questions, they must perforce relate to a central issue in biology: the relationship between social behavior and its systemization, and genetic composition and change in species. Since it is very unlikely that the relationship between intrafemale social behavior and selection is a random one, the analysis of the nature of such relationships becomes directly pertinent. Certainly the emerging body of information about the relationship between female social behavior and kinship networks suggests that the articulation between social networks and genetic networks is nonrandom and that, therefore, broad biological questions about social behavior and genotype are estimably approachable. So, for example, even such apparently nongenetic studies as Stack (1974), Young and Wilmott (1962) and Geiger (1968) may all connect usefully with efforts to recast kinship theory in the context of a social-biological concern with genotype (Fox 1978). Even the persistence of matrilineal patterns in modern sophisticated Paris—patterns which extend from grandmothers through grandchildren (as described by a participant in the symposium, Evelyne Sullerot, in personal communication)—also may reveal how social networks relate to genetic ones.

Needless to say, I am not concerned here with defining a narrow social Darwinian view of the matter, that is, one in which individuals are held to the effort of competing with each other for resources, energy, time, social connections, etc. in order to further their own genetic advantages through their offspring. Rather the opposite is intended by indicating that cooperative structures, which often even hierarchies must be, provide a basis for the interdependence of individuals as they conduct their social and reproductive lives. To maintain these forms of reciprocity, the interaction among females and the pattern these may assume occupy a central role, and so therefore must the scientific study of them.

REFERENCES CITED

CHANCE, M.R.A. and R.R. LARSEN
1976—*The Social Structure of Attention*. New York:Wiley.
COHEN, YEHUDI
1964—*The Transition from Childhood to Adolescence*. Chicago:
Aldine.
DEAG, JOHN M.
1977—Aggression and Submission in Monkey Societies. *Animal Behavior* 25:2.
DUVALL, SUSAN W., I.S. BERNSTEIN, and T.P. GORDON
1976—Paternity and Status in a Rhesus Monkey Group. *Journal of Reproduction and Fertility* 47:25-31.
EATON, G. GRAY
1976—Animal Models and the Study of Human Aggressive Behavior. *JAMAWA* 31:9.
FOX, ROBIN
1972—Alliance and Constraint: Sexual Selection in the Evolution of Human Kinship Systems. In *Sexual Selection and the Descent of Man 1871-1971*, Bernard Campbell, ed. Chicago:Aldine.
1978—The Evolution of the Mind: An Anthropological Approach. In *Evolutionary Biology and Human Social Behavior: An Anthropological Perspective*, Napoleon Chagnon and William Irons, eds. Duxbury, Ma.: Duxbury.
GEIGER, H. KENT
1968—*The Family in Soviet Russia*. Cambridge, Ma.:Harvard University Press.
HAMBURG, D.A.
1963—Emotions in Perspective of Human Evolution. In *Expression of the Emotions in Man*, Peter H. Knapp, ed. New York: International Universities Press.
HAUSFATER, G.
1975—*Dominance and Reproduction in Baboons (Papio Cynocephalus): A Quantitative Analysis*. Contributions to Primatology Series 7. Basel:S. Karger.
HENNIG, MARGARET and ANNE JARDIM
1977—*The Managerial Woman*. New York:Doubleday.
LARSEN, R.R.
1976—On Comparing Man and Ape: An Evaluation of Methods and Problems. *Man* 11:202-219.
LEE, RICHARD B.
1968—What Hunters Do for a Living, or, How To Make Out on

Scarce Resources. In *Man the Hunter,* Richard B. Lee and Irven DeVore, eds. Chicago:Aldine.

LEE, RICHARD B., *et al.*
1977—Kung Ecology. *Science* 197:1233.

MICHAEL, R.P. and J.H. CROOK
1973—*Comparative Ecology and Behaviour of Primates.* New York: Academic.

RAPHAEL, DANA
1975—Women and Power. In *Being Female: Reproduction, Power, and Change,* Dana Raphael, ed. The Hague:Mouton/Chicago:Aldine.

ROSALDO, MICHELLE A. and LOUISE LAMPHERE
1974—*Woman, Culture, and Society.* Stanford:Stanford University Press.

SAHLINS, M.
1972—*Stone Age Economics.* Chicago:Aldine.

STACK, CAROL
1974—*All Our Kin.* New York:Harper and Row.

STEPHENSON, GORDON R.
1975—Social Structure of Mating Activity in Japanese Macaques. In *Symposia of the Fifth Congress of the International Primatological Society,* Vol. 1, J.H. Crook, ed. Tokyo:Japan Science Press.

THIESSEN, D.D.
1976—*The Evolution and Chemistry of Aggression.* Springfield, Ill.: Charles C Thomas.

TIGER, LIONEL
1969—*Men in Groups.* New York:Random House.

1975—Somatic Factors and Social Behavior. In *Biosocial Anthropology,* Robin Fox, ed. London:Wiley/New York:Halsted.

TIGER, LIONEL and JOSEPH SHEPHER
1975—*Women in the Kibbutz.* New York:Harcourt Brace Jovanovich.

WRANGHAM, RICHARD W.
1975—The Behavioral Ecology of Chimpanzees in Gombe National Park, Tanzania. Ph.D. Dissertation, University of Cambridge, England.

WILLIAMS, B.J.
1977—Book review. *Science* 196:761-762.

YOUNG, FRANK W.
1962—The Function of Male Initiation Ceremonies. *American Journal of Sociology* 68:4.

YOUNG, M. and P. WILLMOTT
1962—*Family and Kinship in East London.* London:Penguin.

1

Epistemologies of Sex

SANDRA WALLMAN

PREAMBLE

Behavioral differences between men and women have generally been attributed *either* to natural, and therefore, essential, differences in biology, physiology, genetics *or* to cultural, and therefore non-essential impositions, the fortuitous demands and/or accidents of a social system and the dialectics of history and/or of the human mind. By this logic, the observable phenomena that distinguish men from women must be biological *or* social, natural *or* cultural. The terminology of discourse is inexorably bifid: we talk of biological sex, on the one hand, and social role, on the other. Although some confound the two kinds of factors,[1] most explanations of sex differences may be lumped into one or other of these polarized classes.

For many purposes this formula is both convenient and appropriate. But where the objective is an understanding of the whole human creature, the binary habit is a twofold impediment. First, if we insist on a nature *versus* culture dichotomy, we cannot deal with the fact that (even) that which is to be called nature is a construct of culture; that the classification of a human being as male or female is done (normally, if not always) at birth by other human beings according to their superficial reading of quite superficial body signs; and that this classification (normally, if not always) determines the subse-

21

quent socialization and, to some considerable extent, the behavior of that human being. Second, perhaps consequently, we lack or have lacked a terminology common to both biological and sociological approaches. We have used the same terms to refer to quite different phenomena and have confused each other horribly.

Some solution to the problem of terminology was both prerequisite and consequent to discussion in this symposium. All of us were soon persuaded that a minimum of three levels of sex difference had to be recognized: sex or sex class,[2] gender behavior, and sex role. Thus:

1. Human beings are slotted into sex class male or sex class female and the "folk" classification (nearly always) tallies with the "scientific" distinction between male and female sex.

2. Gender or gender behavior is the social correlate of sex class: being in or having been slotted in a particular sex class, one learns to behave accordingly, to be masculine or feminine according to the norms of a particular culture.

3. Within each culture certain things are done, certain functions performed by men, others by women, and these sex-linked tasks give rise to sex roles.

We still did not know the relative weight of these three sets of factors, but at least we could begin to discuss it.

This is all to the good. Improved communication between the sciences of man is no mean achievement. But returning to my own corner of the problem and the effort to explain degrees of variation in the significance of sex or sex differences within, between, and across cultures, I find I am no further ahead. Certainly, where I am using the materials of others and largely where I am using my own, it remains extremely hard to decide whether the sex differences observed and/or reported are functions of sex class, gender behavior, or sex role. It may be that terminology is the least of our difficulties.

INTRODUCTION

In the explanation of sex difference, social anthropologists have been extraordinarily careful to keep their distance from biologists. The reasons for their doing so are by now common-place: the founding fathers and mothers were not only struck by the significance of cultural factors, they were also constrained as a profession to distinguish themselves from biologists and anxious, for good moral reasons, to correct the errors of vulgar evolutionism.[3] The effect has been to lean heavily on the concept of social role and so to demonstrate that the business of being a woman—relating to other women, to men, to the economic and social system—depends largely if not only on "the position of women," on the way in which "the female role" is defined in each society.

The weight put here on the female side is not added to fit the topic to this symposium: it is striking that sex differences or variations in the balance between men and women are never analyzed from the perspective of "the male role" or "the position of men"; and although all role theorists list sex roles somewhere in their compendia, "the position of men" or "the male role" is not normally mentioned at all. Banton, for example, asks us to consider "What would be the social consequence of allowing an individual to occupy both the female role and the priestly role?" (1965:32-33), but refers later to the probable reaction to a "man filling what is considered to be a woman's job (e.g. nursing)" (Banton 1965:51). To write the second statement in the form of the first makes a very different point: *viz.* "What would be the social consequences of allowing an individual to occupy both the male role and the nursing role?"

The difference in gloss is not simply that "the role of female tends to be less independent of other roles than that of male" (Banton 1965:34), nor that social scientists, being notoriously androcentric, can more readily stereotype and so objectify "the female role." The point to be made is that two peculiar difficulties inhere in the analysis of sex roles. First, while *role* is an explicitly "cultural" concept, even when applied to pre-cultural/

proto-cultural species (Benedict 1969), the conceptualization of *sex* roles involves inexplicit assumptions about the "essential" attributes of each sex class. Second, the concept of "female role" is not equal and opposite to the apparently corrresponding concept of "male role." In combination, it is as though membership in the female sex class constitutes a role, but membership in the male sex class does not (cf. Sullerot 1971:7).

The object of this exercise is to examine the effect of this unstated hypothesis on the analysis of sex difference. I shall begin by posing the reverse, i.e., sex, specifically female sex, does not constitute a role, so that it may be tested in a number of ethnographic situations. I shall try to distinguish the logic of situations in which sex is (only) *perceived to be* a role from those in which it (actually) *is* a role. I shall work towards the conclusion that there is no analytic meaning in such concepts as "the position of women" or "the female role" is society X or society Y, since the inevitable presence of the sex attribute tells us nothing at all about its general social relevance. The phrases, like the attribute to which they refer, must be narrowly qualified by *context* (exactly when and how is sex class *socially* relevant); and by *perception* (in whose eyes is it relevant?).

I shall first try to make clear the ways in which I am using the notions of *situation* and *role,* and shall then deal with some ethnographic material in four sections in such a way as to demonstrate if not to exaggerate the peculiar epistemology of sex difference. It will be obvious that the purview of this paper is the *social* differentiation of male and female. Given the range of contributors to this volume I have neither the temerity nor the need to treat biological and ethological perspectives as such. The conclusion, however, attempts to relate the various "kinds" of human sex difference to each other, and to problems raised in the previous sections. The effort is very tentative, but anomalies in the data demand that it be made.

The contents are:

1. The logic of sex class situations
2. The problem of sex roles
3. The over-sexed peasant

1. THE LOGIC OF SEX CLASS SITUATIONS

Models for the analysis of situation are not wanting in the social sciences. For my purposes the most useful are probably those of Goffman (1959, 1971) and Nadel (1957). Gellner's (1973a) paper underlines the enormous difficulties inherent in circumscribing (or, as he argues it, refusing to circumscribe) the context in which a concept is meaningful. The same difficulties inhere in attempts to define situation: it is hard to know where to stop. Indeed, without explicit criteria of relevance, the tendency is to define a situation in wholly subjective or psychological terms: the situation is *only* what the subject perceives. Jarvie's recent exploration of the notion is very explicit. He itemizes the nonsubjective dimensions of situation and castigates holistic and psychologistic approaches for ignoring their effect, and denying the systematic importance of unintended consequences (Jarvie 1972:3-36; see also Popper 1959, passim; 1972: 78).

It is not a coincidence that scholars in economic anthropology are least prone to this fallacy: they are necessarily concerned with real phenomena, with the perception of those phenomena, and with the consequences of the perception. Firth's various statements of the tasks of the subdiscipline constitute both a plea and a prescription for situational analysis and imply a logic by which the situation can be bounded (Firth 1939:1-31, 352-365; 1951). His latest statement might also be a credo: "There is a structure at all levels—in the phenomena, as in the perceptions which order them and in the concepts which interpret their logical relationships; and it is presumptuous to assign to one level more 'reality' than to another" (Firth 1972:38).

I interpret this to mean that the phenomenon, the actor's perception of the phenomenon, and the observer's perception of the phenomenon are each integral parts of a situation, and that

they act and react on each other in circular—perhaps spiral—
not linear sequence. In a discussion of sex differences neither
the social nor the biological "side" can claim precedence over
the other. Gender is clearly *more than* a mental construct of the
actor and/or the observer, but, in terms of the logic of the situation, it is *not more important than* those constructs. And, in the
time-honored functional formula, a variation in one part constitutes a variation of the whole thing.

2.   THE PROBLEM OF SEX ROLES

Concerning role generally, Banton's formula is conveniently
minimal: Role is "a set of norms and expectations applied to the
incumbent of a particular position" (Banton 1965:29). Being
relatively unspecific, this version allows me the inferences I
want. These are that: roles are performed in and constitute part
of situations rather than whole societies (Nadel 1957); there
may be variations in and conflicting definitions of appropriate
performance (certainly most readably described by Goffman
1959); roles and role systems may be classified and differentiated
according to a number of different criteria (as Banton himself
attempted).

Having said that, it is necessary to take note of the fact that
the concepts of status and role are peculiarly subject to conflicting definitions. Since "they are widely used as basic concepts in
social analysis, and they are used in attempts to solve an enormously wide variety of sociological problems, this need not sur-
prise us at all. The usefulness of a particular version in one
analytic context cannot be expected to carry over into all others
(Wallman 1974a). If there are many versions it is because there
are many problems.

But such proliferation has two important corollaries. Corollary
one: not all the differences are equally useful. Some have been
articulated into approaches as distinct from each other as the
legalistic (which emphasizes the rights and obligations that
comprise a role) and the dramatic (which emphasizes individual performance of a socially scripted part). Others smack of
entirely unhelpful pedantry, i.e., the question of how many roles

make a status, for example, might better be asked of pre-Renaissance theologians than of empirical social scientists. Corollary two: it is appallingly easy to get one's methodological wires crossed, to confuse the parts and the purposes of one role model with the parts and purposes of another.

Against this background, the striking fact that most role theorists have extraordinary trouble with sex roles might be attributed to ordinary methodological confusion. This is entirely feasible: all sciences need better theories. But for our present purposes, a better explanation is suggested when we look at the particular kind of trouble sex roles give. Let me try to demonstrate it very briefly.

Nadel (1957) classes sex roles as "non-relational" and "ascribed." Non-relational means that their performance requires no "other." Not only can you play them by yourself, but they (apparently) require no "other's" perception/interpretation/evaluation of performance. Ascribed roles are "assigned to individuals without reference to their innate differences or abilities" (Banton 1965:29). A sex role then does not have to be performed, and it has nothing to do with innate differences. But if it does not have to be performed, it entails no particular rights or obligations; being non-relational, it entails no opposite number, no audience, no interaction. It is not then a role, socially scripted, it is an attribute, socially passive. But an attribute is (usually?) an innate difference, and sex roles, being ascribed, (should) bear no reference to innate differences. The methodological confusion is compounded.

Banton (1965:33) tries to clear it by differentiating roles along a scale from "basic" to "independent" that "compares the extent to which particular roles can be played independently of other roles." On this scale, sex roles are the most basic and are graphically placed very near to the extreme left-hand end of the continuum. According to him, "A person's sex role usually affects the way people respond to him or her more than does any other role; it is relevant to conduct in a wide range of situations" (1965:33). But he is in the same bind. He says that the sex *role* is relevant in many situations, but must mean that sex class is relevant in many situations. Wherever he refers to the female role or roles (as on pp. 38-41), he refers in effect either to sex class or to roles which are usually performed by females, to what might be called sex-linked roles. (Despite the appealing analogy to sex-linked genes, this is intended to indicate *social* linking. In a smilar sense, *gender behavior* is sex limited.)

It seems to me to be useful to compare the notion of *sex roles* as such with a pair of *sex-linked roles*—roles that imply/require/ are normally associated with a particular sex attribute. For example, a wife is normally—but not quite always—female (one exception might be the male wife of a homosexual male). A husband is normally—but not quite always—male (anthropological literature on "woman marriage" is an obvious source of exceptions).[4] In such cases, the sex-linked role can be understood in terms of the logic of the situation in which it occurs. The phenomenon—sex—is only *one* of the parts integral to the situation. The actors' perception of the phenomenon and the observer's analysis of that perception are also necessary to the role concept, because a role has meaning only within the situational context in which it occurs.

There are sociolegal systems in which sex, specifically female sex, affects rights and obligations. There are also situations in which it is a necessary condition of role performance. But the biological sex attribute, whatever its social significance, cannot *by itself* constitute a role. More generally stated, no physical attribute is a role, although there is, as in Goffman's analysis of stigma (1968), plenty of evidence to show that it may give rise to one. The special problem of sex roles springs from a confusion of these two levels of analysis.

I shall try now to clarify and substantiate these assertions with examples from the ethnographic literature and from my own experience.

3. THE OVERSEXED PEASANT

In our analyses of other societies, particularly of peasant societies, we have a tendency to emphasize differences between the sexes. Some possible reasons for our doing so will be suggested below. But the effect is that we have more or less explicit models of power, labor, and values wielded/performed/held by men or women *because* they are male or female. The appropriateness of these models is widely assumed, and their use tells us a lot about the ideals of the model-builders and of their informants. Very often that is all we want to know. In this context it is not: the understanding of real differences within and between the human sexes is circumscribed if we confuse what is ideal with what is normal, what is ideal in our society with what is ideal in theirs and, particularly, if we accept male ideals about women's behavior in certain situations as a description of the way in which women behave in all situations. And an understanding of the real significance of sex difference will be impossible if our models make sex difference primordial and we assume only one level of sexual differentiation.

With a different emphasis, it is possible to see situations in which class, rank, status, "race," age, kinship, wealth, profession—even mood set—are more significant to the allocation of power, tasks, or opinions than is sex. But the attraction of the sex attribute over these other criteria is the crux of the epistemological problem: sex class does not change with situation. It thus entails a once-for-all social classification of individuals within a particular society and tempts us to confuse the social with the biological fact.[5]

We need to examine the manner and extent to which the *variable* social significance of sex difference reflects or refracts *invariable* biological/ethological differences between male and female. We cannot do this if the conceptual separateness of the two levels is ignored any more than we can if their mutual entailment is denied.

The methodological weakness of simplistic sex models can be illustrated by reference to a very few sources.

The Sexual Division of Power

Under this heading I cannot resist quoting at length the introductory statement of Lebeuf's essay on "The Role of Women in Political Organisation of African Societies." (Note that the title is context—if not situation—specific.) She writes:

By a habit of thought deeply rooted in the Western mind, women are relegated to the sphere of domestic tasks and private life, and men alone are considered equal to the task of shouldering the burden of public affairs. This anti-feminist attitude, which has prevented political equality between the sexes from being established in [Western industrial] countries until quite recently (and even so the equality is more *de jure* than *de facto*), should not allow us to prejudge the manner in which activities are shared between men and women in other cultures. . . . And we are entitled to ask ourselves if it is not an attitude of this kind that is at the bottom of many erroneous ideas about the very real authority exercised by women in African political systems; and whether it has not contributed . . . to the initiation of policies which deprive women of responsibilities which used to be theirs (Lebeuf 1971:93).

The very clear inference here is that we are pushing—or have pushed—*our* particular sexism onto *them* and are measuring their "normal" against our "ideal." Trying to correct this bias, Lebeuf, in the body of the same paper, makes reference to dozens of African societies in which some form of political authority has routinely been allocated to women. Two types of traditional African political systems are contrasted: the nation state in which authority is centered on a single locus; and the noncentralized federations in which authority is diffused across the whole and rests with the heads of the various member lineages.

In systems of the first type, which are characterized by a "pronounced hierarchical structure, most women who either belong to or have affinal ties with the royal lineage enjoy various prerogatives which often have political implications. They are frequently given positions of territorial authority, having one or several villages under their control or full powers over a district—in which latter case succession in the female line may be involved, as with the Bemba" (Lebeuf 1971:107). In the second type, where the political system is based on kinship organization, the political opportunities open to women are not as clear cut, but extend to a large number of individuals. Sometimes women head communities; more commonly their political influence is nonspecific, often a result of "their preponderant role in spiritual matters" (Lebeuf 1971:109).

This reinterpretation of the data is important. But still it begs the central question: Is political power allocated to women *because* they are female, *despite* their being female, or is it allocated without reference to their sex at all? In which cases is female sex a necessary or an efficient criterion? In which is it irrelevant? In most cases it is extremely difficult to tell. Where it is said, for example, that a woman is permitted to inherit the functions of her husband or her father *in the absence of a male heir*, should we call this an asexual appointment (because she is qualified by kinship, not gender); a desexing appointment (because she occupies the position "as if she were a man"); or a sexist appointment in which the woman is put in a position of power so that her menfolk can manipulate it?

Where the political structure actually calls for a queen, she probably has particular ritual functions—either as part of her duties as sole head of state, or as complementary to the non-ritual functions of a king or male chief—the sex class of the royal person is clearly socially significant. But we cannot say that sex class alone makes the role, nor do we know over which spheres and in which situations its significance extends.

The same is true of the reference to the Aba Riots in 1929 (in Ibo country, eastern Nigeria), otherwise known as "the war of the women." The reference reads: "Following upon a rumour that the government was on the point of introducing a tax on women's property, [women] started making demonstrations which . . . spread through . . . two provinces . . . mobilising more than two million people, *very few of whom seem to have been men*" (Lebeuf 1971:113-114, emphasis added). So some were. So a particular sex attribute was not prerequisite to participation in this case. (Presumably not only women stood to lose by the tax.) But was *female* sex prerequisite to leadership? *If* the women were mobilized by those few men, then sex difference parallelled rank difference. But *if* it did, was one characteristic *prior* to the other? Was male sex made *prerequisite* to leadership by differential ability and/or by consensus? Or were the men camp followers, servants? We know that members of both sex classes participated in these political demonstrations. But we do not know how far and in which ways sex class was significant.

Given an underlying assumption that only sex counts, other aspects of the logic of the situation will not be reported. Indeed, they may not have been observed.

Bailey is not using a sex model when he writes of the competition for and manipulation of local level political power in (Bisipara) India. Perhaps *because* he is not using such a model, he recognizes the different significance of sex in two different political spheres. He calls these spheres Structure A and Structure B. It is clear from his description that women wield little (formal?) political power in either one, but for different reasons. In Structure A (roughly, the traditional system) they do not enter the political arena because they are females, and females "are a source of danger to society, a temptation to evil and antisocial behaviour" (Bailey 1969:192). In Structure B (the non-traditional democratic system) they do not enter the arena because they do not have the economic and educational resources necessary for political competition, "and even as voters they often turn out to be the dependents of their husbands" (Bailey 1969:193). Bailey clinches my point in a footnote to the same sentence: "This discussion, of course, applies to *peasant* women. The Indian middle class has produced some formidable female politicians" (Bailey 1969:225; emphasis his).

The Sexual Division of Value/Values

The view of women held in Bailey's Structure A is, if the anthropological literature is indicative, to be found in comparable forms all over the world. As there is said to be a division of power on the basis of sex, so there seems to be a division of value and of values. Which is to say something like: women are qualitatively different from men and therefore they normally do and/or they ideally should react differently in response to the same external stimuli, and they do and/or they should affect the world around them differently from the way in which men do. Such assertions present the greatest of epistemological difficulties: 1) they refer only to symbols, not to tangible phenomena (if the universe may be divided up in this way); and 2) they have the ring of nature, the appeal of natural law. Most of us hold some version of the sexual division of value/values to be self-evidently and properly true. Even those who would wish to sweep away all political and economic inequalities between men and women commonly still nurture an edge of qualitative difference so that (in Ellmann's nice phrase) they can "still enjoy encounters" (1973).

Both because it is "naturally" there, and because—within and between social systems—its boundaries shift, this value difference warrants particular attention here. I shall address it by reference to one of the most intricate of the many division of value models, *Honour and Shame: the Values of Mediterranean Society*. This model has been elegantly and systematically propounded in the now classic volume under that title (Peristiany 1966) and widely used by Mediterraneanists subsequently [see the references to Aswad (1967); Friedl (1967); and Schneider (1970) below].

At first statement, honor and shame are simply "two poles of an evaluation. Honour is at the apex of the pyramid of temporal social values and it conditions their hierarchical order" (Peristiany 1966). But the implications are more fundamental. "Cutting across all other social classifications it divides social beings into two fundamental categories, those endowed with honour, and those deprived of it" (Peristiany 1966). There are no *degrees* of honor and honorability; you either have it, or you do not (i.e., it does not vary with situation but is once-for-all ascribed?). At the same time, however, people seem to be constantly and repeatedly striving to achieve it, maintain it, monopolize it, and their success or failure in doing so is measured by and reflected in the amount of honor that is imputed to them by public opinion (i.e., it does vary with situation and can be achieved by appropriate behavior?).

This kind of contradiction in a value system is quite ordinary: inconsistencies are commonly prerequisite to viability (Gellner 1973a; Leach 1966), and I am willing to believe that the members of these Mediterranean societies may hold both statements true. What *is* problematic however, is the position of women and/or of females in this conceptual universe.

All the contributing authors to the *Honour and Shame* volume identify sexual honor as the bastion of all things honorable, and this is the aspect most enthusiastically taken up by writers subsequently. In each paper it is more or less explicit that women's role in its defense is opposite to that of men: "The honour of a man and a woman . . . imply quite different modes of conduct." More specifically, "a woman is dishonoured . . . with the tainting of her sexual purity, but a man [is] not" (Pitt-Rivers 1966:42). The complementarity of the sexes is expressed in their different roles in the maintenance of their joint (family) honor: "The honour of a man is . . . in the sexual purity of his mother, wife and daughters, and sisters, not in his own" (Pitt-Rivers 1966:45). Which is to say that a woman is dishonored by losing her shame in the way that a man is shamed in losing his honor. Pitt-Rivers writes simply, "Thus honour and shame, when they are not equivalent, are linked exclusively to one sex or the other and are opposed to another" (Pitt-Rivers 1966:43) . . . *"because they derive from natural qualities"* (Pitt-Rivers 1966:45: emphasis added; see also p. 189).

It is impossible here to do justice to the intricate analyses that are given to support this model. I shall instead shamelessly extract the points which are germane to my argument. First, the absolute dichotomy between the sexes which is fundamental to the model is based on assumptions of essential differences between men and women, differences which are therefore neither functions of nor vulnerable to changes in *social* situation. Second, however, while shame is unmanly (because it is womanly) a man who does not manifest it by appropriate modesty and sensitivity to his reputation is not honorable. Third, a person who *has* shame is honorable but he who is *given* shame is dishonored (Pitt-Rivers 1966:43). By these tokens honor is not sex-specific but situation-specific.

In order properly to appreciate the significance of sex, some effort has to be made to separate the phenomenon of sex from the situation in which it sits, to distinguish the personal attribute from the person's performance. In doing so, we must necessarily deal with changes of analytic level as well as changes of context. These "values of Mediterranean society" are inevitably refracted by the perceptions of those who report them and those who read the reports—not, of course, because they observe inefficiently or report dishonestly, but because this is a fact of epistemological life.

Consequently, statements to the effect that the honor and shame model has only a limited importance for the middle class and none for the upper (Pitt-Rivers 1966; Aswad 1967); that the conception of honor has changed in these countries for political, economic, and religious reasons (Baroja 1966); that what is honorable behavior in public is inappropriate, certainly not normal, in private (Friedl 1967); that the whole business is a question of ecology and resource management (Schneider 1970)— such statements are almost impossible to interpret in terms of our present interest. The model makes sex difference primordial, but how can we know its significance without knowing the entire logic of each of these separate situations? To what extent are we talking about a division of value(s) on the "natural" basis of sex at all?

The Sexual Division of Labor

It should be easier to deal with the division of labor but, by and large, it is not. Certainly the tasks of reproduction still are (biologically) sex-limited, but we are no longer sure about the tasks of nurture. It used to be said that these were essentially, and biologically, female tasks; now it seems possible that they are no more than socially, customarily the jobs of women which could just as effectively be done by men. Certainly some tasks are heavier than others and thus are better suited to the (normally? ideally?) stronger physique of the male. But a model of tasks allocated on the basis of sex class may be misleading at the level of ideals and at the level of actual patterns of behavior (cf. Ward 1966). I am referring here neither to cross-cultural differences in the role of women, nor to the economics of machine technology, but to the fact that the priorities of survival, the exigencies of situation take precedence over symbolic norms.

Examples of this happening could probably be found in any peasant society in which the division of labor by sex is said to be ideal and/or normal. Certainly they can in two peasant societies in which I have worked.

In Lesotho, it is not unusual to see women herding, tending, and handling cattle, although Bantu custom forbids them any contact with them (Wallman 1969; cf. Schapera 1937). In the absence of large numbers of men, somebody must do the job and the only options are probably female. There is no shame involved, although it does seem polite to joke about it, as though to acknowledge that one knows this to be a man's job, and one knows this woman is not a man.

In the western Italian Alps, the cutting of hay with a large heavy scythe is a man's job, so much so that the man who gives up doing it seems to be acknowledging sexual as well as economic incompetence. But a woman of any age who is widowed or has an invalid husband can and will cut the hay, with the same instrument, with comparable efficiency, and without a sense of parody or shame. In the fields men and women often work together, sometimes actually switching tasks to break the monotony or to ease their backs. There is a desperately short growing season in these high regions and no one can afford to disqualify labor on the grounds of sex, even though they may describe and even perceive tasks as being appropriate to one sex class or the other.

Since both these peoples are urban-oriented and familiar at first or second hand with nonpeasant norms, the contrasts of a still-traditional Islamic group may make a more trenchant point.[6]

The unambiguous ideal in Dajebel Khroumir (in northwest Tunisia) is a division of labor by sex. However, the more peasant one is (in pejorative local terms, the more stupid; in ecological terms, the more constrained), the less notice one takes of this ideal in real life. When necessary, men and women work in the fields together, sometimes doing the same tasks. When this happens, the next level caveat is that the men and women who work together should be kin. And where exigency presses still harder, the proprieties can be observed and honor saved simply by turning one's back towards unrelated members of the opposite sex. So much for the tasks of agriculture. The slaughter of animals is even more stringently sex-linked. Women, according to the conscious model, must not/cannot/do not do it. But if an animal is to be slaughtered and there is no man available at the appropriate time, then a woman will put the knife in the hand of even the tiniest boy and, putting her own hand over his, make the first fatal cut on the throat of the animal by his agency. From then on the task may be completed by the woman alone. Perhaps more correctly, from then on the sex class of the slaughterer is irrelevant.

The report that a particular society allocates different tasks to men and women tells us nothing about the significance of sex class in particular work situations. Whose perception of the division of labor are we dealing with? If this is a conscious model, is it of the whole society, or of a particular interest group? How do people live with the values they espouse if, and when, situations make ideal behavior impossible? What options do they have at the level of values and at the level of action? The extent to which the observer shares the conscious model of his informants will affect the posing and the answering of such questions. And, in this respect, since we are dealing with sex differences, does the sex of the observer count?

4. THE ASEXUAL ETHNOGRAPHER

In social anthropology the effect of the observer's sex is now quite commonly referred to, but only rarely is it specifically analyzed. Where it is mentioned at all, it is mentioned by women, and tends to have been made into a role, i.e., a female ethnographer is better able to study women simply by being female.

An interesting exception on both counts is Edwin Ardener's essay which attempts to divide "the problem of women" into a technical and an analytical part. This division is less feasible than he would maintain. I would, for example, be unwilling to estimate how much of the distortion of over-sexed peasant model is based on technical and how much on analytical confusion. Following Ardener's distinction, however, most of the discussion in this section is concerned with the first aspect: to what extent are the ethnographic difficulties of dealing with women affected by the sex class of the ethnographer? Among these problems he includes accessibility, language competence, and what appears to be, or to be his particular view of, gender behavior (". . . they giggle when young, snort when old, reject the question, laugh at the topic . . ."). But his dissection of the second, the analytical aspect, is inescapably germane. Briefly:

1. Women are biologically not men, and it would be surprising if they bounded themselves against nature in the same way that men do.
2. Ethnographic models of a society are male models, bounding men from women and women from nature in an essentially male way (which may mean simply "as men do"), because "they tend to be models derived from the male portion of that society" (Ardener 1972:136).
3. "Because of an interesting failure in the functionalist observational model, statements *about* observation were always added to the ethnographer's own observation" (Ardener 1972:139).

In other words, indigenous male statements about the world were necessarily part of the ethnographic reality observed and reported—whatever the sex of the ethnographer.

This is an interesting argument and one to which I have done meager justice here. It is even possible that Ardener is right in suggesting that only an emphasis on myth and belief may enable and/or force us to recognize and reconcile "a man's sector and a woman's sector" and so to solve both the indigenous and the anthropological problems of women (Ardener 1972:145 ff.). But belief is only observed through action—verbal or behavioral; the separation of technical and analytical problems is difficult in any science (Popper 1965), and social anthropology is said to have a particular tendency to confuse the two (Jarvie 1964; Fox 1973:3-40).

It is therefore not surprising (although it is disappointing) that we should expect to correct the androcentric bias of the empirical social sciences simply by putting more women in the field. Not only are women ethnographers expected to pay relatively more attention to women in the societies they study (which indeed they often do), but a female ethnographer is expected to be more warmly and openly received by these women than a man would be and so, of course, to learn more about them. The assumption here again is that sex class is of overriding significance.

But there is direct evidence to the contrary in the experience of many female ethnographers (Powdermaker 1967; Bowen 1954; Golde 1970; Paulme 1971). A female ethnographer is perceived by her female subjects as an ethnographer, not as a man perhaps, but not as a woman either. If her sex class is recognizably female, her gender behavior is wrong. She normally does too many strange things, plays too many strange roles, for her sex to be womanhood. Paulme writes:

> When African women see a female foreigner making a direct approach for information to the men of the village, starting discussions with them, entering places and even attending ceremonies to which they, as women, are not admitted, they show no interest in her at all at first. But, once their curiosity is aroused, they tend to be ironical and severely critical: how can a woman, whose proper tasks are looking after the home and the children, behave in a way that seems to deny her very nature? . . . And there can be no doubt as to which side she is on: has she not lent a sympathetic ear to the men's complaints? . . . And when the foreigner finally comes to visit the women, she will be met with reserve or even open hostility, and as often as not will find her efforts rewarded by a refusal to admit her" (Paulme 1971:1-2).

At this stage, in this situation, the woman ethnographer is perceived by women as a stranger, perhaps a threat. Later, when she is better known and the suspicion is softened a bit by habit, she may move into the role of acquaintance, curious (in both senses), but no longer threatening. Now the local women can afford to be patronizing. The outsider is not competent at doing what has to be done here (which in itself is unwomanly) and occupies herself with fruitless and unpleasant tasks. Paulme (1971), Richards (1939), and Bowen (1954) each report overhearing expressions of pity, even horror at the drudgery of ethnographic work. "That girl makes me tired with her everlasting paper and pencil: what sort of a life is that?" (Paulme 1971:2). I have the impression that this reaction is very common, even in so-called non-primitive settings. I also suspect that it might as commonly be elicited by a man.

The point at which the ethnographer moves into the status of a friend—but a strange friend—is likely to be much later in the relationship, unless it is precipitated by a particularly dramatic or surprising event (Powdermaker 1967:113; and my own experience below). There will still be situations in which one's role is defined otherwise—both by oneself and/or by the now friendly informants—even if only on the basis of a different time-table of work or a relatively nonpartisan stand on some important community issue. Again, I think variations in this process are not, at least not directly, related to the sex class of the ethnographer.

I do not want to argue that being female in the field does not make a difference, only that the difference is not predictable or consistent, nor is it based on sex alone. Many other variables are involved. Some are functions of historical and/or professional era: What sort of relationship is currently fashionable between the native culture and the observer culture? What kind of professional norms has the anthropologist internalized? Others are functions of the culture being studied: What is the local view of strangers, researchers, women? Is there an existing niche, a role for a "researcher-female-stranger" (Golde 1970:14) and is it defined in the same way by everybody? (Those of us who have worked in colonies governed by our own compatriots may have had more adjustment problems with them than with the people being studied.)

In some settings, it seems to be an advantage to be female or, at least, not to be male. Powdermaker (1967:108-114) suggests that fieldwork is invariably easier for a woman alone than for a man alone, on the grounds that a woman ethnographer has access to women's matters (in a way that a strange male does not?) and to men's matters also (in a way that indigenous women do not?). I could ask no stronger support for the contention that female ethnographers are asexual. Mead (1970:325) reports that in the Pacific Islands women outsiders may more easily live as part of established households; Creyghton (in a personal communication) suggests that Arab countries are better studied by women, not because of sexual freedoms or constraints, but because of women's ascribed innocence in political affairs. And especially in communities with experience of sexually preda-tory male strangers—traders, missionaries, administrators, an-thropologists—it is less threatening not to be male. The point is not that stranger women are sexually less predatory (although in-deed they may be), but that "the fact that an anthropological field worker is a man is less easily masked—for the village women, that is—than is the fact that the strange, remote, equip-ment-burdened anthropologist is a woman for the men" (Mead 1970:322)—(i.e. ethnographic fieldwork behavior is more like male than like female gender behavior?).

These are cultural reactions to female (nonmale?) strangers as a general category. There will be further variation according to the social and physical characteristic of particular females and to the kind of inquiry they are or seem to be making. Lan-guage competence and degree of cultural strangeness must count; so does physiognomy, whether in terms of perceived beauty and vulnerability or of race (cf. Marshall 1970:167-191; and my observation below). Certainly (perceived) age makes an impression: in many societies even native women "become men" after menopause, and Mead writes that "women field workers [tend to] have an easier time the older they look or are willing to look" (Mead 1970:322; Silverman 1967).[7]

The interpretation of these latter statements is problematic since the people's perceptions of the fieldworker become almost impossible to dissociate from her perceptions of herself. The self that is perceived by others has to be sent to be received, and although certainly the "little behavioral warning lights which indicate the place the individual will have in the under-takings to follow" (Goffman 1971:399) are not always viable in cross-cultural situations, the female fieldworker may more or less deliberately play down her sex.

Many of those who have written on the topic of women in the field refer to the emotional needs, anxieties, and tensions that are or may be suffered by women enthographers. Yet it is seldom clear if they are making sex class statements that apply to all women in field situations or if they are making role statements that refer to the disruption of a particular set of cultural or subcultural habits and expectations.

Even Mead, whose analysis is more than usually sensitive to such nuances, is not unambiguous on this point: "where men may chafe under continence enforced by the exigencies of fieldwork, what women miss deeply are strong personal relationships and tenderness. This can be somewhat compensated . . . with babies and small children . . . a resource that male field-workers *who also miss tenderness* can seldom take advantage of . . ." (Mead 1970:323, emphasis added). But where she contrasts the problems of women "who have made a masculine identification in childhood" with those "who have lived their whole lives in intense relationships with others" (Mead 1970: 328-329), she is clearly not talking about male/female sex difference but about masculine/feminine roles.

One last variable that complicates this aspect of the gender/ role question is the company in the field of significant others from the woman fieldworker's own milieu. Whether these are members of a team or members of the nuclear family, and whether they are loved or not, they will affect subjective and objective perceptions of the fieldworker and will alter the material structure of the field situation. The functions of husbands and children in field settings are especially crucial and especially enigmatic. Their effects are personal, idiosyncratic, but they are nonetheless governed by and a part of the total logic of a particular field situation.

I shall pursue some of these points with notes on my own field experience in several different settings. I do not hope to arrive at a formula which will allow us to measure the significance of female sex in and about female enthographers. But by holding the female ethnographer constant, it may be possible to appreciate the extent of our epistemological difficulties. Comparative personal ethnography has been done before, I think explicitly only by women (cf. Fischer 1970; Mead 1970). My justification for this sketchy attempt is that I can act as my own informant.

5. ONE ETHNOGRAPHER × THREE PRESENTATIONS
   OF SELF × N SITUATIONS

Case A (1963) "Our White"

ETHNOGRAPHER. Female, white, aged in late twenties. Middle
class. British. Highly educated. No religion. Mated but not
married. Childless. Unaccompanied.

SETTING. Lesotho, Southern Africa. British (Colonial) Protec-
torate. Small, stark, mountainous country. Population about
700,000. All but 2,000 are Bantu, black. Nearly half the men
absent at any one time to work in white apartheid state of South
Africa which surrounds Lesotho. Women do most of the agricultural tasks and officially head some households.
In the lowland village, 100-odd households, 500-odd people,
wattle and daub huts. Field station one such hut. No piped
water for drinking or sanitation. Little topsoil. No meat. Maize
diet.
Poor subsistence maize farming. School often on alternate days.
Far off. Relatively high literacy for women, not men. A few thin
cows, much cherished. Many thinner dogs. Bark only at whites.
In the administrative center, stretches of tar road, small hos-
pitals, courts, trading stores. The administration (some British,
some Boers, some Basuto) living in varying degrees of sturdy
stone modern house. Smiling black servants. Trees. Gardens
with rich watered lawns. British club. Tennis, bridge, horse
riding, natural science club. Some dedication. Children over
eight away at school in Britain or South Africa. Many sleek,
bounding dogs. Bark only at blacks.

COMBINATION. In both the Basuto village and the British colonial
settings, "whiteness" the most (often) significant characteristic
of the ethnographer.
For the Basuto villagers whiteness meant power, distance, un-
friendliness, wealth, patronage. No vulnerability, commensality,
or physical labor. Stereotype escaped by inappropriate behavior
in these three areas. Crisis when sick in public. Later, not white,
but "our white," not "Madam," but "Miss." Not "Mmè" (mother)

but "Aussie" (big sister). Interaction with men and women. More with women—but more women around. (No sexual overtures, no sexual jokes.)

For the British administration whiteness meant closeness, affinity, solidarity, obligation. Strong objections to white woman moving into, staying in village. Suggestion that standards should be kept by proper food and drink (meat for, cognac after dinner); by living in the center and driving in every day, etc. Distress when advice not taken. Later irritation. Some gossip. A communist? A *kafir boetie?*[8] Countered by male professional associates responding to professional norms and/or the sanctions of gallantry. (Some sexual overtures, no sexual jokes.)

Case B (1971-73) "The Mother of Those Children"

ETHNOGRAPHER: Female, white, aged in late thirties. Middle class. British. Highly educated. No religion. Mated and married. Four children. Accompanied on first excursion by children; on second excursion by husband and children.

SETTING. Small cluster of villages in western Italian Alps. Isolated, sometimes quite cut off in winter. Ancient stone houses. Cold water supply in some. No central heating, no sanitary plumbing except in the house of the priest. Large church with own order of nuns. Very active. Population depleted except in high summer when emigrants return from France to take ancestral air. Old population. Field station in largest village. Ordinary abandoned house. In same village small local school to grade six. Twenty pupils, two classrooms, two teachers. One hotel (summer only), two other bars. Two general shops. Eight television sets, some in public places. Cows, pasture and hay for cows, exercise for cows etc. main economic preoccupations. Men and women herd, hoe, plant, walk, etc. together. Husbands and wives, or brothers and sisters. Even unrelated men and women if one working for the other. Two—maybe three—months exhausting work, the rest of the year in the stalls with the cows for much of the day and, for many, at night. Out of season, some men and some women work in lowlands. For FIAT mostly.

COMBINATION. *First season:* The most significant feature is the sudden arrival of four children. The person with them apparently the mother, although less dark, less like Italians. No father. Maybe a creche come up for the air? Priest finds out there is a father but working away. Also that the family not Catholic. Those poor children. Some effort made to enfold them. Not resisted, successful in some non-verbal externals. For the priest the level of education significant. Because of it he wanted to be friends. But the lack of religion made this problematic: not even a Protestant? Only half a Jew? Problem solved for him by the children who being (all) of mixed race and (some) "foundlings" could be taken as evidence of the true Christian spirit. And *Serietà.* Interaction with men and women possible. (No sexual overtures. No sexual jokes.) Impeded by domestic chores, mud, food-getting, etc. Donations of food for the children offered and accepted. Domestic help not offered. Not asked.
Second season: For the villagers the most significant thing now seems to be that it is the second season. In spite of the difficulties, you brought the children back? *Brava.* Secondarily significant is that this time there is the father whose strange race is accounted for by the children, and whose strange preoccupation (with insects) by education. This research season is longer, but seems physically less hard, socially warmer. The children attend the village school, learn the language, make friends and enemies. Crisis when eldest child mocked at school trying to read in Italian. Local children report event to their parents. Some indifferent, some "wept." The latter now declare themselves our friends, the former make comments about the trials of parenthood. Now interaction with a few couples and families in couples or family groups. (No sexual overtures, a lot of sexual jokes.) Now allowed to work in fields with friends as friends—something which the highly educated (*professori*) cannot do.

It is to me clear that being of the sex class female was in neither of these cases significant *of itself.* Its significance was prescribed and altered by other elements of the situation, with roles played or perceived in particular contexts. The ethnographer was not, in effect, constant in these two cases—most importantly perhaps in the playing of (locally) sex-linked or sex-limited roles. I cannot know what difference it would have made to be in Italy entirely alone, or without a husband on the second trip, nor the way in which domesticity would have affected the ethnographer as subject or as object in the Lesotho case. It seems to have been pertinent, however, that the ethnographer's gender behavior was more "natural" in the Italian than in the Sotho setting, both because English culture is less exotic to northern Italy than to Lesotho, and because the presence of those "others" necessary to sex-linked or sex-limited roles allowed their performance. It may be that the sex class of the ethnographer is less significant to interaction than the (possible?) appropriateness of (her) gender behavior to a particular research setting.

Case C (1965-1974) "The Female Professor"

This case is not strictly comparable, but it is relevant to the general gender/role topic and particularly to the following section. Two settings are involved, one North American, the other European[9] and while I am convinced that the setting is significantly different and alters others' perception of me, I cannot be sure that the third element in the situation, myself, is not also significantly different. These comments are then speculative ethnography. Objectively, the ethnographer remains roughly as before: female, white, aged young-to-middle. Middle class. British. Highly educated. No religion. Mated and married. Accompanied by husband and children.

In the North American context, at the level of interaction, it seems normatively important that one is female (or married female, or married female with young children) and a professor. University colleagues and administrators are proud or distressed about it, but they notice. Some deal with it by joking or avoidance, others by perceptual hlonipha.[10] Although official policy has recently begun to be nondiscriminatory, a female academic is still likely to be perceived as competing on a different hierarchy, for other prizes. It is not said of male professors that they are mated, married, with children: women professors in North America are commonly interviewed about it.

In the European context, there are no protestations of equality or democracy. There are still settings in which women are paid less than men. But not women professors. More important, in European academic contexts there is no joking or avoidance behavior entailed by the sex class of (female) academicians.

The (female) sex attribute seems to have a less limpet-like significance and to create less anxiety in Europe than it does in North America. There are situations whose logic denies it significance, and academic situations are a case in point. This may mean that women *as women* do not constitute a threat in the European professional hierarchy, whatever threat they may present as professors. In (traditional?) European society, whether feminist or anti-feminist, neither men nor women are constrained to *perform* their sex class to the extent that they are in (ideal?) North America. The sex attribute can be assumed. It is not *of itself* a role.

6. THE NORTH AMERICAN PERVERSION: GENDER BEHAVIOR IDEALIZED

Having to this point taken the tack that sex is not a role, and that the assumption that it is has distorted our understanding of sex difference, I shall in this section reverse direction and consider a setting in which it *is* a role. This is the phenomenon which I am calling the North American perversion.

The peculiar epistemology of sex in North American culture is (probably) a product of its history and its consumer technology. Crucial features are shared by other industrial societies; others are unique to, or at least much more pronounced in, industrial North American society. In this sense, North America is the apotheosis of modernity and progress, its "perversion" increasingly normal.

There are two separate and somewhat contradictory statements made about industrial society in regard to the position of women and/or significance of female sex class. The first is that industrialization deprived women of productive/economic roles which they played (and still do play) in nonindustrial, agricultural settings. The second is that industrial countries offer more options to women than do nonindustrial countries, and form the progressive spearhead of sexual equality. Both these statements are true in particular contexts of time and class.

> The process of eliminating women from economically active positions affected different social groups in different ways, as does the complementary process of bringing them back into paid jobs. . . . [But] habits of thought that belong to past phases of these complex developments, and frequently to particular social groups, [have] become established as absolutes in situations where they no longer apply (Myrdal and Klein 1956:1-2).

One such "absolute" is the sex-linking (which is to say the maleness) of many economic roles. This is reflected in legal discrimination and in virtually all Indo-European languages, although of course not all occupational titles are post-nineteenth century, and not all these languages indicate occupational gender to the same extent or in the same way. On the level of action, the extent to which a particular sex-link is perceived as essential to the performance of a particular role varies with class, country, context, etc.

For example, my perceptions of policeman, bus driver, and matador roles have altered palpably and in succession over the last few years—the first two because I have seen women performing them and find it increasingly less anomalous, the last less firmly because only on the basis of a single newspaper article about a successful young Spanish woman matador.[11] I suspect that some part of my perceptual malaise in this case springs from the fact that so "liberated" a creature should exist in *Spain*, but sex class is significant to it because it is the "wrong" one.

It is possible that, when large numbers of women enter the ranks of a profession in which maleness is fundamental to its image as well as to its organization, a different image of the female version will evolve, and a separate organizational hierarchy to match. The formation of separate women's divisions in various police forces, for example, deals with anomalies of gender by forming a new profession instead of converting the old to an asexual or no longer sex-linked form. Significantly, the idealized media versions of female police persons are aggressively feminine.[12]

Another anachronistic "absolute" is the opposition (for women) of the home role and the work role and, by corollary, the methodologically curious inference that women play only two roles. The Myrdal and Klein volume (1956) is actually called *Women's Two Roles: Home and Work.* It seeks to make analyses and recommendations that will demonstrate that these two roles need not be opposed, that both can be played by the same woman—if only at different life stages—and that it is demographically and economically appropriate for this to happen in industrial society. While this study is not the latest or last word on the subject (cf. Sullerot 1971), the dual role model remains popular. Nor is its application confined to industrial society. Analyses of the position of women and the female role in nonindustrial societies are made with the same perceptual framework (LeVine 1966) and distort the significance of sex as much as do models which over-emphasize the sex class of the peasant in relation to power, values, and work.

The North American perversion is related to this point. The inference that follows this dualistic home/work model is that the "home role" is the female bit, the "work role" the nonfemale bit. Females out of the house therefore must work to be female.[13] Their sex is context specific *as a role is.* Change the context and in some sense femaleness is cast in doubt, both for the woman herself, for other women, and for men. To ease anomaly, sex must be *performed* as a role is.

There are a number of ways in which the peculiarity of sex in prototypical North American society has been or can be represented. We may note that there is an opposition to organized day care and other forms of surrogate motherhood quite unwarranted by the evidence of any detrimental effect in the children (cf. Ellmann 1973), and apparently quite unmatched in other cultures. This anxiety is handily attributable to a need to *do* motherhood because it is necessary to demonstrate femaleness.

We may observe that there is an extraordinary importance attached to the secondary characteristic of female sex, the cosmetic aspects of gender. And that what is cosmetic in the consumer society is buyable, achievable. And that when it is bought, achieved, it is (briefly) an index of success. (Only briefly because the culture of consumption must stimulate but never satisfy, and because the body degenerates anyway.)

We may also observe that failure in this area, failure "to be sexy," entails more than economic loss, although that is inevitable: it entails very often an existential crisis—failure as a woman, as a female, as a human being. There is little doubt that aging, particularly for women, is toughest in North America (compare Lessing [1973] with de Beauvoir [1971]).

Segal imputes these anxieties equally to both sex classes in North America, thus laying an emphasis on males. He begins a chapter called "The Solitary Sex" with the statement: "The relationship of American men to American women increasingly astonishes not only foreigners, but Americans themselves" (Segal 1970:46). He attributes these astonishing male/female relationships to "a widespread concern with sexual identity. . . . American parents go in dread of rearing children whom their neighbors will regard as aberrations. . . . [Their] anxiety . . . cannot fail to transmit itself to the children, and not seldom promotes the very condition against which it is directed." Homosexuality is feared, despised—and rampant[14]—and "a sense of strayed sexual purpose" is everyone's lot (Segal 1970:47). Segal's analysis does not pretend to be scientific and may exaggerate the case, but it is irresistibly appropriate to my argument: prototypical North Americans work at achieving, maintaining, demonstrating maleness or femaleness in a way that nobody else does.

In the terminology of this symposium, two things may be said of the North American case. Firstly, in no other setting is sex class a role so much of the time. Secondly, its characteristic difference appears in *gender behavior*—the level of sexual dimorphism intermediate to sex class and role. While the precise extent to which gender behavior is an (innate) function of sex class or is an (imposed) function of culture remains problematic, it is clear that male and female gender behaviors are systematically differentiated in all cultures. "American" gender behavior, however, is characterized by a peculiar compulsion to define, teach, learn, and perform it appropriately.

In this process the mass media of communication must be crucial: they permit these forms to be both idealized and perfectly demonstrated. The correlation is persuasive: the preoccupation with gender behavior in North America is allowed if not entailed by its advanced communication technology. The insights achieved through the analysis of television soap opera[15] and through the dissection of large numbers of pictorial advertisements (Goffman 1978) are striking in this context precisely *because* they are culture bound. Not only would the recording of such elaborated forms of gender behavior be impossible without the camera, they could neither have developed nor been propagated without a prevalence of television sets and popular magazines. Nor, perhaps, would they have their present existential significance in North America.

These speculations suggest that gender behavior becomes increasingly more self-conscious and sex class more like a *role* with each advance in communication technology, and that the rest of the world will follow the "American" lead in this respect as in so many technological others. But whatever path(s) social evolution takes, a one-to-one relationship between technology and social forms is not indicated: the logic of social situations is more complicated and more interesting than that (Wallman 1974b). There is, however, a sense in which "developed" societies *are* more sex class discriminating than the "developing," in which (industrial) Americans are consistently more sex class conscious and perhaps, by corollary, more sex conscious than (nonindustrial) Africans.

While the evidence for this is no more than inferential, the possible reasons for the contrast are important. Special stresses of superurban life have been cited (Morris 1971; Segal 1970) as have the discrepant forms and timing of industrialization, different class structures, and a less sexist division of industrial labor (Myrdal and Klein 1956; Paulme 1971). Very obviously, of course, there is money in the "American" version of sex class consciousness: a striving towards ideal forms is a great spur to the consumerism on which industrial capitalism has been said to depend (Galbraith 1958). But if this relationship between the economic system and sexual differentiation is imputed differently, the contrast between the (industrial) American and the (non-industrial) African versions make more than superficial sense. Thus, the proportional decrease in sex-linked or sex-limited roles allowed by industrial technology is matched by increasing pre-occupation with the details of gender behavior—which is allowed by the same technology. Otherwise put, the blurring of male/female differentiation at one level provokes the sharpening of differentiation at another. In these terms the "American" case is far from perverse.

7. CONCLUSION

I have tried to indicate the ways in which our particular epistemology of sex prevents an understanding of the social systems of ourselves and others by masking variations in the significance of being female, and to demonstrate that this significance in fact varies with technology, setting, class, context, task, rank, race, age, profession, kinship, wealth, and economics —with any or all of the other dimensions of a situation of which it can form only a part. By implication, the importance of distinguishing between females, women, and human-beings-who-happen-to-be-female and/or women is underlined: our epistemological difficulties also distort the facts of sex differentiation.

At the level of observation, the general conclusions are all rather obvious. They are nonetheless vital to any consideration of female groups, female hierarchies, female difference. First, the plain presence of a number of female people together does not constitute a group of women playing a (the) woman's role. Second, a hierarchy of human females may be ranked on grounds related neither to sex nor sexuality. Third, women appearing in a heterosexual hierarchy may or may not have different roles from men in the same hierarchy; sex class may or may not be pertinent to the ranking. Fourth, the assertion that a group of eight men is necessarily different from a group of seven men and one woman is only true at the level of sex class (cf. Banton 1965:51), as is the assertion that "a cluster of females" is other than "a group of people." And last, the behavior of a female person is not invariably perceived as gender behavior, nor is it necessarily a function of sex class.

But we are here concerned with identifying and accounting for any systematic differences between the behaviors of women and of men, resisting the tendency to treat social and biological explanations in mutually exclusive frames. A conventional evolutionary inference is therefore drawn to relate biological and social differentiation between the sexes and to account for contradictions at the level of situation.

Two propositions about the human species can be stated with reasonable confidence. The first is that biological differences between males and females are immutable insofar as they are essential to the reproduction and so the survival of the species. The second is that man makes culture—which is to say that human behavior is uniquely flexible, that "it is natural for man to be unnatural" (Fox 1973:47). As an animal there are a limited number of things he can and must do; as a *cultural* animal "he can vary enormously the way in which he does them" (Fox 1973:48).

The human genetic blueprint entails that the sexes are biologically different and that they are systematically differentiated. Behavioral distinctions between men and women are therefore drawn in all social systems but (the species being flexible and adaptive) they are drawn very differently from one system to another. Each social system has evolved/is evolving its particular pattern of sex differentiation—by task allocation, behavioral style, perception of difference, etc. But an ideal pattern is not always feasible and may not even be normal: the exigencies of situations quite commonly entail an other-than-ideal performance. Any systematic pattern is therefore, by the same ingenuity, made potentially flexible. Hence, it is not inappropriate for normal males to perform tasks normally defined as female or for normal females to behave in a masculine manner (in the terms of any one society) *where the logic of the situation demands it.*

This logic is not idiosyncratic. "Anti-sexual" behavior will be neither aberrant nor abhorrent where a context of exigency is agreed between the actor and any observer. Where the premises of exigency are socially prescribed, it is likely that a "wrong" performance will be signalled and so explained by some symbolic formula (like the Arab woman's use of the small boy's hand, or the ceremony of "woman marriage", etc.). Likewise, it may be that the common and comfortable definition of such a situation is not possible without one (as the case of the female professor).

I can only conclude that male and female behavior will be systematically differentiated (in any one society) and/but that the behavior of women and men (in that society) will not invariably take the "proper" form. This epistemological bind is compounded by elaborations and compensations of (gender) behavior invented to cover exigencies that we may not have recognized to begin with, and by the absurdly difficult need to know the context to which a particular item pertains.

NOTES

[1] Ortner (1974) has analyzed an important aspect of this confusion. See also Gellner's (1973b) handling of the same problem in relation to a different topic.

[2] In ordinary English usage, "sex" denotes "sexual activity" more often than it does "sex class." Throughout this essay it is used in the latter sense.

[3] See Gellner (1973a) and Tiger (1970) for discussions of the moral and historical factors. Fox (1973:311-349) deals with the implications.

[4] *Woman marriage* has been defined as "a custom whereby a woman may go through a rite of marriage with another woman and thereby she stands in the place of a father (*pater*) to the offspring of the wife, whose physical father (*genitor*) is an assigned lover" (Radcliffe-Brown and Forde 1962:4).

[5] It is sometimes argued that the same applies to kinship and age criteria. This is not so. Kinship ties—kin class—may be ignored, avoided, or denied in any kind of society, depending on the logic of a particular situation involving kinsmen; their significance is actually very fluid (Wallman 1974b). Age categories are probably firmer—but very obviously not for individuals, only for social systems. At the level of individuals, only the sex attribute is irrevocable.

[6] This example was given to me by Dr. Marilou Creyghton of the University of Amsterdam. It is based on her own field observations.

[7] In this context it occurs to me to wonder whether, in societies where menstruation is considered polluting or ritually dangerous,

any community interest is taken in the menstrual cycle of foreign women fieldworkers. The form or absence of such interest might be an indicator of the perceived significance of the fieldworker's sex. I have not seen such information reported anywhere, but it is not possible to say whether it is not reported out of modesty, or because the matter never arose. In my own case, the matter has never arisen.

[8] *Kafir boetie,* literally translated, is Afrikaans for "little brother of the Kafir," the South African equivalent of "nigger lover" in the United States.

[9] The first is the University of Toronto, the second the University of Amsterdam. I am indebted to both these institutions for the opportunity to make these observations and for secretarial help in successive stages of this paper.

[10] *Hlonipha* is a Zulu term referring to a woman's obligation to avoid the use of words containing syllables appearing in the name of her father-in-law.

[11] "Taking the bull by the horns in the name of women's lib," which appeared in *The Times* (London), December 5, 1973.

[12] Two serial dramas on American television—"Policewoman" (NBC) and "Get Christie Love" (ABC)—are indicative. So too is the item "Police Drama: Women are on the case" and its appearance in *Ms* magazine (October 1974:104 and 108).

[13] They must also work to keep their men from being unmanned by the move (see Sullerot 1971; Segal 1970; and Morris 1971:87-101). A non-American male associate has observed that the corresponding anxiety besets the North American male in the female domain. Hence, the work role is the male bit, the home role the nonmale and therefore potentially threatening bit.

[14] Clearly there is homosexuality elsewhere too, perhaps even in greater percentage numbers than in North America. The point is that nowhere in the modern world does it generate the same anxiety.

[15] These are the product of a seminar, "Culture and Communication," convened by T.F.S. McFeat in the Department of Anthropology, University of Toronto. They have not yet been published but were reported to me in a personal communication.

REFERENCES CITED

ARDENER, EDWIN
    1972—Belief and the Problem of Women. In *The Interpretation of Ritual: Essays in Honour of A.I. Richards,* J.S. La Fontaine, ed. London:Tavistock.

ASWAD, BARBARA
1967—Key Roles of Noble Women in a Middle-Eastern Plains Village. *Anthropological Quarterly* 40(1):139-152.

BAILEY, F.G.
1969—*Stratagems and Spoils*. Oxford:Blackwell.

BANTON, M.
1965—*Roles*. London:Tavistock.

BENEDICT, BURTON
1969—Role Analysis in Animals and Man. *Man* 4(2):203-214.

BOWEN, E.S.
1954—*Return to Laughter*. New York:Harper and Row.

CARO BAROJA, JULIO
1966—Honour and Shame: A Historical Account of Several Conflicts. In *Honour and Shame: The Values of Mediterranean Society*, J.G. Peristiany, ed. London:Weidenfeld and Nicolson.

DE BEAUVOIR, SIMONE
1971—The Age of Discretion. In *The Woman Destroyed*, Simone de Beauvoir. London:Fontana/Collins. (Translated by P. O'Brien.)

ELLMANN, M.
1973—Women's Work. *New York Review*, Nov. 1:18-19.

FIRTH, RAYMOND
1939—*Primitive Polynesian Economy*. London:George Routledge.
1951—*Elements of Social Organisation*. London:Watts.
1972—The Sceptical Anthropologist?: Social Anthropology and Marxist Views on Society. *Proceedings of the British Academy* 58. London:Oxford University Press.

FISCHER, ANN
1970—Field Work in Five Cultures. In *Women in the Field*, Peggy Golde, ed. Chicago:Aldine.

FOX, ROBIN
1973—*Encounter with Anthropology*. New York:Harcourt Brace Jovanovich.

FRIEDL, E.
1967—The Position of Women: Appearance and Reality. *Anthropological Quarterly* 40(1):97-108.

GELLNER, ERNEST
1973a-Concepts and Society. In *Cause and Meaning in the Social Sciences*, Joseph Agassi and I.C. Jarvie, eds. London:Routledge and Kegan Paul.
1973b-Nature and Society in Social Anthropology. In *Cause and*

Meaning in the Social Sciences, Joseph Agassi and I.C. Jarvie, eds. London:Routledge and Kegan Paul.

GOFFMAN, ERVING
1959—*The Presentation of Self in Everyday Life.* New York: Doubleday.

1968—*Stigma.* Middlesex, England:Penguin.

1971—*Relations in Public.* New York:Basic Books.

1978—Gender Display. In *Female Hierarchies,* Lionel Tiger and Heather T. Fowler, eds. Chicago:Aldine.

GOLDE, PEGGY, ed.
1970—*Women in the Field.* Chicago:Aldine.

JARVIE, I.C.
1964—*The Revolution in Anthropology.* London:Routledge and Kegan Paul.

1972—*Concepts and Society.* London:Routledge and Kegan Paul.

LEACH, EDMUND
1966—Virgin Birth. *Proceedings of the Royal Anthropological Institute,* pp. 39-49.

LEBEUF, ANNIE M.D.
1971—The Role of Women in the Political Organization of African Societies. In *Women of Tropical Africa,* Denise Paulme, ed. Berkeley:University of California Press. (Translated by H.M. Wright.)

LESSING, DORIS
1973—*The Summer Before the Dark.* London:Jonathan Cape.

LEVINE, R.A.
1966—Sex Roles and Economic Change in Africa. *Ethnology* 5:186-193.

MARSHALL, GLORIA
1970—In a World of Women: Field Work in a Yoruba Community. In *Women in the Field,* Peggy Golde, ed. Chicago:Aldine.

MEAD, MARGARET
1949—*Male and Female: A Study of the Sexes in a Changing World.* New York:Morrow.

1970—Field Work in the Pacific Islands 1925-1967. In *Women in the Field,* Peggy Golde, ed. Chicago:Aldine.

MORRIS, DESMOND
1971—*The Human Zoo.* New York:Dell.

MYRDAL, ALVA and VIOLA KLEIN
1956—*Women's Two Roles: At Home and Work.* London:Routledge and Kegan Paul.

NADEL, S.F.
　1957—*The Theory of Social Structure*. Glencoe, Ill.:Free Press.
ORTNER, SHERRY B.
　1974—Is Female to Male as Nature is to Culture? In *Woman, Culture, and Society*, Michelle Z. Rosaldo and Louise Lamphere, eds. Stanford:Stanford University Press.
PAULME, DENISE, ed.
　1971—*Women of Tropical Africa*. Berkeley:University of California Press. (Translated by H. M. Wright.)
PERISTIANY, J.G., ed.
　1966—*Honour and Shame: The Values of Mediterranean Society*. London:Weidenfeld and Nicolson.
PITT-RIVERS, J.
　1966—Honour and Social Status. In *Honour and Shame: The Values of Mediterranean Society*, J. Peristiany, ed. London: Weidenfeld and Nicolson.
POPPER, KARL
　1959—*The Logic of Scientific Discovery*. London:Hutchinson.
　1965—The Unity of Method in the Natural and Social Sciences. In *Philosophical Problems in the Social Sciences*, David Braybrooke, ed. New York:Macmillan.
　1972—*Objective Knowledge: An Evolutionary Approach*. Oxford: Clarendon.
POWDERMAKER, H.
　1967—*Stranger and Friend*. London:Secker and Warburg.
RADCLIFFE-BROWN, A.R. and DARYLL FORDE, eds.
　1962—*African Systems of Kinship and Marriage*. International African Institute Series. London:Oxford University Press.
RICHARDS, A.I.
　1939—*Land, Labour, and Diet in Northern Rhodesia: An Economic Study of the Bemba Tribe*. International African Institute Series. London:Oxford University Press.
RIEGELHAUPT, JOYCE
　1967—Portuguese Peasant Women: Informal and Formal Political and Economic Roles. *Anthropological Quarterly* 40(1): 109-126.
SCHAPERA, I., ed.
　1937—*The Bantu Speaking Tribes of South Africa*. London:Routledge and Kegan Paul.
SCHNEIDER, JANE
　1970—Of Vigilance and Virgins: Honour, Shame, and Access to Resources in Mediterranean Societies. *Ethnology* 10(1): 1-24.

SEGAL, RONALD
1970—*America's Receding Future*. Middlesex, England:Pelican.
SILVERMAN, SYDEL
1967—The Life Crises as a Clue to Social Function. *Anthropological Quarterly* 40(1):127-138.
SULLEROT, EVELYNE
1971—*Woman, Society, and Change*. New York:McGraw-Hill. (Translated by Margaret S. Archer.)
TIGER, LIONEL
1970—*Men in Groups*. New York:Random House.
WALLMAN, SANDRA
1969—*Take Out Hunger: Two Case Studies of Rural Development in Basutoland*. London School of Economics Monographs on Social Anthropology Series. London:Athlone.
1974a-Status and the Innovator. In *Choice and Change: Essays in Honour of Lucy Mair*, John Davis, ed. London School of Economics Monographs on Social Anthropology Series 50. London:Athlone.
1974b-Kinship, A-Kinship, Anti-Kinship. In *The Compact: Selected Dimensions of Friendship*, Elliott Leyton, ed. Newfoundland: Memorial University, Institute for Social and Economic Research.
WARD, BARBARA
1966—Sociological Self-Awareness: Some Uses of the Conscious Model. *Man* 1(2):201-215.

2

Gender Display

ERVING GOFFMAN

I

Take it that the function of ceremony reaches in two directions, the affirmation of basic social arrangements and the presentation of ultimate doctrines about man and the world. Typically these celebrations are performed either by persons acting to one another or acting in concert before a congregation. So "social situations" are involved—defining these simply as physical arenas anywhere within which persons present are in perceptual range of one another, subject to mutual monitoring—the persons themselves being definable solely on this ground as a "gathering."

It is in social situations, then, that materials for celebrative work must be found, materials which can be shaped into a palpable representation of matters not otherwise packaged for the eye and the ear and the moment. And found they are. The divisions and hierarchies of social structure are depicted microecologically, that is, through the use of small-scale spatial metaphors. Mythic historic events are played through in a condensed and idealized version. Apparent junctures or turning points in life are solemnized, as in christenings, graduation exercises, marriage ceremonies, and funerals. Social relationships are addressed by greetings and farewells. Seasonal cycles are given dramatized boundaries. Reunions are held. Annual vacations and, on a lesser scale, outings on weekends and evenings are assayed, bringing immersion in ideal settings. Dinners and parties are given, becoming occasions for the expenditure of resources at a rate that is above one's mundane self. Moments of festivity are attached to the acquisition of new possessions.

In all of these ways, a situated social fuss is made over what might ordinarily be hidden in extended courses of activity and the unformulated experience of their participants; in brief, the individual is given an opportunity to face directly a representation, a somewhat iconic expression, a mock-up of what he is supposed to hold dear, a presentation of the supposed ordering of his existence.

A single, fixed element of a ceremony can be called a "ritual"; the interpersonal kind can be defined as perfunctory, conventionalized acts through which one individual portrays his regard for another to that other.

II

If Durkheim leads us to consider one sense of the term ritualization, Darwin, in his *Expression of Emotion in Man and Animals,* leads us, coincidentally, to consider quite another. To paraphrase Julian Huxley (and the ethological position), the basic argument is that under the pressure of natural selection certain emotionally motivated behaviors become formalized—in the sense of becoming simplified, exaggerated, and stereotyped—and loosened from any specific context of releasers, and all this so that, in effect, there will be more efficient signalling, both inter- and intra-specifically (Huxley 1966:250). These behaviors are "displays," a species-utilitarian notion that is at the heart of the ethological conception of communication. Instead of having to play out an act, the animal, in effect, provides a readily readable expression of his situation, specifically his intent, this taking the form of a "ritualization" of some portion of the act itself, and this indication (whether promise or threat) presumably allows for the negotiation of an efficient response from, and to, witnesses of the display. (If Darwin leads here, John Dewey, and G.H. Mead are not far behind.)

The ethological concern, then, does not take us back from a ritual performance to the social structure and ultimate beliefs in which the performer and witness are embedded, but forward into the unfolding course of socially situated events. Displays thus provide evidence of the actor's *alignment* in a gathering, the position he seems prepared to take up in what is about to happen in the social situation. Alignments tentatively or indicatively establish the terms of the contact, the mode or style or formula for the dealings that are to ensue among the individuals in the situation. As suggested, ethologists tend to use the term communication here, but that might be loose talk. Displays don't communicate in the narrow sense of the term; they don't enunciate something through a language of symbols openly established and used solely for that purpose. They provide evidence of the actor's alignment in the situation. And displays are important insofar as alignments are.

A version of display for humans would go something like this: Assume all of an individual's behavior and appearance informs those who witness him, minimally telling them something about his social identity, about his mood, intent, and expectations, and about the state of his relation to them. In every culture a distinctive range of this indicative behavior and appearance becomes specialized so as to more routinely and perhaps more effectively perform this informing function, the informing coming to be the controlling role of the performance, although often not avowedly so. One can call these indicative events displays. As suggested, they tentatively establish the terms of the contact, the mode or style or formula for the dealings that are to ensue between the persons providing the display and the persons perceiving it.

Finally, our special concern: If gender be defined as the culturally established correlates of sex (whether in consequence of biology or learning), then gender displays refers to conventionalized portrayals of these correlates.

III

What can be said about the structure of ritual-like displays?

1) Displays very often have a dialogic character of a statement-reply kind, with an expression on the part of one individual calling forth an expression on the part of another, the latter expression being understood to be a response to the first.

These statement-response pairs can be classified in an obvious way. There are symmetrical and asymmetrical pairs: mutual first-naming is a symmetrical pair, first-name/sir is an asymmetrical one. Of asymmetrical pairs, some are dyadically reversible, some not: the greetings between guest and host, asymmetrical in themselves, may be reversed between these two persons on another occasion; first-name/title, on the other hand, ordinarily is not reversible. Of dyadically irreversible pairs of rituals, some pair parts are exclusive, some not: the civilian title a male may extend a female is never extended to him; on the other hand, the "Sir" a man receives from a subordinate in exchange for first-name, he himself is likely to extend to *his* superordinate in exchange for first-name, an illustration of the great chain of corporate being.

Observe that a symmetrical display between two individuals can involve asymmetries according to which of the two initially introduced the usage between them, and which of the two begins his part of the mutual display first on any occasion of use.

And symmetry (or asymmetry) itself can be misleading. One must consider not only how two individuals ritually treat each other, but also how they separately treat, and are treated by, a common third. Thus the point about symmetrical greetings and farewells extended between a male and a close female friend is that he is very likely to extend a *different* set, albeit equally symmetrical, to her husband, and she, similarly, a yet different symmetrical set to his wife. Indeed, so deeply does the male-female difference inform our ceremonial life that one finds here a very systematic "opposite number" arrangement. For every courtesy, symmetrical or asymmetrical, that a woman shows to almost anyone, there will be a parallel one—seen to be the same, yet different—which her brother or husband shows to the same person.

2) Given that individuals have work to do in social situations, the question arises as to how ritual can accommodate to what is thus otherwise occurring. Two basic patterns seem to appear. First, display seems to be concentrated at beginnings and endings of purposeful understandings, that is, at junctures, so that, in effect, the activity itself is not interfered with. (Thus the small courtesies sometimes performed in our society by men to women when the latter must undergo what can be defined as a slight change in physical state, as in getting up, sitting down, entering a room or leaving it, beginning to smoke or ceasing to, moving indoors or outdoors, suffering increased temperature or less, and so forth.) Here one might speak of "bracket rituals." Second, some rituals seem designed to be continued as a single note across a strip of otherwise intended activity without displacing that activity itself. (Thus the basic military courtesy of standing at attention throughout the course of an encounter with a superior—in contrast to the salute, this latter clearly a bracket ritual.) One can speak here of a "ritual transfix" or "overlay." Observe that by combining these two locations—brackets and overlays—one has, for any strip of activity, a *schedule* of displays. Although these rituals will tend to be perceived as coloring the whole of the scene, in fact, of course, they only occur selectively in it.

3) It is plain that if an individual is to give and receive what is considered his ritual due in social situations, then he must—whether by intent or in effect—style himself so that others present can immediately know the social (and sometimes the personal) identity of he who is to be dealt with; and in turn he must be able to acquire this information about those he thus informs. Some displays seem to be specialized for this identificatory, early-warning function: in the case of gender, hair style, clothing, and tone of voice. (Handwriting similarly serves in the situation-like contacts conducted through the mails; name also so serves, in addition to serving in the management of persons who are present only in reference.) It can be argued that although

ritualized behavior in social situations may markedly change over time, especially in connection with politicization, identificatory stylings will be least subject to change.

4) There is no doubt that displays can be, and are likely to be, multivocal or polysemic, in the sense that more than one piece of social information may be encoded in them. (For example, our terms of address typically record sex of recipient and also properties of the relationship between speaker and spoken to. So, too, in occupational titles ["agentives"]. In the principal European languages, typically a masculine form is the unmarked case; the feminine is managed with a suffix which, in addition, often carries a connotation of incompetence, facetiousness, and inexperience.[1]) Along with this complication goes another. Not only does one find that recognition of different statuses can be encoded in the same display, but also that a hierarchy of considerations may be found which are addressed sequentially. For example, when awards are given out, a male official may first give the medal, diploma, prize, or whatever, and then shake the hand of the recipient, thus shifting from that of an organization's representative bestowing an official sign of regard on a soldier, colleague, fellow citizen, etc., to a man showing regard for another, the shift in action associated with a sharply altered facial expression. This seems nicely confirmed when the recipient is a woman. For then the second display can be a social kiss. When Admiral Elmo R. Zumwalt, then chief of U.S. naval operations, officiated in the ceremony in which Alene Duerk became the first female admiral in the U.S. Navy's history (as director of the Navy Nurse Corps), he added to what was done by kissing her full on the lips (*International Herald Tribune* 1972). So, too, a female harpist after just completing Ginastera's Harp Concerto, and having just shaken the hand of the conductor (as would a male soloist), is free (as a male is not) to strike an additional note by leaning over and giving the conductor a kiss on the cheek. Similarly, the applause she receives will be her due as a musician, but the flowers that are brought onstage a moment after speak to something that would not be spoken to in a male soloist. And the reverse sequence is possible. I have seen a well-bred father raise his hat on first meeting his

daughter after a two-year absence, *then* bend and kiss her. (The hat-raise denoted the relationship between the sexes—presumably "any lady" would have induced it—the kiss, the relationship between kin.)

5) Displays vary quite considerably in the degree of their formalization. Some, like salutes, are specified as to form and occasion of occurrence, and failure to so behave can lead to specific sanctions; others are so much taken for granted that it awaits a student of some kind to explicate what everyone knows (but not consciously), and failure to perform leads to nothing more than diffuse unease and a search for speakable reasons to be ill-tempered with the offender.

6) The kind of displays I will be concerned with—gender displays—have a related feature: their apparent optionality. In the case, for example, of male courtesies, often a particular display need not be initiated; if initiated, it need not be accepted, but can be politely declined. Finally, when failure to perform occurs, irony, nudging, and joking complaint, etc., can result—sometimes more as an opportunity for a sally than as a means of social control. Correlated with this basis of looseness is another: for each display there is likely to be a set of functional equivalents wherewith something of the display's effect can be accomplished by alternative niceties. At work, too, is the very process of ritualization. A recipient who declines an incipient gesture of deference has waited until the intending giver has shown his desire to perform it; the more the latter can come to count on this foreclosure of his move, the more his show of intent can itself come to displace the unfolded form.

7) Ordinarily displays do not in fact provide a representation in the round of a specific social relationship but rather of broad groupings of them. For example, a social kiss may be employed by kin-related persons or cross-sex friends, and the details of the behavior itself may not inform as to which relationship is being celebrated. Similarly, precedence through a door is available to mark organizational rank, but the same indulgence is accorded guests of an establishment, the dependently young, the aged and infirm, indeed, those of unquestionably strong social position and

those (by inversion courtesy) of unquestionably weak position. A picture, then, of the relationship between any two persons can hardly be obtained through an examination of the displays they extend each other on any one type of occasion; one would have to assemble these niceties across all the mutually identifying types of contacts that the pair has.

There is a loose gearing, then, between social structures and what goes on in particular occasions of ritual expression. This can further be seen by examining the abstract ordinal format which is commonly generated within social situations. Participants, for example, are often displayed in rankable order with respect to some visible property—looks, height, elevation, closeness to the center, elaborateness of costume, temporal precedence, and so forth—and the comparisons are somehow taken as a reminder of differential social position, the differences in social distance between various positions and the specific character of the positions being lost from view. Thus, the basic forms of deference provide a peculiarly limited version of the social universe, telling us more, perhaps, about the special depictive resources of social situations than about the structures presumably expressed thereby.

8) People, unlike other animals, can be quite conscious of the displays they employ and are able to perform many of them by design in contexts of their own choosing. Thus instead of merely "displacing" an act (in the sense described by ethologists), the human actor may wait until he is out of the direct line of sight of a putative recipient, and then engage in a portrayal of attitude to him that is only then safe to perform, the performance done for the benefit of the performer himself or third parties. In turn, the recipient of such a display (or rather the target of it) may actively collaborate, fostering the impression that the act has escaped him even though it hasn't—and sometimes evidentially so. (There is the paradox, then, that what is done for revealment can be partially concealed.) More important, once a display becomes well established in a particular sequence of actions, a section of the sequence can be lifted out of its original context, parenthesized, and used in a quotative way, a postural

resource for mimicry, mockery, irony, teasing, and other sportive intents, including, very commonly, the depiction of make-believe scenes in advertisements. Here stylization itself becomes an object of attention, the actor providing a comment on this process in the very act through which he unseriously realizes it. What was a ritual becomes itself ritualized, a transformation of what is already a transformation, a "hyper-ritualization." Thus, the human use of displays is complicated by the human capacity for reframing behavior.

In sum, then, how a relationship is portrayed through ritual can provide an imbalanced, even distorted, view of the relationship itself. When this fact is seen in the light of another, namely, that displays tend to be scheduled accommodatively during an activity so as not to interfere with its execution, it becomes even more clear that the version ritual gives us of social reality is only that—not a picture of the way things are but a passing exhortative guide to perception.

IV

Displays are part of what we think of as "expressive behavior," and as such tend to be conveyed and received as if they were somehow natural, deriving, like temperature and pulse, from the way people are and needful, therefore, of no social or historical analysis. But, of course, ritualized expressions are as needful of historical understanding as is the Ford car. Given the expressive practices we employ, one may ask: Where do these displays come from?

If, in particular, there are behavioral styles—codings—that distinguish the way men and women participate in social situations, then the question should be put concerning the origins and sources of these styles. The materials and ingredients can come directly from the resources available in particular social settings, but that still leaves open the question of where the formulating of these ingredients, their *styling*, comes from.

The most prominent account of the origins of our gender displays is, of course, the biological. Gender is assumed to be an extension of our animal natures, and just as animals express their sex, so does man: innate elements are said to account for the behavior in both cases. And indeed, the means by which we initially establish an individual in one of the two sex classes and confirm this location in its later years can be and are used as a means of placement in the management of domestic animals. However, although the signs for establishing placement are expressive of matters biological, why we should think of these matters as essential and central is a cultural matter. More important, where behavioral gender display does draw on animal life, it seems to do so not, or not merely, in a direct evolutionary sense but as a source of imagery—a cultural resource. The animal kingdom—or at least certain select parts of it—provides us (I argue) with mimetic models for gender display, not necessarily phylogenetic ones. Thus, in Western society, the dog has served us as an ultimate model of fawning, of bristling, and (with baring of fangs) of threatening; the horse a model, to be sure, of physical strength, but of little that is interpersonal and interactional.[2]

Once one sees that animal life, and lore concerning that life, provides a cultural source of imagery for gender display, the way is open to examine other sources of display imagery, but now models for mimicry that are closer to home. Of considerable significance, for example, is the complex associated with European court life and the doctrines of the gentleman, especially as these came to be incorporated (and modified) in military etiquette. Although the force of this style is perhaps declining, it was, I think, of very real importance until the second World War, especially in British influenced countries and especially, of course, in dealings between males. For example, the standing-at-attention posture as a means of expressing being on call, the "Sir" response, and even the salute, became part of the deference style far beyond scenes from military life.

For our purposes, there is a source of display much more relevant than animal lore or military tradition, a source closer to home, a source, indeed, right in the home: the parent-child relationship.

V

The parent-child complex—taken in its ideal middle-class version—has some very special features when considered as a source of behavioral imagery. First, most persons end up having been children cared for by parents and/or elder sibs, and as parents (or elder sibs) in the reverse position. So both sexes experience both roles—a sex-free resource. (The person playing the role opposite the child is a mother or older sister as much or more than a father or elder brother. Half of those in the child role will be male, and the housewife role, the one we used to think was ideally suitable for females, contains lots of parental elements.) Second, given inheritance and residence patterns, parents are the only authority in our society that can rightly be said to be both temporary and exerted "in the best interests" of those subordinated thereby. To speak here—at least in our Western society—of the child giving something of equivalence in exchange for the rearing that he gets is ludicrous. There is no appreciable quid pro quo. Balance lies elsewhere. What is received in one generation is given in the next. It should be added that this important unselfseeking possibility has been much neglected by students of society. The established imagery is economic and Hobbesian, turning on the notion of social exchange, and the newer voices have been concerned to show how parental authority can be misguided, oppressive, and ineffective.

Now I want to argue that parent-child dealings carry special value as a means of orienting the student to the significance of social situations as a unit of social organization. For a great deal of what a child is privileged to do and a great deal of what he must suffer his parents doing on his behalf pertains to how adults in our society come to manage themselves in social situations. Surprisingly the key issue becomes this: *What mode of handling ourselves do we employ in social situations as our means of demonstrating respectful orientation to them and of maintaining guardedness within them?*

It might be useful, then, to outline schematically the ideal middle-class parent-child relationship, limiting this to what can occur when a child and parent are present in the same social situation.

It seems to be assumed that the child comes to a social situation with all its "basic" needs satisfied and/or provided for, and that there is no good reason why he himself should be planning and thinking very far into the future. It is as though the child were on holiday.

There is what might be called orientation license. The child is tolerated in his drifting from the situation into aways, fugues, brown studies, and the like. There is license to flood out, as in dissolving into tears, capsizing into laughter, bursting into glee, and the like.

Related to this license is another, namely, the use of patently ineffective means to effect an end, the means expressing a desire to escape, cope, etc., but not possibly achieving its end. One example is the child's hiding in or behind parents, or (in its more attenuated form) behind his own hand, thereby cutting his eyes off from any threat but not the part of him that is threatened. Another is "pummeling," the kind of attack which is a half-serious joke, a use of considerable force but against an adversary that one knows to be impervious to such an effort, so that what starts with an instrumental effort ends up an admittedly defeated gesture. In all of this one has nice examples of ritualization in the classical ethological sense. And an analysis of what it is to act childishly.

Next, protective intercession by parents. High things, intricate things, heavy things, are obtained for the child. Dangerous things—chemical, electrical, mechanical—are kept from him. Breakable things are managed for him. Contacts with the adult world are mediated, providing a buffer between the child and surrounding persons. Adults who are present generally modulate talk that must deal with harsh things of this world: discussion of business, money, and sex is censored; cursing is inhibited; gossip diluted.

There are indulgence priorities: precedence through doors and onto life rafts is given the child; if there are sweets to distribute, he gets them first.

There is the notion of the erasability of offense. Having done something wrong, the child merely cries and otherwise shows contrition, after which he can begin afresh as though the slate had been washed clean. His immediate emotional response to being called to task need only be full enough and it will be taken as final payment for the delict. He can also assume that love will not be discontinued because of what he has done, providing only that he shows how broken up he is because of doing it.

There is an obvious generalization behind all these forms of license and privilege. A loving protector is standing by in the wings, allowing not so much for dependency as a copping out of, or relief from, the "realities," that is, the necessities and constraints to which adults in social situations are subject. In the deepest sense, then, middle-class children are not engaged in adjusting to and adapting to social situations, but in practicing, trying out, or playing at these efforts. Reality for them is deeply forgiving.

Note, if a child is to be able to call upon these various reliefs from realities, then, of course, he must stay within range of a distress cry, or within view—scamper-back distance. And, of course, in all of this, parents are provided scenes in which they can act out their parenthood.

You will note that there is an obvious price that the child must pay for being saved from seriousness.

He is subjected to control by physical fiat and to commands serving as a lively reminder thereof: forced rescues from oncoming traffic and from potential falls; forced care, as when his coat is buttoned and mittens pulled on against his protest. In general, the child's doings are unceremoniously interrupted under warrant of ensuring that they are executed safely.

He is subjected to various forms of nonperson treatment. He is talked past and talked about as though absent. Gestures of affection and attention are performed "directly," without engaging him in verbal interaction through the same acts. Teasing and taunting occur, dealings which start out involving the child as a coparticipant in talk and end up treating him merely as a target of attention.

His inward thoughts, feelings, and recollections are not treated as though he had informational rights in their disclosure. He can be queried on contact about his desires and intent, his aches and pains, his resentments and gratitude, in short, his subjective situation, but he cannot go very far in reciprocating this sympathetic curiosity without being thought intrusive.

Finally, the child's time and territory may be seen as expendable. He may be sent on errands or to fetch something in spite of what he is doing at the time; he may be caused to give up territorial prerogatives because of the needs of adults.

Now note that an important feature of the child's situation in life is that the way his parents interact with him tends to be employed to him by other adults also, extending to nonparental kinsmen, acquainted nonkin, and even to adults with whom he is unacquainted. (It is as though the world were in the military uniform of one army, and all adults were its officers.) Thus a child in patent need provides an unacquainted adult a right and even an obligation to offer help, providing only that no other close adult seems to be in charge.

Given this parent-child complex as a common fund of experience, it seems we draw on it in a fundamental way in adult social gatherings. The invocation through ritualistic expression of this hierarchical complex seems to cast a spate of face-to-face interaction in what is taken as no-contest terms, warmed by a touch of relatedness; in short, benign control. The superordinate gives something gratis out of supportive identification, and the subordinate responds with an outright display of gratitude, and if not that, then at least an implied submission to the relationship and the definition of the situation it sustains.

One afternoon an officer was given a call for illegal parking in a commercial area well off his sector. He was fairly new in the district, and it took him a while to find the address. When he arrived he saw a car parked in an obviously dangerous and illegal manner at the corner of a small street. He took out his ticket book and wrote it up. As he was placing the ticket on the car, a man came out of the store on the corner. He approached and asked whether the officer had come in answer to his call. When the patrolman said that he had, the man replied that the car which had been bothering him had already left and he hoped the patrolman was not going to tag his car. "Hey, I'm sorry, *pal* but it's already written."

"I expected Officer Reno, he's usually on 6515 car. I'd appreciate it, Officer, if next time you would stop in before you write them up." The patrolman was slightly confused. . . .

He said politely and frankly, "Mister, how would it look if I went into every store before I wrote up a ticket and asked if it was all right? What would people think I was doing?" The man shrugged his shoulders and smiled. "You're right, son. O.K., forget it. Listen stop in sometime if I can help you with something." He patted the patrolman on the shoulder and returned to his business (Rubinstein 1973:161-162).

Or the subordinate initiates a sign of helplessness and need, and the superordinate responds with a volunteered service. A *Time* magazine story on female police might be cited as an illustration:

Those [policewomen] who are there already have provided a devastating new weapon to the police crime-fighting arsenal, one that has helped women to get their men for centuries. It worked well for diminutive Patrolwoman Ina Sheperd after she collared a muscular shoplifter in Miami last December and discovered that there were no other cops—or even a telephone—around. Unable to summon help, she burst into tears. "If I don't bring you in, I'll lose my job," she sobbed to her prisoner, who chivalrously accompanied her until a squad car could be found (1972:60).[3]

It turns out, then, that in our society whenever a male has dealings with a female or a subordinate male (especially a younger one), some mitigation of potential distance, coercion, and hostility is quite likely to be induced by application of the parent-child complex. Which implies that, ritually speaking, females are equivalent to subordinate males and both are equivalent to children. Observe that however distasteful and humiliating lessers may find these gentle prerogatives to be, they must give second thought to openly expressing displeasure, for whosoever extends benign concern is free to quickly change his tack and show the other side of his power.

VI

Allow here a brief review. Social situations were defined as arenas of mutual monitoring. It is possible for the student to take social situations very seriously as one natural vantage point from which to view all of social life. After all, it is in social situations that individuals can communicate in the fullest sense of the term, and it is only in them that individuals can physically coerce one another, assault one another, interact sexually, importune one another gesturally, give physical comfort, and so forth. Moreover, it is in social situations that most of the world's work gets done. Understandably, in all societies modes of adaptation are found, including systems of normative constraint, for managing the risks and opportunities specific to social situations.

Our immediate interest in social situations was that it is mainly in such contexts that individuals can use their faces and bodies, as well as small materials at hand to engage in social portraiture. It is here in these small, local places that they can arrange themselves microecologically to depict what is taken as their place in the wider social frame, allowing them, in turn, to celebrate what has been depicted. It is here, in social situations, that the individual can signify what he takes to be his social identity and here indicate his feelings and intent—all of which information the others in the gathering will need in order to manage their own courses of action—which knowledgeability he in turn must count on in carrying out his own designs.

Now it seems to me that any form of socialization which in effect addresses itself to social situations as such, that is, to the resources ordinarily available in any social situation whatsoever, will have a very powerful effect upon social life. In any particular social gathering at any particular moment, the effect of this socialization may be slight—no more consequence, say, than to modify the style in which matters at hand proceed. (After all, whether you light your own cigarette or have it lit for you, you can still get lung cancer. And whether your job termination interview is conducted with delicacy or abruptness, you've still lost your job.) However, routinely the question is that of whose opinion is voiced most frequently and most forcibly, who makes the minor ongoing decisions apparently required for the co-ordination of any joint activity, and whose passing concerns are given the most weight. And however trivial some of these little gains and losses may appear to be, by summing them all up across all the social situations in which they occur, one can see that their total effect is enormous. The expression of subordina-nation and domination through this swarm of situational means is more than a mere tracing or symbol of ritualistic affirmation of the social hierarchy. These expressions considerably constitute the hierarchy; they are the shadow *and* the substance.[4]

And here gender styles qualify. For these behavioral styles can be employed in any social situation, and there receive their small due. When mommies and daddies decide on what to teach their little Johnnys and Marys, they make exactly the right choice; they act in effect with much more sociological sophisti-cation than they ought to have—assuming, of course, that the world as we have known it is what they want to reproduce.

And behavioral style itself? Not very stylish. A means of mak-ing assumptions about life palpable in social situations. At the same time, a choreography through which participants present their alignments to situated activities in progress. And the styl-ings themselves consist of those arrangements of the human form and those elaborations of human action that can be dis-played across many social settings, in each case drawing on local resources to tell stories of very wide appeal.

VII

I conclude with a sermon.

There is a wide agreement that fishes live in the sea because they cannot breathe on land, and that we live on land because we cannot breathe in the sea. The proximate, everyday account can be spelled out in ever increasing physiological detail, and exceptional cases and circumstances uncovered, but the general answer will ordinarily suffice, namely, an appeal to the nature of the beast, to the givens and conditions of his existence, and a guileless use of the term "because." Note, in this happy bit of folk wisdom—as sound and scientific surely as it needs to be—

the land and sea can be taken as there prior to fishes and men, and not—contrary to Genesis—put there so that fishes and men, when they arrived, would find a suitable place awaiting them.

This lesson about the men and the fishes contains, I think, the essence of our most common and most basic way of thinking about ourselves: an accounting of what occurs by an appeal to our "natures," an appeal to the very conditions of our being. Note, we can use this formula both for categories of persons and for particular individuals. Just as we account for the fact that a man walks upright by an appeal to his nature, so we can account for why a particular amputee doesn't by an appeal to his particular conditions of being.

It is, of course, hardly possible to imagine a society whose members do not routinely read from what is available to the senses to something larger, distal, or hidden. Survival is unthinkable without it. Correspondingly, there is a very deep belief in our society, as presumably there is in others, that an object produces signs that are informing about it. Objects are thought to structure the environment immediately around themselves; they cast a shadow, heat up the surround, strew indications, leave an imprint; they impress a part picture of themselves, a portrait that is unintended and not dependent on being attended, yet, of course, informing nonetheless to whomsoever is properly placed, trained, and inclined. Presumably this indicating is done in a malleable surround of some kind—a field for indications— the actual perturbations in which is the sign. Presumably one deals here with "natural indexical signs," sometimes having "iconic" features. In any case, this sort of indicating is to be seen neither as physical instrumental action in the fullest sense, nor as communication as such, but something else, a kind of by- production, an overflowing, a tell-tale soiling of the environment wherever the object has been. Although these signs are likely to be distinct from, or only a part of, the object about which they provide information, it is their configuration which counts, and the ultimate source of this, it is felt, is the object itself in some independence of the particular field in which the expression happens to occur. Thus we take sign production to be situa- tionally phrased but not situationally determined.

The natural indexical signs given off by objects we call animal (including, and principally, man) are often called "expressions," but in the sense of that term here implied, our imagery still allows that a material process is involved, not conventional symbolic communication. We tend to believe that these special objects not only give off natural signs, but do so more than do other objects. Indeed, the emotions, in association with various bodily organs through which emotions most markedly appear, are considered veritable engines of expression. As a corollary, we assume that among humans a very wide range of attributes are expressible: intent, feeling, relationship, information state, health, social class, etc. Lore and advice concerning these signs, including how to fake them and how to see behind fakeries, constitute a kind of folk science. All of these beliefs regarding man, taken together, can be referred to as the doctrine of natural expression.

It is generally believed that although signs can be read for what is merely momentarily or incidentally true of the object producing them—as, say, when an elevated temperature indicates a fever—we routinely seek another kind of information also, namely, information about those of an object's properties that are felt to be *perduring, overall,* and *structurally basic,* in short, information about its character or "essential nature." (The same sort of information is sought about classes of objects.) We do so for many reasons, and in so doing presume that objects (and classes of objects) have natures independent of the particular interest that might arouse our concern. Signs viewed in this light, I will call "essential," and the belief that they exist and can be read and that individuals give them off is part of the doctrine of natural expression. Note again, that although some of these attributes, such as passing mood, particular intent, etc., are not themselves taken as characteristic, the *tendency* to possess such states and concerns is seen as an essential attribute, and conveying evidence of internal states in a particular manner can be seen as characteristic. In fact, there seems to be no incidental contingent expression that can't be taken as evidence of an essential attribute; we need only see that to respond in a particular way to particular circumstances is what might be expected in general of persons as such or a certain kind of person or a particular person. Note, any property seen as unique to a particular person is likely also to serve as a means of characterizing him. A corollary is that the absence in him of a particular property seen as common to the class of which he is a member tends to serve similarly.

Here let me restate the notion that one of the most deeply seated traits of man, it is felt, is gender; femininity and masculinity are in a sense the prototypes of essential expression—something that can be conveyed fleetingly in any social situation and yet something that strikes at the most basic characterization of the individual.

But, of course, when one tries to use the notion that human objects give off natural indexical signs and that some of these expressions can inform us about the essential nature of their producer, matters get complicated. The human objects themselves employ the term "expression," and conduct themselves to fit their own conceptions of expressivity; iconicity especially abounds, doing so because it has been made to. Instead of our merely obtaining expressions of the object, the object obligingly gives them to us, conveying them through ritualizations and communicating them through symbols. (But then it can be said that this giving itself has unintended expressive features: for it does not seem possible for a message to be transmitted without the transmitter and the transmission process blindly leaving traces of themselves on whatever gets transmitted.)

There is, straight off, the obvious fact that an individual can fake an expression for what can be gained thereby; an individual is unlikely to cut off his leg so as to have a nature unsuitable for military service, but he might indeed sacrifice a toe or affect a limp. In which case "because of" becomes "in order to." But that is really a minor matter; there are more serious difficulties. I mention three.

First, it is not so much the character or overall structure of an entity that gets expressed (if such there be), but rather particular, situationally-bound features relevant to the viewer. (Sometimes, for example, no more than that the object is such a one and not another.) The notion of essence, character, structure, is, one might argue, social, since there are likely to be an infinite number of properties of the object that could be selected out as the central ones, and, furthermore, often an infinite number of ways of bounding the object from other ones. Thus, as suggested, an attribute which allows us to distinguish its possessor from those he is seen amongst is likely to enter strongly in our characterization of him.

Second, expression in the main is not instinctive but socially learned and socially patterned; it is a socially defined category which employs a particular expression, and a socially established schedule which determines when these expressions will occur. And this is so even though individuals come to employ expressions in what is sensed to be a spontaneous and unselfconscious way, that is, uncalculated, unfaked, natural. Furthermore, individuals do not merely learn how and when to express themselves, for in learning this they are learning to be the kind of object to which the doctrine of natural expression applies, if fallibly; they are learning to be objects that have a character, that express this character, and for whom this characterological expressing is only natural. We are socialized to confirm our own hypotheses about our natures.

Third, social situations turn out to be more than a convenient field of what we take to be natural expression; these configurations are intrinsically, not merely incidentally, a consequence of what can be generated in social situations.

So our concern as students ought not to be in uncovering real, natural expressions, whatever they might be. One should not appeal to the doctrine of natural expression in an attempt to account for natural expression, for that (as is said) would conclude the analysis before it had begun. These acts and appearances are likely to be anything but natural indexical signs, except insofar as they provide indications of the actor's interest in conducting himself effectively under conditions of being treated in accordance with the doctrine of natural expression. And insofar as natural expressions of gender are—in the sense here employed—natural and expressive, what they naturally express is the capacity and inclination of individuals to portray a version of themselves and their relationships at strategic moments—a working agreement to present each other with, and facilitate the other's presentation of, gestural pictures of the claimed reality of their relationship and the claimed character of their human nature. The competency to produce these portraits, and interpret those produced by others, might be said to be essential to our nature, but this competency may provide a very poor picture of the overall relationship between the sexes. And indeed, I think it does. What the relationship between the sexes objectively is, taken as a whole, is quite another matter, not yet well analyzed.

What the human nature of males and females really consists of, then, is a capacity to learn to provide and to read depictions of masculinity and femininity and a willingness to adhere to a schedule for presenting these pictures, and this capacity they have by virtue of being persons, not females or males. One might just as well say there is no gender identity. There is only a schedule for the portrayal of gender. There is no relationship between the sexes that can so far be characterized in any satisfactory fashion. There is only evidence of the practice between the sexes of choreographing behaviorally a portrait of relationship. And what these portraits most directly tell us about is not gender, or the overall relationship between the sexes, but about the special character and functioning of portraiture.

One can say that female behavioral style "expresses" femininity in the sense of providing an incidental, gratuitous portrait. But Durkheim recommends that such expression is a political ceremony, in this case affirming the place that persons of the female sex class have in the social structure, in other words, holding them to it. And ethologists recommend that feminine expression is an indication of the alignment a person of the female sex class proposes to take (or accept) in the activity immediately to follow—an alignment which does not merely express subordination but in part constitutes it. The first points out the stabilizing influence of worshipping one's place in the social scheme of things, the second, the substantial consequences of minor allocations. Both these modes of functioning are concealed from us by the doctrine of natural expression; for that doctrine teaches us that expressions occur simply because it is only natural for them to do so—no other reason being required. Moreover, we are led to accept as a portrait of the whole something that actually occurs at scheduled moments only, something that provides (in the case under question) a reflection not of the differential nature of persons in the two sex classes but of their common readiness to subscribe to the conventions of display.

Gender displays, like other rituals, can iconically reflect fundamental features of the social structure; but just as easily, these expressions can counterbalance substantive arrangements and compensate for them. If anything, then, displays are a symptom, not a portrait. For, in fact, whatever the fundamental circumstances of those who happen to be in the same social situation, their behavioral styles can affirm a contrary picture.

Of course, it is apparent that the niceties of gender etiquette provide a solution for various organizational problems found in social situations—such as who is to make minor decisions which seem better lost than unresolved, who is to give way, who to step forward, who is to follow, who to lead, so that turns, stops, and moving about can be coordinated, and beginnings and endings synchronized. (In the same way, at the substantive level, the traditional division of labor between the sexes provides a workable solution to the organization of certain personal services, the ones we call domestic; similarly, sex-biased linguistic practices, such as the use of "he" as the unmarked relative pronoun for "individual"—amply illustrated in this paper—provide a basis for unthinkingly concerted usage upon which the efficiency of language depends.) But just why gender instead of some other attribute is invoked to deal with these organizational problems, and how well adapted gender is for doing so, is an open question.

In sum, gender, in close connection with age-grade, lays down more, perhaps, than class and other social divisions an understanding of what our ultimate nature ought to be and how and where this nature ought to be exhibited. And we acquire a vast corpus of accounts to be used as a source of good, self-sufficient reasons for many of our acts (particularly as these determine the allocation of minor indulgences and deprivations), just as others acquire a sovereign means of accounting for our own behavior. Observe, there is nothing superficial about this accounting. Given our stereotypes of femininity, a particular woman will find that the way has been cleared to fall back on the situation of her entire sex to account to herself for why she should refrain from vying with men in matters mechanical, financial, political, and so forth. Just as a particular man will find that his failure to exert priority over women in these matters reflects on him personally, giving him warrant for insisting on success in these connections. (Correspondingly, he can decline domestic tasks on the general ground of his sex, while identifying any of his wife's disinclination here as an expression of her particular character.) Because these stereotypes begin to be applied by and to the individual from the earliest years, the accounting it affords is rather well implanted.

I have here taken a functionalist view of gender display and have argued that what, if anything, characterizes persons as sex-class members is their competence and willingness to sustain an appropriate schedule of displays; only the content of the displays distinguishes the classes. Although this view can be seen as slighting the biological reality of sex, it should not be taken as belittling the role of these displays in social life. For the facilitation of these enactments runs so deeply into the organization of society as to deny any slighting view of them. Gender expressions are by way of being a mere show; but a considerable amount of the substance of society is enrolled in the staging of it.

Nor should too easy a political lesson be drawn by those sympathetic to social change. The analysis of sexism can start with obviously unjust discriminations against persons of the female sex class, but analysis as such cannot stop there. Gender stereotypes run in every direction, and almost as much inform what supporters of women's rights approve as what they disapprove. A principal means men in our society have for initiating or terminating an everyday encounter on a sympathetic note is to employ endearing terms of address and verbal expressions of concern that are (upon examination) parental in character and profoundly asymmetrical. Similarly, an important ritual available for displaying affectionate concern, emphasizing junctures in discourse, and marking differential conversational exclusiveness is the laying on of the hand, ordinarily an unreciprocatable gesture of male to female or subordinate male.

In all of this, intimacy certainly brings no corrective. In our society in all classes the tenderest expression of affection involves displays that are politically questionable, the place taken up in them by the female being differentiated from and reciprocal to the place taken up by the male. Cross-sex affectional gestures choreograph protector and protected, embracer and embraced, comforter and comforted, supporter and supported, extender of affection and recipient thereof; and it is defined as only natural that the male encompass and the female be encompassed. And this can only remind us that male domination is a very special kind, a domination that can be carried right into the gentlest, most loving moment without apparently causing strain—indeed, these moments can hardly be conceived of apart from these asymmetries. Whereas other disadvantaged groups can turn from the world to a domestic scene where self-determination and relief from inequality are possible, the disadvantage that persons who are female suffer precludes this; the places identified in our society as ones that can be arranged to suit oneself are nonetheless for women thoroughly organized along disadvantageous lines.

And indeed, reliance on the child-parent complex as a source of display imagery is a means of extending intimate comfortable practices outward from their source to the world, and in the wake of this domestication, this only gentling of the world we seem to have, female subordination follows. *Any* scene, it appears, can be defined as an occasion for the depiction of gender difference, and in any scene a resource can be found for effecting this display.

As for the doctrine of expression, it raises the issue of professional, as well as folk, analysis. To accept various "expressions" of femininity (or masculinity) as indicating something biological or social-structural that lies behind or underneath these signs, something to be glimpsed through them, is perhaps to accept a lay theory of signs. That a multitude of "genderisms" point convergently in the same direction might only tell us how these signs function socially, namely, to support belief that there is an underlying reality to gender. Nothing dictates that should we dig and poke behind these images we can expect to find anything there—except, of course, the inducement to entertain this expectation.

NOTES

[1] See the thorough treatment of "feminizers" in Conners (1971).

[2] An important work here, of course, is Darwin's *Expression of Emotions in Man and Animals*. In this treatise a direct parallel is drawn, in words and pictures, between a few gestures of a few animals—gestures expressing, for example, dominance, appeasement, fear—and the same expressions as portrayed by actors. This study, recently and rightly resurrected as a classic in ethology (for indeed, it is in this book that displays are first studied in detail in everything but name), is generally taken as an elucidation of our animal natures and the expressions we consequently share with them. Now the book is also functioning as a source in its own right of cultural beliefs concerning the character and origins of alignment expressions.

[3] I leave unconsidered the role of such tales in *Time*'s fashioning of stories.

[4] A recent suggestion along this line can be found in the effort to specify in detail the difference between college men and women in regard to sequencing in cross-sexed conversation. See Zimmerman and West (1975), Fishman (n.d.), and West and Zimmerman (n.d.). The last discusses some similarities between parent-child and adult male-female conversational practices.

REFERENCES CITED

CONNERS, KATHLEEN
    1971—Studies in Feminine Agentives in Selected European Languages. *Romance Philology* 24(4):573-598.
FISHMAN, PAMELA
    n.d.—Interaction: The Work Women Do. Paper presented at the American Sociological Association Meetings, August 25-30, 1975, San Francisco.
HUXLEY, JULIAN
    1966—A Discussion on Ritualization of Behaviour in Animals and Man. *Philosophical Transactions of the Royal Society of London*, Series B, No. 772, Vol. 251:247-526.

INTERNATIONAL HERALD TRIBUNE
   1972—*International Herald Tribune*, June 3-4.
RUBINSTEIN, JONATHAN
   1973—*City Police*. New York:Farrar, Straus and Giroux.
TIME
   1972—*Time*, May 1, p. 60.
WEST, CANDACE and DON H. ZIMMERMAN
   n.d.—Women's Place in Conversation: Reflections on Adult-Child
      Interaction. Paper presented at the American Sociological
      Association Meetings, August 25-30, 1975, San Francisco.
ZIMMERMAN, DON H. and CANDACE WEST
   1975—Sex Role, Interruptions and Silences in Conversation. In
      Language and Sex: Differences and Dominance, Barrie
      Thorne and Nancy Henley, eds. Rowley, Ma.:Newbury
      House.

3

The Biological Basis of Female Hierarchies

ERNST W. CASPARI

The subject of this symposium has two aspects that may be discussed from a biological point of view: the problem of sexual dimorphism and the problem of social hierarchy. As far as the first problem is concerned, I shall discuss the genetic basis of sex determination and the developmental and biochemical mechanisms by which differences characterizing the two sexes are produced. Regarding the second problem, we know that social rank order exists in all organisms with a social organization. For purposes of the present conference this can be discussed under two headings: 1) the relative ranks of males and females in social organizations; and 2) the social hierarchies present amongst females, both in societies consisting of males and females, and in unisexual societies. Finally, I should like to discuss the population-genetic and evolutionary implications of sexual dimorphism and of a hierarchic organization among females, and make some remarks on the possible importance of the resulting mating patterns in human evolution. These remarks will not be exhaustive, since the last topic will be covered more thoroughly by other speakers, particularly Drs. Zihlman and Tanner.

I want to thank Professor F. Anders of the Institute of Genetics, Justus Liebig University, Giessen, Germany, for reading the manuscript and making numerous valuable suggestions. I am also obliged to the editor, Dr. Lionel Tiger, for his constructive criticism.

GENETIC BASIS OF SEXUAL DIMORPHISM

It has been pointed out in an earlier article (Caspari 1965) that the existence of two sexes is a general characteristic of living organisms, including bacteria. The generalization has in the meantime become more complicated due to work on fungi; for present purposes it is sufficient to state that in most organisms, two sexes can be distinguished on the basis of the contribution of cytoplasm to the fertilized ovum, the cell resulting from the sexual process. The female cell contributes most or all of the cytoplasm while both sexes contribute nuclear material, forming in animals a complete nucleus.

Sexual processes are extremely widespread. In higher animals, asexual reproduction is unusual and exceptional (identical twin formation in humans is a form of asexual reproduction), and the sexual process has become the primary mechanism of reproduction, without losing its more general function—the recombination of genes. In the human, copulation, a preliminary step in sexual reproduction, has assumed the function of pair bonding and has in this way become an important factor in social · organization and physiological functioning.

In animals and plants a bewildering variety of sex-determining mechanisms, genetic and environmental, exists. For most mammals, the situation is simple: sex determination is always genetic and involves the presence of two X chromosomes in the female, and one X and one Y chromosome in the male.[1] The sex-determining agent in this mechanism in mammals is the presence or absence of a Y chromosome: XO organisms are infertile females in humans, fertile females in the mouse; XXY humans are sterile males, XYY humans fertile males (whether or not they are more likely to show antisocial behavior than normal XY males has not been decided on the evidence available). Thus, presence or absence of a Y chromosome decides whether a fertilized egg cell will develop into a male or a female. In some marsupials the Y chromosomes in the male (and one X chromosome in the female) are lost early in development, while in other female mammals including humans, only one X chromosome remains active in somatic cells.[2] This difference in chromosomal constitution leads in the embryo to a series of developmental steps which result in the formation of male and female sex glands, respectively. Subsequent to the differentiation of the sex glands, the accessory parts of the genital system develop, still in the embryonic stage. These are, for instance, uterus and vagina in the female; vas deferens, prostate, seminal vesicle, and penis in the male. In the complete absence of sex glands, the female structures are formed. The development of the male structures and the disappearance of the embryonic female structures depend on the action of hormones produced by the male embryo.

In later development, in all organisms there arise a number of secondary differences between the sexes which are known as secondary sex characters. All the differences between the two sexes of the same species are described by the term *sexual dimorphism*. Many characters affected by sexual dimorphism are to a certain degree involved in sexual functioning, such as recognition of the sexes, mating activity, feeding and protection of progeny, etc. In many cases, however, the function of a sexually dimorphic character is by no means apparent, and in such cases explanations for their (functional) existence have sometimes been proposed. We will show later on that a functional significance may not exist, and cannot always be postulated, in all cases of sexual dimorphism.

Many of the secondary sexual characters in vertebrates depend in their development and expression on sex hormones. Hormones are special substances produced in the metabolism of an organ that are released into the blood stream and affect certain other organs in specific ways. There are thus organs that produce the hormones; for the sex hormones these are the primary sex organs—the testes, ovaries, and to a lesser extent, the adrenal glands. There are in addition the target organs, those that react to the sex hormones with specific activities and differentiations. The chemical constitution of the sex hormones of vertebrates has been well established: all belong to the class of substances called steroids.

In the female mammal the presence of two sex hormones, estrogen and progesterone, is responsible for the appearance of the estrus cycle. In the first half of this cycle, estrogen hormones circulate in the blood. At the height of the cycle—the so-called estrus period—ova are shed from the ovary into the Fallopian tube. Since the ova are short-lived, mating has to take place within a short time of estrus for fertilization to occur. Consequently, in most mammals, estrus is easily recognizable, and females copulate only while they are in estrus. In some primates, such as the chimpanzee and baboon, the females possess a *sexual skin* which becomes engorged conspicuously during estrus; but possession of a sexual skin is not general amongst primates. After the estrus period the estrogen level drops briefly, and progesterone, another steroid hormone produced in the ovary, assumes a high level. It continues to be produced if fertilization has occurred, but in the absence of an embryo both hormones drop to a low level, and the uterine epithelium is sloughed off. This estrus cycle is under the feedback control of hormones released by the pituitary gland, situated beneath the brain. The estrus cycle occurs generally among mammals including humans.

Two special features of the human estrus cycle are important. First of all, the estrus period itself is externally not conspicuous, though some physiological indicators, such as a slight rise in body temperature, exist. The human female can copulate outside the estrus period, even though, as in other mammals, only copulation during the estrus period leads to fertilization. A second characteristic of the human cycle is the very conspicuous menstruation indicating the time after the reduction of sex hormones in the circulation. While sloughing off of epithelium occurs in all mammals at this time of the cycle, a true menstruation appears only in Old World monkeys and seems to be particularly conspicuous in humans.

The aspects of hormonal control of secondary sex characters and sexual behavior briefly reviewed above have been known for 30 to 40 years. In the last decade, research in the action of sex hormones has taken a different direction (Jensen and De-Sombre 1973; O'Malley and Means 1974). It has been concerned with the fact that certain *target tissues* react to a particular sex hormone, while others do not. For example, in young female mammals, such as rats, goats, and sheep, the female sex hormone estradiol is taken up by the target organs uterus, vagina, and pituitary gland, but not by other organs. This is due to the fact that the cells of these target organs contain in their cytoplasm specific receptor proteins that combine specifically with the hormones. These receptor-hormone complexes are transported to the nucleus of the target cell where they become bound to the genetic material—the DNA and its associated proteins, which presumably control the action of the DNA. In this way, the activity of the genes of the target cell is affected by sex hormones in specific ways, specific for the hormone-receptor complex involved and for the specific target cell in which it acts. Specific messenger RNA's are formed, which result in the production of specific proteins and cellular differentiations.

Sexual dimorphism thus acquires an additional dimension: in addition to the primary sex organs (testes and ovaries) and the hormones they produce, there appears a third variable—the reaction of the target organs to the sex hormones. One implication is that a normal level of sex hormones does not guarantee a normal reaction of the target organs: the reaction of the target organs may be affected independently of the hormone level.

Ohno (1972) has pointed out that sexual differentiation is genetically a very simple character not requiring an elaborate mechanism of genetic control. Only two genetic control mechanisms must be assumed: 1) the primary sex difference, consisting of the development of male and female sex glands and their hormones; and 2) the reactivity of the target cells. The former is initiated by the Y chromosome mechanism. The latter is controlled by a separate gene which has been called *Tfm* because its mutation *tfm* results in a specific abnormal condition called *testicular feminization*. Testicular feminization has been particularly studied in the mouse (Lyon and Hawkes 1970; Ohno 1972). Organisms, including humans, showing this condition are by all external criteria complete but sterile females. Humans with the *tfm* mutation have female external genitalia and breasts and are in general regarded as females. Genetically they are, however, males, possessing one X and one Y chromosome, and their sex glands are small but clearly recognizable testes which remain in the body cavity. In mutant *tfm* organisms, unlike both males and females, the target organs do not react to testosterone, the male sex hormone; thus the female external characteristics are developed. Ohno assumes that *tfm* inhibits the activity of genes normally stimulated by the hormone.

This simplicity of genetic control has two consequences which should be pointed out: there is usually no difficulty in establishing the genetic sex of an individual from external inspection. The simplicity of the primary control mechanism makes it unlikely and rare that intermediate states are produced. Secondly, the chromosomal sex determination mechanism results in about equal numbers of males and females in a population.

The simplicity of primary sex determination, however, is modified by a number of complicating factors. The first one is the fact that the actualization of the simple control mechanisms involves a number of steps, biochemical and developmental, each of which is in turn dependent on further specific genes. Mutation of these genes may therefore affect particular developmental steps and inhibit or reduce the formation of particular hormones. Two examples in which the synthesis of sex hormones is affected by gene mutations, with special effects on sexual development, will be given here.

In a village in the Dominican Republic there has been found a hereditary form of male pseudohermaphroditism. At birth the affected babies have externally no penis or scrotum and a blind vagina-like pouch, and are therefore diagnosed as females. At puberty they undergo a normal male development, the penis and scrotum develop, and they become normal fertile males. The biochemical explanation is that the embryonic development of the male structures depends on two chemically very similar hormones, testosterone and dihydrotestosterone. The former is converted into the latter by an enzyme, steroid 5 α-reductase. In embryonic development, testosterone induces the formation of the epididymis, vas deferens, and seminal vesicle, while dihydrotestosterone is needed for a normal development of the penis and scrotum, and reduction of the vaginal pouch. If, by a mutation, the reaction testosterone → dihydrotestosterone is blocked, the latter structures do not develop, and the person appears at birth superficially female. The changes going on at puberty are controlled by testosterone, and thus, at that time, the persons become functional and fertile males. It is of interest from the point of view of this symposium that all these pseudo-hermaphrodites as adults assume completely male psychosexual orientation and gender roles, even though most of them have been reared as females. This is an argument in favor of considering both the type of sexual drive and of gender role preference as being determined by testosterone (Imperato-McGinley *et al.* 1974).

Another instructive example is the genetic condition known as adrenogenital syndrome. In this case, the formation of cortisol and related hormones in the adrenal cortex is partly blocked by reduction or lack of enzymes necessary for their synthesis. Since the adrenal cortical hormones are steroids, they are chemically closely related to sex hormones. Thus, it occurs that some of their precursors and their derivatives act similarly to testosterone. If a step leading to cortical hormones is partly blocked, and the precursors accumulate, they may exert a masculinizing effect. The condition results, therefore, in masculinization, i.e., the development of male characters in females and the early development of sexual characters in young males (Stempfel and Tomkins 1966).

Thus the mechanisms by which the sex hormones are synthesized and by which the sex organs develop are under the control of a great number of genes, whose mutation may result occasionally in abnormal sexual development.

Many sexual dimorphisms, however, cannot be simply explained by direct action of the sex chromosomes, the synthesis of sex hormones, and the reaction of cells to sex hormones. They depend on additional genes and gene products, and such genes influencing sexually dimorphic characters have indeed been found. The relations of the genes controlling these characters to the sex determining mechanisms are varied and have, therefore, received different names.

The location of a gene on the sex chromosome X or Y causes a particular manner of transmission which is called *sex-linked*. *A priori*, it might appear logical to assume that genes affecting sexual characters should be sex-linked. For instance, genes responsible for male characters may be assumed to be carried in the Y chromosome, while female characters might be based on heterozygosity of a gene in the X chromosome. Actually very few characters controlled by genes in the Y chromosome have been identified. In the fly *Drosophila*, no Mendelian genes affecting characters of the animal have been localized in the Y chromosome, but the Y chromosome is apparently active in the differentiation of sperm, since deletions in the Y chromosome may inhibit the production of viable sperm (Hess and Meyer 1968). In man, several characters limited to males have been ascribed to the Y chromosome but only one of them, the appearance of hair on the outer rim of the ear seems to be well supported (Dronamraju 1960). In the large pedigrees described by Dronamraju, all males derived from the original ancestor are affected. However, some doubts have been expressed on the complete Y chromosome dependence of this character, since it is variable in its expression, particularly depending on age at appearance.

Sex-linked recessive genes located in the X chromosome are quite frequent in humans and animals. They are recognized by the fact that a character controlled by a sex-linked recessive is transmitted from mother to sons and never from a father to sons. Conditions due to X chromosome-linked genes occur more frequently in males than in females, and in rare conditions may be found only in males. The characters concerned usually have no relation to sexual functions, and it has been suggested that their location in the sex chromosome is accidental; various anomalies of color vision and some conditions controlling blood clotting are the best known conditions in humans. It should, however, be pointed out that the above mentioned gene *tfm*, which controls the reaction of target organs to the male sex hormone, has been shown to be located in the X chromosome in the mouse; the same probably applies to other mammals, including human beings.

The majority of genes affecting sexually dimorphic characters are located in the autosomes (non-sex chromosomes). A few examples from different organisms will be given. Sexual dimorphism affecting the color of the wing is quite frequent in butterflies and moths (Lepidoptera). In this group of organisms the male is XX and the female XY. In the diurnal butterflies, the female may be polymorphic, i.e., have several types of wing colors, while in moths either male or female may be polymorphic. In the gypsy moth *Porthetria (Lymantria) dispar,* the female has a whitish wing while the male wing is brown. Color mutations affecting the male wing are known but do not affect the white female wing at all. Only in the male parts of the mosaic wings of intersexes may these genes become expressed (Goldschmidt 1920, 1955). This is a special case of a widespread phenomenon that the phenotypic expression of many genes, both dominant and recessive, may be restricted to one sex. Such conditions are called *sex-limited* genetic conditions. Sex-limited conditions may be affected by autosomal or sex-linked genes.

All the cases in Lepidoptera in which one sex shows a different color pattern than the other can be explained as being due to genes with sex-limited expression. The genetic basis can be investigated only in cases where one sex shows polymorphism. The field of genetic polymorphism in Lepidopterans has been reviewed by Sheppard (1961) and by Ford (1964). It can be concluded from the evidence that the genetic basis of wing color polymorphisms in Lepidoptera is usually not simple, that frequently several genes are involved, but that sex-linked genes do not play a major role and contribute only in exceptional cases.

The mechanism of sex control of dimorphic characters is most easily analyzed in genetically simple cases. An example is the "hen-feathering" of the Sebright Bantam breed of chickens. The roosters of this breed have the same type of feathers as the hens, so that they cannot be told by their feathers from the females. This character has been shown to be determined by a dominant autosomal gene (Morgan 1920). The mechanism by which this gene acts has been analyzed by Danforth and Foster (1929) by skin transplantations between the sexes and between normal and hen-feathered breeds. It turned out that normal and hen-feathered breeds do not differ from each other with respect to their sex hormones. Castration of the Sebright Bantam cock, like the normal cock, induces it to develop male feathers. The autosomal gene in question thus does not affect the male sex hormone, nor does it inhibit the ability of the feather follicles to produce male feathers. Rather, it changes the competence of the feather follicles in such a way as to form female feathers in the presence of both male and female hormones. It is important to realize that females of the Sebright Bantam breed also carry the gene for hen-feathering and can transmit it to their offspring. But they cannot express it phenotypically because they are hen-feathered anyway. The gene is a sex-limited one.

Some sex-limited characters have been thoroughly investigated genetically because of their economic importance. Milk production in cattle and egg production in chickens are traits that can be observed only in females. There exist many genetic factors controlling the quantity and quality of the milk produced by cows or the number and size of eggs laid by chickens, and the importance of knowledge about these genetic factors is obvious. These, like all genes, are transmitted through the male as well as the female, but selection for these characters is complicated because the phenotypes for milk and egg production cannot be observed in the bull and rooster. In the old times, males were therefore selected on the basis of "show points," i.e., characters thought to be correlated with the transmission of genes for high productivity, and on the basis of their pedigrees, the production records of their dams and granddams. Nowadays almost all breeding programs use progeny-tested bulls and roosters (males that are first test bred to females), and only those giving progeny of high productivity are used for further breeding. From the point of view of our topic, it is sufficient to emphasize that these are also genes, which are expressed only in one sex, causing sex-limited phenotypes.

Although sex-limited conditions occur in humans, they have not been the object of intensive study. There are, for instance, differences between races, populations, and individuals in the strength and pattern of facial hair in the male. But, as far as I know, no systematic genetic investigations of this character have been carried out.

There exist on the other hand, genes that are expressed in different frequencies and with different intensities in the two sexes. Phenotypic conditions of this type are called *sex-controlled* characters. I want to mention three examples from humans: pattern baldness, gout, and stuttering. All of them are considerably more frequent in males than in females, and the first two were originally described as monogenic, sex-controlled characters. Pattern baldness was first regarded as due to a single Mendelian gene which is dominant in males but recessive in females. In other words, in males the heterozygote is bald, while the heterozygous female possesses hair. Investigations by Harris (1946) have indicated that the situation is more complex. More than one genetic condition leading to pattern baldness seems to be involved: at least one which induces baldness in relatively young males, and another which induces the condition in older males. Actually, women with pattern baldness are very rare, and it may be that the condition is never expressed in the absence of male sex hormone.

Gout is a metabolic disturbance that primarily results in an elevation of the uric acid level in the blood. The condition is certainly familial and genetic, but pedigrees do not support the assumption of a single gene responsible for the condition. While in many cases increased uric acid level does not lead to any disturbances, in others insoluble uric acid becomes deposited in the joints, leading to the well-known symptoms of the disease. This disease occurs in both sexes, but much more frequently in males than in females. It has been suggested that at least one reason consists in the fact that normal males have a considerably higher uric acid level in the blood than normal females. Therefore, a relatively small rise may surpass the level of solubility of uric acid in males (Smyth, Cotterman, and Freyberg 1948; Hauge and Hervald 1955). But additional factors may be involved in this sex difference.

Similarly, stuttering is familial and has in many cases a genetic basis, but occurs two to four times more frequently in males than in females (Kant and Ahuja 1970; Van Riper 1971).

The case of gout is informative in another aspect. There are biochemical differences between the two sexes. These differences are indicated in this case by the level in normal humans of uric acid in the blood, which has no relation to sexual function, and in which the genetic or biochemical basis for the sexual dimorphism is not known. The difference must be assumed to be another instance of differential action of the same genes in the sexes. This seems to be a very frequent phenomenon and leads to the fact that in most species the sexes differ statistically in many biochemical and quantitative characters. It is the exception rather than the rule that the two sexes of a species are statistically identical with respect to a variable quantitative character. This is an expression of the phenomenon that the action of many genes is affected by other genes. Furthermore, since organisms are integrated systems, many genes, after their usually simple primary actions, have secondary (pleiotropic) effects due to the effects of other genes (Caspari 1952).

Thus it can be understood that while the genetic determination and regulation of the primary sex differences are simple, the differences have secondary consequences that extend to many aspects of biochemistry, physiology, and development. Sexual dimorphisms are frequently dependent on autosomal genes, which show different degrees of penetrance and expressivity depending on the sex of the carrier. Some of these effects in vertebrates may be mediated by differential reactions of the cells to the sex hormones. But direct reactions of the cells to sex differences certainly occur, as shown by the fact that where sex hormones are lacking in insects, sexual dimorphism is at least as widespread as it is in vertebrates.

BIOLOGICAL BASIS OF SOCIAL DOMINANCE

Many species of higher animals live in organized groups. Solitary animals exist: the woodchuck, a species of marmot, leads a solitary life in a territory which it defends against all other animals of the same species. Its contacts with cospecific organisms are restricted to the association of male and female during the copulatory period and the association between mother and young (Barash 1974). Such extremely solitary habits are rare among primates; they are in general gregarious, with the possible exception of the orangutan, in which single males or females accompanied by one young are frequently observed (Rodman 1973).

In gregarious animals we usually find a social organization based on a hierarchic dominance order. A social order based on dominance was first described in the chicken (Schjelderup-Ebbe 1922). Since the society of the barnyard chicken consists typically of one male and a flock of females, it is in the main the social organization of the females that has been investigated. This organization is a linear hierarchy: the social status of the members is unambiguously defined by a linear order of dominance and subordination. It is best observed by their pecking behavior, and the work *peck order* has become generally accepted in the language to designate a hierarchic order. In this case it is unclear whether the male should be regarded as dominant over all the females or as being separate and not belonging to the hierarchic order at all. The fact that the status of a female in the hierarchy can be modified by injection of male or female hormones (Allee, Collias, and Lutherman 1939; Allee and Collias 1941) may be an argument in favor of the first alternative.

Hierarchic organizations have been observed in all social animals, but it is not always a straight linear order. Furthermore, the criteria according to which the social status of an individual is judged may be different depending on the species observed. Criteria may involve position within the aggregate of individuals in movement and at rest, advantage in food acquisition, territoriality, advantages in mate selection, and many other activities. Usually, different criteria observed in the same species are correlated with each other, but the correlation is not always perfect. The direct observation of the encounter of two individuals in which one assumes the dominant and the other the subordinate position may be the best criterion; but even then, it is sometimes difficult to identify correctly the subordinate and the dominant position in a nonhuman organism. There may arise, therefore, differences between observers in the interpretation of organization patterns of a species.

In spite of these limitations, a large body of knowledge on the social organization of animals has been accumulated. Social organization is not restricted to vertebrates, but is also found in some insects and crustaceans. In the wasp *Polistes gallicus,* for instance, Pardi (1948) described a linear order of hierarchy among the females in a colony, similar to the peck order in a flock of chickens. Dominance order is established by fighting, and the most dominant female will finally survive and become established as the queen of the hive. Amongst the workers, infertile females, a hierarchy becomes established primarily according to age, and when the queen is lost, the most dominant worker will develop fertile ovaries. Males are always subordinate to females.

Amongst vertebrates, social organization is frequent and varied. Even within a closely related group of species, various types of organizational patterns can be found, as was shown for instance in marmots (Barash 1974) and baboons (Nagel 1971). Even different local populations of the same species may show considerable differences in social organization, as shown by Yoshiba (1968) for the Indian langur. It is therefore dangerous to generalize from observations on only a few species. But a number of facts and observations may be cited which may have a bearing on the topic of this symposium.

Unisexual societies of females are observed quite frequently in ungulates. It should be mentioned that cases of all-female societies have also been observed in primates, more specifically in the more primitive primates, the prosimians.

More interesting are primate societies consisting of both sexes. Here we can study the dominance relations between males and females as well as of females among each other. It is a rather frequent finding in primates that males are dominant over females, and the young are subordinate to adults of both sexes. It is furthermore a general rule that amongst primates, males are larger than females, and it has been claimed that the degree of male dominance may be correlated with the degree of the dimorphism in size. These rules certainly apply to the best investigated species—the chimpanzee, different species of baboons, and macaques. In the gibbon, males are only slightly larger than females, and this genus lives in monogamous associations with little indication of social dominance. In the orangutan, on the other hand, the dimorphism in size is extreme and, still, little evidence for social dominance has been observed where male and female live in association (Rodman 1973). In some South American monkeys, the female is larger than the male, but little is known about the social organization of the species in question (Crook 1972).

Much attention has been given in the ethological literature to the dominance order of males, their interactions with each other, and its ecological meaning. Dominance relations among females have been comparatively neglected. Their existence has been demonstrated in social carnivores (Scott and Fuller 1965; Rabb, Woolpy, and Ginsburg 1967) and in quite a number of primate species.[3]

The mechanism of establishing dominance has been described in a few cases and the ecological and genetic consequences discussed. In the wolf, for instance, Rabb, Woolpy, and Ginsburg (1967) have shown that the dominant female maintains its position by threats and occasional fighting, and that she tries to inhibit subordinate females from copulation. On the other extreme, the female of lowest rank sometimes does not reproduce and may act as a dry nurse for the offspring of other females. In all primates studied, the dominance rank of the mother has a great effect on the social standing of her offspring, both male and female. This fact was discovered in the Japanese macaque by Kawamura (1958) and has since been confirmed and elaborated by Koyama (1967), Norikoshi (1974), and others. The same situation has been described for the rhesus monkey (Koford 1963) and for the chimpanzee (Goodall 1971). At least in the females of the two macaque species, rank of the mother is one of the most prominent determinants in the social position of a female; others may include age, birth order, and for estrous and pregnant females, the dominance rank of her consort (Altmann 1962). It should be noted that none of these determinants of dominance in these females depends on physical or behavioral characters of the individual.

The situation seems to be more complex in males. Here, too, the influence of social rank of the mother is important in young males, and in many cases persists throughout life. However, among males threatening and fighting play a role in the substitution in the dominance order. Fighting has also been described in female primates, e.g., the chimpanzee (Goodall 1971), the Patas monkey (Hall, Boelkins, and Goswell 1965), and the gelada baboon (Kummer 1971b). But in two of these cases, disturbed social situations in captivity were involved. Fighting of primate females plays, as far as we know, little or no role in the establishment of dominance order.

The primate species whose social structure has been most thoroughly investigated is the Japanese macaque (Yamada 1966; Koyama 1967; and Stephenson 1974). Both males and females show, with few exceptions, a linear hierarchical rank order. The investigators divide the adult monkeys within a troop into three rank order classes for each sex. We will call these classes high, medium, and low (the authors use different terms). The males of high rank, usually few in number, are individually dominant over all other members of the group, male and female. The more numerous high ranking females are subordinate to high ranking males, but dominant over males of medium and low rank. The low ranking males and females are usually located at the periphery of the group.

Rank in males is primarily dependent on age. In females, the most important factor determining rank is matriarchal lineage, as mentioned above (Kawamura 1958; Koyama 1967). Within a particular matriarchal line, the youngest sister is usually dominant over her older sisters. This system is further complicated by the phenomenon of *dependent rank* (Kawai 1958). Daughters frequently take a rank immediately below their mothers when the mothers are present; in their absence they hold a much lower rank. Similarly, in the presence of the highest ranking male, the other males of high rank may be subordinate to some of the high ranking females. Finally, the rank of a low ranking individual may be modified by a special personal relationship to a high ranking male (Stephenson 1974). Thus, an individual may be sometimes in a high rank class and at other times in a low one, depending on the social constellation. Furthermore, it is not correct, at least in this species, that females are generally subordinate to adult males. Some high ranking females may be dominant to all males except the highest ranking male, at least under some social conditions. The complexity of social relations in this species suggests that continuing observation may reveal more complex relationships in other primates as well.

The genetic basis of social dominance has been best investigated in the house mouse (Scott 1966). The fighting of male mice has been thoroughly studied. Many factors affecting the agonistic behavior of the mouse have been investigated. It has been shown that different inbred strains show, among other factors, different degrees of aggressiveness, different modes of behavior in fighting, and different probabilities of success. All these "strain-specific" characters, however, can be greatly modified by early experience, experience in previous fights, and other experiential and environmental factors. The main evidence for the influence of genetic differences on agonistic behavior consists in the demonstration of strain differences. Little attempt has been made to analyze these differences by breeding tests, and selection experiments have given ambiguous results.

The ecological meaning of agonistic behavior in the male mouse seems to be well established: as in many other species, it leads to the establishment of social dominance. As a result of success, a male will occupy a larger territory as shown by the deposition of urine (Bronson and Marsden 1973). It is furthermore known that a territory is occupied by a small group of mice which inbreeds closely (Selander 1970; Klein and Bailey 1971). A group consists of a dominant male, several females, several subordinate males, and young. It should be expected from this social pattern that selection for genes favoring social dominance of the male would operate in the mouse.

Agonistic behavior has also been observed in female rats and mice, and was early reported by Fredericson (1952). Female rats and mice who are nursing young defend their nests against strangers. In addition, nonmaternal females show agonistic behavior toward each other. This behavior is observed more frequently in wild mice than in inbred laboratory strains. A genetic basis for this character is indicated by the fact that selection in positive and negative directions has been successful (Hyde and Ebert 1976). It has been reported by Tollman and King (1956) that injection of male hormones into castrated females does not modify their typical fighting behavior, even though their copulatory behavior is changed. The ecological meaning of nonmaternal fighting in females is unknown; more specifically it is not known whether agonistic behavior in females results in the formation of a female hierarchy.

Finally, it may be appropriate to report a nongenetic consequence of female dominance in fish, which has been described by Robertson (1972). In the wrasse (*Labroides dimidiatus*), the male controls a territory and, in it, a number of females who establish smaller subterritories. The male patrols his territory, worrying and biting the females and driving away all other males who approach. The females themselves defend their subterritories against each other and establish a hierarchy among themselves. If the male dies and no other male takes over the territory within a short time, the dominant female develops within about 24 hours into a complete and functional male, taking over all the functions of the original male. Such sex inversion occurs also in other relatives of *Labroides* who start life as females and may be transformed into males naturally or by injection of androgenic hormones (Reinboth 1975). But *Labroides* is the only species in which this sex inversion is a consequence of social dominance. It may be suggested that in these females the production of androgenic hormones is suppressed by the constant worrying from the male, and that the hormones are released as soon as the male is removed. Important in our present context is the fact that the stimulus determining the sex is behavioral and is based on the hierarchy amongst the females. It shows that the ecological importance and meaning of hierarchy may be very different amongst different species and that caution is indicated in transferring conclusions from one species to the other.

This is necessary to keep in mind in drawing conclusions from the social behavior of animal species to that of human beings. In particular, Yoshiba (1968) and Kummer (1971a) have called attention to the great variety of social organizations found in primates. Even closely related species and different geographic populations of the same species may show considerable differences in social organization and dominance relations. These differences may in part be correlated with ecological conditions, but not all differences can be explained in this way. It must be emphasized that few generalizations apply to all primates and that it is thus dangerous to extrapolate from one species to another.

We can perhaps state as a general conclusion of our discussion of animal societies that, in societies consisting of both sexes, the two are never equal in the sense that the individuals form a society regardless of sex and obtain status within the society independent of their sex. Males and females have different functions, and in many cases either the male (Polistes) or the female (chimpanzee, baboon) is the subordinate sex; in other cases (chicken, perhaps wolf), it is doubtful whether the relations between the sexes can be expressed in terms of dominance and subordination rather than in terms of different functions. In other species different rank classes of males and females may exist, and the rank of a particular individual may not be absolute but may depend on temporary social conditions. The only known cases of possible equality among Old World primates are represented by animals living in very small groups, such as gibbons and orangutans. In many New World monkeys, however, the social differentiation of the sexes is not pronounced or is missing.

The concept of dominance has a much clearer meaning within one sex. In all cases discussed, there appears to be evidence for a hierarchy amongst the males, and a separate hierarchy amongst the females. Usually, more is known about the male dominance order, partly because it is more conspicuous and partly, I am afraid, due to prejudice on the part of the observers.

The organization of human society is so different from that of any known organisms that one may ask whether much can be gained for an understanding of human society from the study of animal societies. Beach (1974) emphasized the great difference between the mating behavior of animals and human sexuality. The term *sexuality* in Beach's terminology refers to the fact that in humans, besides the sexual dimorphism discussed in the first part of this paper, we observe gender roles and gender identity. Human society is much more complex than that of any animal. The roles of a human individual are more varied in that a person occupies a status not in one society, but in a number of different and overlapping social groups. Gender is an expression of the fact that in every human society certain behavioral roles are ascribed to males and females. Beach's term *gender identity* refers to the fact that a human being perceives himself or herself in terms of gender. While in different societies the gender roles may be quite differently defined, they encompass the totality of human functioning in society and are not restricted to sexual activities and the care and protection of the young. The existence of gender sharply distinguishes all human societies from any animal society. On the other hand, it must be emphasized that the gender roles are never completely arbitrary, since the genders are identified as the two biological sexes. As shown in the case of pseudohermaphroditism mentioned above (Imperato-McGinley, *et al.* 1974), when a mistake in the identification of biological sex is discovered, the individual concerned may change his social gender. It is not possible for gender roles to be incompatible with the biological capacities of the sexes; and, as pointed out earlier, the differences between the sexes include a large array of biochemical, physiological, and morphological characters not connected with the reproductive function. This is due to the interaction and pleiotropic effects of gene-controlled processes. It is frequently difficult, in concrete cases of individual characters to decide whether a difference between the sexes in humans is due to genetic conditions, to societal influences based on gender roles, or an interaction between the two.

It is, for instance, a common observation that in humans the male is bigger than the female. Most biologists will assume that this difference is determined by the biological difference between sexes. The argument is that larger size of the male is general amongst the Old World primates, and genetically determined sexual dimorphism in size is very frequent in animals. But if one wishes to hold the opinion that the difference in size in humans is due to differences in gender roles in early life, this statement cannot be easily falsified, since it is impossible to raise a human being without a gender role. Cases in which a gender different from the true sex has been ascribed to individuals at birth are not decisive, since all of them involve abnormalities in the development of sexual structures in the first place.

It is important to realize that the existence of gender roles is one of the aspects that distinguishes human from animal societies and contributes to the richer and more complex structure of human societies. Beach emphasizes that the origin of gender must be sought in the evolution of the human species, and offers many suggestions and ideas about this topic. He points out that the existence of gender roles was probably necessary for the emergence of the nuclear family and enhanced cooperation in childrearing and other economic activities. However, a clear understanding of the phylogenetic origin of gender will not be possible until we know more about the social structure of our prehuman ancestors.

In the beginning we stated that the sexual function, originally genic recombination, was modified in the evolution of animals to encompass also reproduction. In the evolution of human beings it has assumed a third function, social bonding through copulation. Finally, sexual dimorphism has led to the introduction of gender, which forms the basis of the complexity and adaptability of human societies. It is, however, characteristic for all these steps that the earlier functions have not been lost in the process of acquiring the new one. Though we are most conscious of their gender roles in the overt behavior of the sexes, reproduction, genetic recombination, and fertilization are still dependent on the function of the two sexes in the original way.

EVOLUTIONARY IMPLICATIONS OF SEXUAL DIMORPHISM AND FEMALE HIERARCHIES

The question of the evolutionary origin of sexual dimorphism was first raised by Charles Darwin (1871) with particular emphasis on the fact that some of these dimorphic characters, such as the brilliant plumage of some male birds, make the organism conspicuous and for this reason vulnerable to predation. He, therefore, proposed his theory of sexual selection, that certain sexually dimorphic characters give a reproductive advantage to their carriers, and are thus favored by selection. It should be considered that Darwin's distinction of natural and sexual selection would nowadays be regarded more as the extremes of a continuum, since we regard survival, fertility, and fecundity as components of natural selection. Therefore, Darwin's sexual selection would constitute a special mechanism affecting one component of natural selection—the probability of an individual to produce offspring (Campbell 1972).

In order to discuss the evolutionary origin of sexual dimorphism, we must return to its genetic basis as presented in the first section. We have seen that most of the genes involved in sexual dimorphism are autosomal and occur in the same frequencies in both sexes; they must therefore act differently in the male and female organism. Darwin's conclusion, expressed in modern terms, says that a gene acting in a particular way in one sex will be favored by selection if its carriers will be more readily accepted by the other sex or possess for other reasons a reproductive advantage. In other words, a gene must have acted to produce a dimorphism before it can become the object of sexual selection.

That this may indeed be the case becomes persuasive if we look at the example of pattern baldness in humans. As stated earlier, it is a secondary sexual character depending on autosomal sex-controlled genes that are polymorphic in the population. At the present time it appears that it is neither selected for nor against in human populations. Why it has arisen in the first place, and how the polymorphism is maintained are unknown. But it may be added that the large number of genetic polymorphisms in natural populations is an unsolved problem of population genetics widely discussed at the present time. More important is the fact that bald areas of the skin are very widespread as secondary sexual characters among primates; an example is the bald chest of the male gelada baboon. In adult chimpanzees, the head frequently becomes bald, but in this instance the character appears in both sexes. It would be actually easy to establish baldness as a general secondary sex character in man if for some reason baldness would result in a reproductive advantage for affected males. As far as I know this is not true in any human society, and the different frequencies of baldness found in different human populations have not yet been explained. If a polymorphism for sex-controlled genes exists in a population, the genes may be subject to selection, and in this way a sexual dimorphism may become established.

It must now be considered whether sexual dimorphism is itself a consequence of natural selection. Sexual dimorphism in size is very widespread in animals with separate sexes. In primates and in mammals in general, the male is usually larger than the female, though there are exceptions. In insects, the female is frequently larger than the male. In the fruit fly *Drosophila melanogaster*, the favorite experimental subject of genetics, the female weighs about 1 mg and the male 0.9 mg. In experiments on the inheritance of size it is therefore usual to measure females and males separately. An attempt to understand the genetic basis of this sexual dimorphism has been made in selection experiments with *Drosophila*. Bird and Schaffer (1972), using wing length as an indication of size, selected for families that showed large and small differences between the wing lengths of the sexes. Such a selection experiment is in principle different from the usual selection experiment where the largest or smallest males and females are chosen to select for size. The character sexual dimorphism in size does not appear in any one individual, but selection must be based on families. The experiment of Bird and Schaffer was successful. They succeeded in establishing lines with high and low degrees of sexual dimorphism within 15 generations. In the course of this selection experiment, wing length was reduced in both sexes, possibly due to inbreeding. In the selection for high sexual dimorphism, the wing length of males decreased more steeply than that of the females, resulting in a higher degree of sexual dimorphism. In the low sexual dimorphism line, the wings of females were reduced more than those of the males. The genes involved in this selection are partly located in the autosomes, but also in the X chromosomes. This experiment shows that the degree of sexual dimorphism is dependent on genes that may be affected by selection. They are not genes affecting size *per se*—it goes down uniformly in the experiment—but they affect the strength of the growth reaction to the male and female genotypes.

The existence of such genes that act differently in males and females makes it difficult to predict the outcome of selection exerted on one sex only. Theories have been proposed that the evolution of high intelligence and the emotional control in primates may be due to selection acting on males only (Chance and Mead 1953). The young males have to balance their sexual desire against the fear of the dominant male. Etkin (1954) criticized this theory on the basis that selection acting only on male intelligence would not be expected to raise female intelligence too. I have in turn criticized Etkin's statement, because it implies that there are separate genes for male and female intelligence. I have also expressed the expectation that selection in one sex only would select for the same genes as selection in both sexes but proceed more slowly (Caspari 1972). I was thus surprised when a paper by Palenzona and Alichio reported (1973) that males and females of *Drosophila* reacted indeed differently to selection for wing length. These authors selected for short wing length (not sexual dimorphism with respect to wing length) and chose for breeding the smallest animals of one sex, taking the mate of the other sex at random. It turned out that selection on females was more effective than selection on males. Unfortunately the authors have published measurements from females only, so that the effect of this selection on sexual dimorphism is not clear. In any case, the experiment shows that, in characters showing sexual dimorphism, it is possible to select for exactly those genes that react differently on the sex of its carriers, and thus select in part for different genes if one sex only is subject to selection. In other words, there are genes affecting wing length in general and other genes—earlier called sex-controlled and sex-limited genes—affecting wing length more in one sex than in the other, or even in one sex only.

This model applies to at least some behavioral characters in mammals. It was mentioned above that Ebert and Hyde (1976) were able to establish by selection lines of mice with high and

low scores for female aggressive behavior. In the fifth generation of selective breeding these strains were tested for male
aggressive behavior. It turned out that male agonistic behavior
did not correlate with female agonistic behavior in these lines.
In other words, just as in the *Drosophila* experiment, the character (in this case, aggressiveness) is determined at least in part
by different genes in males and females (Hyde and Ebert 1976).

We are now in a position to ask whether female hierarchies
may have an influence on the genetic structure of populations. It
becomes clear that no general statement can be made. The case
of fish, in which sex determination is dependent on the female
hierarchy, may appear at first sight a bizarre exception, one of
those curiosities that natural historians enjoy. But in actuality
the social organization and the mating pattern of each species
is unique, and therefore female hierarchies will have different
effects in different species, and may affect reproduction, territoriality, access to food, or other factors. There are apparently
cases in which low social status in the female affects adversely
the probability of reproduction, as has been stated for the wolf.
But in those primates investigated there is little evidence that
social status, be it high or low, has a major effect on the probability that a female will have progeny. In those Old World
primates with multiple-male societies, females arouse sexual
interest in males whenever they are in estrus. In some cases,
attempts of other individuals, males as well as females, to interfere with copulation have been described. In the Indian langur,
harassment by females occurs in South-Indian populations with
no female hierarchy, while in North-Indian populations, which
do show female hierarchy, harassment of copulating couples is
carried out by the subdominant males and not by the females
(Yoshida 1968). Only in one-male groups of the gelada baboon
have attempts at harassment of copulation by a dominant female
been observed (Kummer 1971b). The general evidence seems to
support the assumption that rank in females is not a major factor
in their ability to copulate and reproduce.

In the Japanese macaque, Stephenson (1974) has demonstrated
a correlation between the social ranks of mates. High ranking
females were observed mating almost exclusively with high

ranking males and females of medium rank with males of high and medium rank, while low ranking females mate preferentially with males of medium rank (see above discussion on Japanese macaque). This is apparently accomplished by means of choices made by both the male and the female partner, and by harrassment of lower ranking males by higher ranking males during attempts at mating. The high ranking males, in addition, mate most frequently with females that have not yet conceived, suggesting that they produce in any one season more offspring than the medium and low ranking males. This does not appear to be true for the females, since females of different ranks conceive and produce offspring. Thus, high ranking males may indeed, in this species, be favored by selection, but not high ranking females. Since, in addition, in both sexes, rank is not primarily based on characters that may be assumed to be genetically determined, these investigations give little support to the assumption that female hierarchy in the Japanese macaque offers a selective advantage to higher ranking individuals.

There exists, however, some evidence that number of offspring produced and the probability of raising the offspring to adulthood may be affected by social rank. Drickamer (1974), in a careful study of a rhesus monkey population in Puerto Rico, found that high ranking females have their first young at an earlier age than lower ranking females, and that a larger percentage of high ranking females gave birth per year than low ranking females. The mechanism for this difference has not been investigated. High ranking females may start estrus at an earlier age, or have it more frequently, or low ranking females may have a higher number of miscarriages. There is also some evidence that infants born to high ranking mothers show a higher survival rate than infants born to low ranking mothers. Rank in the female hierarchy may therefore indeed affect Darwinian fitness, at least in the population investigated.

It remains, however, doubtful whether this advantage can result in genetic changes in the population. As mentioned earlier, female hierarchy in primates depends primarily on transmission by kinship, and not on the individual characters of the females. Establishment of female dominance by fighting and threatening has been observed in captive populations (Chance 1963), but these were unorganized groups of zoo animals trying to establish a social organization. Under natural conditions, personal characteristics of a female may be important when it joins another troop. But under usual conditions, social rank in females seems to be established by social and environmental factors, and differential reproduction of high and low ranking females would thus have little or no influence on the composition of the gene pool of the next generation.

It must be concluded that in Old World primates, and probably also in other organisms, male and female hierarchy have very different properties. They may differ in mechanism of establishment, in function, and in population-genetic consequences. This is suggested by the findings in the Indian langur mentioned above, where the males in all populations show a dominance order while the females may show no hierarchy at all. In males it is generally accepted that personal characteristics such as strength, ability to form alliances, and fighting ability are instrumental in the establishment of high social rank. There is also good evidence in many primates that high ranking males copulate more frequently and more successfully than low ranking males. If, therefore, the characters leading to the establishment of high social rank have a genetic component—a point demonstrated for the mouse but not primates—the genes involved in the establishment of dominance would be favored by selection. In the female, where social rank is primarily dependent on kinship relations, there is little reason to assume that genetically determined characters are involved in the establishment of social dominance. Thus, even if high ranking females are reproductively more successful than low ranking females, it would have little consequence on the composition of the gene pool.

It should, in addition, be considered that many genes are sex-controlled, i.e., they produce a different phenotype in males than in females. It cannot therefore be assumed without further evidence that genes controlling characters that favor social dominance in males would produce a similar character in females.

Finally, it should be stated that the functions of male and female rank order in primates are quite different. One of the principal functions of high ranking primate males seems to be the defense of the group. This may be accomplished by fighting the predator, as for instance in baboons; by drawing the attention of the predator away from the females and young, as in the Patas monkey; or by other means. The main function of the female rank order seems to be the transmission of their own rank order to their progeny. In this way, a rank order becomes established very early in life in the play groups of the young, and contributes to the establishment of an organization in the young in which every individual knows its standing, and no pronounced fighting is necessary. This order can apparently to a certain degree be modified in later life, more so in the male than in the female. But the female rank order has thus the function of establishing the ordered structure of the group without much agonistic activity.

It could be argued that both male and female hierarchy have, in primate societies, distinct and important functions, and that these functions themselves should have a positive Darwinian fitness value. This question opens a difficult field of inquiry, since it asks for fitness not at the individual but at the population level. This question is difficult to attack, and not necessary for our present considerations. It should, however, be mentioned that the ability of the females themselves to transfer their social rank to their offspring must have been acquired in the course of evolution, and thus be genetically controlled. The mechanism of transfer of social hierarchy clarifies this question. The infants form play groups very early, and the mothers support their own young in encounters occurring during play. A dominant mother will, in such events, be more efficient than a more submissive one. It is thus this aspect of maternal behavior, the tendency of mothers to support their young against other infants in play situations, that is responsible for the transmission of social rank. Whether this maternal behavior has a genetic basis has not been investigated.

A few words should be added about the evolution of the human hierarchic systems. Since the remainder of this book will be devoted to this question, it is not necessary to summarize it here. But a few remarks should be made on the evolutionary origin of human hierarchies, male and female.

We do not know much about the social organization of our prehuman ancestors, to whit *Homo erectus* or *Australopithecus.* There is no reason to assume that they had the same social organization at all times, or that even at the same time different populations of the same species had the same social pattern. But many people assume that the *Australopithecines* lived in relatively small groups in the open savannah and obtained part of their food by social hunting. Social hunting by males is found in the chimpanzee (Goodall 1971) and living in the open savannah in the baboons and the gelada. Therefore the social patterns found in these organisms are frequently taken as analogies.

It is usually assumed that early hominids lived in relatively small bands, and that hunting was restricted to the males. Some reasonable conclusions can be drawn from these assumptions. The bands are assumed to be multiple-male groups, since in hunting relatively large prey, several males must cooperate. We may also assume that a dominance order existed among the males, since this is a widespread characteristic of Old World primates and modern humans. The question arises now whether these bands were true multiple-male groups in the sense meant by Kummer (1971a), with all males having access to the females, or whether for purposes of copulation they were divided into one-male subgroups, as is found in the hamadryas baboon and the gelada. The latter situation must have arisen at some stage in evolution, since it is at present the prevalent human pattern of organization. Whether these one-male groups were polygynic or monogamous cannot be decided. But it is important to realize that a polygynic organization would give a high degree of Darwinian fitness to the polygynic males, who are frequently assumed to be the dominant ones, while monogamy would not necessarily have this consequence. Furthermore, in a polygynic situation, a hierarchy among females becomes very likely, while in monogamous organizations a hierarchy between the females is possible but not necessary.

It should be emphasized that these remarks on the role of sexual dimorphism in human evolution are highly speculative. They are based on comparisons with the social organization of living Old World primates and human societies. It has been a repeated experience in the past that hypotheses based on such a slender basis turned out to be incorrect and had to be reassessed on the basis of additional evidence. Nevertheless, we may state that, on the basis of our knowledge of sexual dimorphism and the social organization of Old World primates, the possibilities for the organization of prehuman hominids are limited, and that we may safely assume a type of social organization that has changed over time. How far social organization has affected the direction taken by morphological and psychological evolution cannot be known at our present state of knowledge. It is particularly hard to decide how and when the typically human character of gender roles arose.

SUMMARY

1. The determination of the existence of two sexes in mammals is genetically simple: it involves the X-Y chromosome mechanism determining the primary sex organs and the production of sex hormones, and the *tfm* gene controlling the competence of cells to react to the sex hormones. Complications arise because the sex hormones themselves are the result of chains of synthetic biochemical reactions that are under genic control, and because many genes—sex-controlled and sex-limited genes—act differently in male and female organisms. The existence of sex-controlled genes forms the basis of many sexual dimorphisms, the fact that in many biochemical, physiological, and morphological characters, the two sexes differ phenotypically, even though they are genotypically identical.

2. In social organisms, the two sexes differ in their social functions. They are either in a dominance relationship toward each other, or they form independent parts of society. Within one sex, there is usually a clear-cut dominance hierarchy in which each individual has his status; the function of the organism in society may depend on its sex and its status within the hierarchy of its sex. In human beings, in addition to genetic sex, there exist gender roles specifying the behavior of males and females expected in society. The existence of gender roles distinguishes human society profoundly from that of nonhuman primates, but the gender roles probably evolved from the sexual

dimorphism affecting behavioral characters present in prehuman ancestors.

3. Sexual dimorphisms are subject to selection, showing that there is a genetic basis for the existence of sexual dimorphism. Furthermore, once polymorphism for a sex-controlled character exists, it may become established by sexual selection, resulting in an additional sexually dimorphic character. While male hierarchy in many species affects the transmission of genes, there is little evidence that female hierarchies have a comparable effect, except for a case observed in the wolf. Its primary function in primates concerns rather the organization of the society, and the transmission of the social rank order to the next generation. Female hierarchy in primates is thus important for the smooth organization of primate societies. While some speculations on the social organization of prehuman hominids can be made, it is difficult to decide whether a female hierarchy existed and what role it may have played in human evolution.

NOTES

[1] In some insectivores and marsupials two Y chromosomes are found.

[2] Rare XX male humans have been described in the medical literature. Their origin is unexplained (Marinello, *et al.* 1977). For other articles on sex determination, see Ohno (1967) and Mittwoch (1967).

[3] For research on dominance order in chimpanzees, see Goodall (1971); in different species of macaques, Kawamura (1958), Koford (1963), and other workers; in Indian langurs, Jay (1965); and in gelada baboons and many others, Kummer (1971a, 1971b).

REFERENCES CITED

ALLEE, W.C. and N.E. COLLIAS
    1941—The Influence of Estradiol on the Social Organization of Flocks of Hens. *Anatomical Record* 75(Supplement):130.
ALLEE, W.C., N.E. COLLIAS, and C.Z. LUTHERMAN
    1939—Modification of the Social Order in Flocks of Hens by Injection of Testosterone Propionate. *Physiological Zoology* 12:412-440.

ALTMANN, S.A.
1962–A Field Study of the Sociobiology of Rhesus Monkeys, *Macaca mulatta. Annals of the New York Academy of Sciences* 102:338-435.

BARASH, D.P.
1974–The Evolution of Marmot Societies: A General Theory. *Science* 185:415-420.

BEACH, F.
1974–Human Sexuality and Evolution. In *Reproductive Behavior,* W. Montagna, ed. New York:Plenum.

BIRD, M.A. and H.E. SCHAFFER
1972–A Study of the Genetic Basis of Sexual Dimorphism for Wing Length in *Drosophila melanogaster. Genetics* 72:475-487.

BRONSON, F.H. and H.M. MARSDEN
1973–The Preputial Gland as an Indicator of Social Dominance in Male Mice. *Behavioral Biology* 9:625-628.

CAMPBELL, B., ed.
1972–*Sexual Selection and the Descent of Man, 1871-1971.* Chicago:Aldine.

CASPARI, E.W.
1952–Pleiotropic Gene Action. *Evolution* 6:1-18.

1965–The Evolutionary Importance of Sexual Processes and of Sexual Behavior. In *Sex and Behavior,* Frank Beach, ed. New York:Wiley.

1972–Sexual Selection in Human Evolution. In *Sexual Selection and the Descent of Man, 1871-1971,* B. Campbell, ed. Chicago:Aldine.

CHANCE, M.R.A.
1963–The Social Bond of Primates. *Primates* 4:1-22.

CHANCE, M.R.A. and A.P. MEAD
1953–Social Behavior and Primate Evolution. *Symposia of the Society for Experimental Biology* 7:395-439.

CROOK, J.H.
1972–Sexual Selection, Dimorphism and Social Organization in the Primates. In *Sexual Selection and the Descent of Man, 1871-1971,* B. Campbell, ed. Chicago:Aldine.

DANFORTH, C.H. and F. FOSTER
1929–Skin Transplantation as a Means of Studying Genetic and Endocrine Factors in the Fowl. *Journal of Experimental Zoology* 52:443-470.

DARWIN, C.
1871—*The Descent of Man and Selection in Relation to Sex.* London:John Murray.

DRICKAMER, L.C.
1974—A Ten-Year Summary of Reproductive Data for Free-Ranging *Macaca mulatta. Folia Primatologica* 21:61-80.

DRONAMRAJU, K.R.
1960—Hypertrichosis of the Pinna of the Human Ear, Y-Linked Pedigrees. *Journal of Genetics* 57:230-244.

EBERT, P.D. and J.S. HYDE
1976—Selection for Agonistic Behavior in Wild Female *Mus musculus. Behavior Genetics* 6:291-304.

ETKIN, W.
1954—Social Behavior and the Evolution of Man's Mental Faculties. *American Naturalist* 88:129-142.

FORD, E.B.
1964—*Ecological Genetics.* London:Methuen.

FREDERICSON, E.
1952—Aggressiveness in Female Mice. *Journal of Comparative and Physiological Psychology* 45:254-257.

GOLDSCHMIDT, R.
1920—*Mechanismus und Physiologie der Geschlechtsbestimmung.* Berlin:Bornträger.
1955—*Theoretical Genetics.* Berkeley:University of California Press.

GOODALL, J. (VAN LAWICK)
1971—*In the Shadow of Man.* Boston:Houghton Mifflin.

HALL, K.R.L., R.C. BOELKINS, and M.J. GOSWELL
1965—Behavior of Patas Monkey, *Erythrocebus patas* in Captivity, With Notes on the Natural Habitat. *Folia primatologica* 3:22-49.

HARRIS, H.
1946—Heredity and Premature Baldness in Man. *Annals of Eugenics* 13:172-181.

HAUGE, M. and B. HERVALD
1955—Heredity in Gout and Hyperuricemia. *Acta Medica Scandinavia* 152:247-257.

HESS, O. and G.F. MEYER
1968—Genetic Activities of the Y Chromosome in *Drospophila* during Spermatogenesis. *Advances in Genetics* 14:171-223.

HYDE, J.S. and P.D. EBERT
1976—Correlated Response in Selection for Aggressiveness in Female Mice. I. Male Aggressiveness. *Behavior Genetics* 6:421-427.

IMPERATO-McGINLEY, J., L. GUERRERO, T. GAUTIER, and R.F. PETERSON
  1974—Steroid 5-reductase Deficiency in Man: An Inherited Form of Male Pseudohermaphroditism. *Science* 186:1213-1215.

JAY, P.
  1965—The Common Langur of North India. In *Primate Behavior: Field Studies of Monkeys and Apes*, I. DeVore, ed. New York:Holt, Rinehart and Winston.

JENSEN, E.V. and E.D. DeSOMBRE
  1973—Estrogen-Receptor Interaction. *Science* 182:126-134.

KANT, K. and Y.R. AHUJA
  1970—Inheritance of Stuttering. *Acta medica auxologica* 2:179-191.

KAWAI, M.
  1958—On the Rank System in a Natural Troop of Japanese Monkeys. I. The Basic and Dependent Rank. *Primates* 1:111-113.

KAWAMURA, S.
  1958—Matriarchal Social Ranks in the Minoo B Troop: A Study of the Rank System of Japanese Monkeys. *Primates* 1:149-156.

KLEIN, J. and D.W. BAILEY
  1971—Histocompatibility Differences in Wild Mice: Further Evidence for the Existence of Deme Structure in Natural Populations of the House Mouse. *Genetics* 68:287-297.

KOFORD, C.B.
  1963—Rank of Mothers and Sons in Bands of Rhesus Monkeys. *Science* 141:356-357.

KOYAMA, N.
  1967—On Dominance Rank and Kinship of a Wild Japanese Monkey Troop in Arashiyama. *Primates* 8:189-216.

KUMMER, H.
  1971a-*Primate Societies: Group Techniques of Ecological Adaptation*. Chicago:Aldine.

  1971b-Immediate Causes of Primate Social Structures. *Proceedings of the Third International Congress of Primatology*, volume 3, H. Kummer, ed. Basel:S. Karger.

LYON, M.F. and S.G. HAWKES
  1970—X-linked Gene for Testicular Feminization in the Mouse. *Nature* 227:1217.

MARINELLO, N.Y., *et al.*
  1977—An XX Man: Unexpected Ascertainment, Endocrinologic Findings and Autopsy. *Annals of Internal Medicine*. Forthcoming.

MITTWOCH, U.
1967–*Sex Chromosomes.* New York:Academic.

MORGAN, T.H.
1920–The Genetic Factor for Hen-Feathering in the Sebright Bantam. *Biological Bulletin* 39:257-259.

NAGEL, U.
1971–Social Organization in a Baboon Hybrid Zone. *Proceedings of the Third International Congress of Primatology,* volume 3, H. Kummer, ed. Basel:S. Karger.

NORIKOSHI, K.
1974–The Development of Peer-Mate Relationships in Japanese Macaque Infants. *Primates* 15:39-46.

OHNO, S.
1967–*Sex Chromosomes and Sex-Linked Genes.* New York: Springer.
1972–Simplicity of Mammalian Regulatory Systems Inferred by Simple Gene Determination of Sex Phenotypes. *Nature* 234: 134-137.

O'MALLEY, B.W. and A.R. MEANS
1974–Female Steroid Hormones and Target Cell Nuclei. *Science* 183:610-620.

PALENZONA, D.L. and R. ALICHIO
1973–Differential Response to Selection on the Two Sexes in *Drosophila melanogaster. Genetics* 74:533-542.

PARDI, E.
1948–Dominance Order in *Polistes gallicus. Physiological Zoology* 21:1-13.

RABB, J.B., J. WOOLPY, and B.E. GINSBURG
1967–Social Relationship in a Group of Captive Wolves. *American Zoologist* 7:305-311.

REINBOTH, R.
1975–Spontaneous and Hormone-Induced Sex-Inversion in Wrasses (LABRIDAE). *Pubblicazioni della Stazione Zoologica di Napoli* 39(Supplement):550-573.

ROBERTSON, E.D.R.
1972–Social Control of Sex Reversal in Coral-Reef Fish. *Science* 177:1007-1009.

RODMAN, P.S.
1973–Population Composition and Adaptive Organization among Orangutans of the Kutai Reserve. In *Comparative Ecology and Behavior of Primates,* R.P. Michael and J.H. Crook, eds. New York:Academic.

SCHJELDERUP-EBBE, T.
  1922—Beiträge zur Socialpsychologie des Haushuhns. *Zeitschrift für Psychologie* 88:225-252.
SCOTT, J.P.
  1966—Agonistic Behavior of Mice and Rats: A Review. *American Zoologist* 6:683-701.
SCOTT, J.P. and J.L. FULLER
  1965—*Genetics and the Social Behavior of the Dog.* Chicago:University of Chicago Press.
SELANDER, R.K.
  1970—Biochemical Polymorphism in Populations of the House Mouse and Old-Field Mouse. *Symposia of the London Zoological Society* 26:73-91.
SHEPPARD, P.M.
  1961—Some Contributions to Genetics Resulting from the Study of the Lepidoptera. *Advances in Genetics* 10:165-216.
SMYTH, C.J., C.W. COTTERMAN, and R.H. FREYBERG
  1948—The Genetics of Gout and Hyperuricemia—An Analysis of 19 Families. *Journal of Clinical Investigation* 27:749-759.
STEMPFEL, R.S. and G.M. TOMKINS
  1966—Congenital Virilizing Hyperplasia (The Adrenogenital Syndrome). In *The Metabolic Basis of Inherited Disease* (second edition), S.B. Stanbury, J.B. Wyngarden, and D.S. Fredrickson, eds. New York:McGraw-Hill.
STEPHENSON, G.R.
  1974—Social Structure of Mating Activity in Japanese Macaques. In *Symposia of the Fifth Congress of the International Primatological Society* 1, J.H. Crook, ed. Tokyo:Japan Science Press.
TOLLMAN, J. and J.A. KING
  1956—The Effects of Testosterone Propionate on Aggression in Male and Female C57BL/10 Mice. *British Journal of Animal Behavior* 6:147-149.
VAN RIPER, C.
  1971—*The Nature of Stuttering.* Englewood Cliffs:Prentice-Hall.
YAMADA, M.
  1966—Five Natural Troops of Japanese Monkeys on Shodashima Island. I. Distribution and Social Organization. *Primates* 7:315-362.
YOSHIDA, K.
  1968—Local and Intertroop Variability in Ecology and Social Behavior of Common Indian Langurs. In *Primates: Studies in Adaptation and Variability,* P. Jay, ed. New York:Holt, Rinehart and Winston.

4

Female Hierarchy: An Evolutionary Perspective

VIRGINIA ABERNETHY

Mothering has been a function of the female through all of primate history. This does not imply that males do not assist in infant and child care, but only that females have usually been occupied with this for most of their adult lives. Moreover, from the point of view of species survival, adequate maternal performance is a *sine qua non*. Therefore, in approaching the ethological question of what kind of social adaptation is innately female, it is certainly relevant to examine the effect that particular types of organizations have on a woman's sense of competence as a mother.

In this paper we summarize research that links social network with sense of maternal competence and discuss its implications for female hierarchies. Finally, the relevance of these findings for female behavior in other hierarchical contexts is explored.

A study carried out with middle and upper-middle class New England women, all of whom had at least one preschool age child showed that there was a strong statistical association $(r = .47, P < .01)$ between having a tight social network and feeling comfortable in performance of the maternal role, including such dimensions as enforcing discipline, giving love, and maintaining poise and ego integrity in the face of a child's demands (Abernethy 1973).

Social network refers to the pattern of linkages by which a nuclear family is articulated with a larger society (Bott 1957).

123

Networks can be located along a continuum from tight to loose. From the point of view of a focal person, a tight network exists when its members (friends or relatives external to the household) all know and see each other fairly regularly. Theoretically, inchoosing is maximized in this type of network (Figure 1).

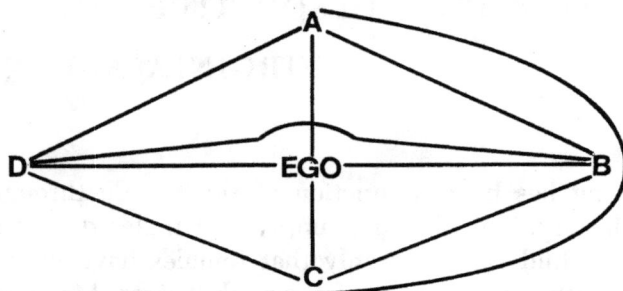

FIGURE 1. *Tight network*

The contrasting type, a loose network, exists when ego's closest associates rarely meet among themselves and may even be unacquainted. In the extreme case, there are no known loops in the network (Figures 2 and 3).

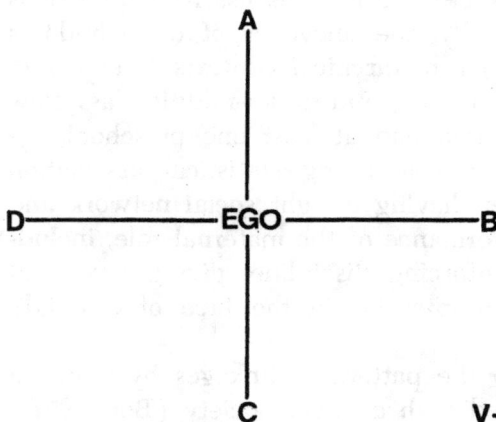

FIGURE 2.

FIGURE 3.

Empirically, the definitional properties of networks are associated with a cluster of other variables. Thus, in addition to the criterion that net members be acquainted, a tight social network tends to be characterized by frequent contact between members, short distances between their residences, and inclusion of one's mother in the network.

These four network components—density of relationships, activity level, localization, and kinship—are not only substantially intercorrelated but also are very good individual predictors of a woman's sense of competence in management of the maternal role. Tight networks appear to facilitate physical sharing of childcare responsibilities. They also provide not only consensual validation of childrearing values and techniques but also positive feedback from significant others, which enhances the mother's self-image as a total person. In contrast, women in loose networks appear to be uncertain of their childrearing goals and of the means for operationalizing any plan. They often feel engulfed by children's needs, particularly the need for affection. Moreover, they find it difficult to make reciprocal childcare arrangements with friends because there is no communality of expectations about appropriate behavior, either among mothers or their children.

Thus, it appears that nonworking suburban or urban mothers are most likely to enjoy their children and to feel that they are doing a good job as a mother when they are located in a specific kind of social structure. Moreover, the data suggest that the essential elements of the favorable milieu are kinship and neighborhood association, both of which are identified within the tight social network constellation.

The validity of such conclusions is intuitively obvious when one considers that the tight network is modern society's closest approximation to conditions in a traditional social structure and probably to humanoid troop structure as well. Moreover, the evolutionary success of man suggests that significant benefits accrue to this social adaptation for childrearing.

Thus, study of the behavior of mothers in tight social networks is especially relevant to the problem of understanding female hierarchies. *If predisposition to form hierarchies is part of the*

*female genetic endowment, this should be expressed and pre-
sumably be observable in the tight social networks of women
who are mothers of young children.*

After such an introduction, it seems unfortunate to admit that
I know of no systematic observations having been made on this
phenomenon precisely. However, the near absence of material on
female hierarchies may be instructive. For example, in a detailed
work such as Beatrice Whiting's *Mothers of Six Cultures* (1965),
there is minimal evidence of hierarchical structures even in a
society, the Rajputs of India, where daughters-in-law live under
the close scrutiny of their husband's mother and are tyrannized
by her. Here, daughters-in-law escape to separate compounds
as soon as they have enough children, enough influence over
their husbands, or when the level of bickering reaches degrees
intolerable to everyone (Whiting 1965).

However, despite the reasonable possibility that results might
be negative, the existence of hierarchies within the context of
women's childcare functions is a theoretically important area for
the study of what is innately female.

Before turning to a more speculative portion of this discussion, it may be well to clarify what will be understood by the
word *hierarchy*. In its simplest sense, a hierarchy is a group of
persons arranged in order of rank, grade, class, etc. It is this
principle of ranking with its implications of subordination and
dominance, and the corollary, control of others, that appear to
be its central element. It should also be noted that power within
a hierarchy depends not only upon the objective force or sanctions that can be applied from above, but also upon the acknowl-
edgment on the part of subordinates that the higher authority is
legitimate, i.e., a hierarchy is the repository of legitimate power
distributed in decreasing amounts from the upper to the lower
levels of the organization.

With this definition as a guide, the balance of the paper will
include: 1) speculation on logical considerations that bear on the
genetic predisposition to form female hierarchies; 2) enumera-
tion of such female hierarchies as can be observed in our society;
and 3) female functioning within a hierarchy.

Focusing on genetic predisposition of women to form hierarchies, a fundamental question becomes: What is the utility of a hierarchy in performance of the female functions of procreation and rearing young? That is, do female hierarchies bestow a selective advantage on the individual or the group?

The nonhuman primate data are ambiguous on this question: first, because most reports suggest that female hierarchies are difficult to identify and unstable; and second, because there is also evidence that sons of high ranking females are most likely themselves to achieve a dominant status within the troop. Are there, then, some females that are higher ranking than others, or are there not? If there are, it appears that the male offspring of such mothers are slightly better off. And in a troop structure where a limited number of dominant males inseminates the majority of females, there is thus a higher than expected probability that the genes of a high ranking female will be passed on to her grand-offspring.

However, one questions whether this factor could itself have exerted sufficient selective force to override other dimensions which militate against the emergence of female predispositions to form hierarchies. Among these is the female reproductive cycle which, during the later stages of pregnancy and shortly after parturition, makes it more difficult for an individual to maintain status if challenged. An interesting feature of the primate data, however, is that mothers of newborn infants are never challenged. This is the time when they have highest status, and they get it without a fight (Goodall 1965). There clearly is selective advantage in this: mother and infant receive the most care and protection at the time when it is most essential for the newborn's survival.

As the infant matures the mother's status wanes. And in all probability her position has been preempted by mothers of infants younger than her own so that she is inhibited from regaining it by aggressive behavior. Thus, the data suggest that to a large extent biologic rhythms, and not intrinsic character traits of the individual, determine female rankings among nonhuman primates. In this probably lies a major countervailing pressure against selection for the development of female hierarchies. Little advantage from fighting for rank accrues to the individual because her preeminence will not last. It gives way before the contradictory behavior which appears to have been most consistently selected: protection of that valuable and vulnerable member of the troop, the newborn.

For the female nonhuman primate, status appears to be legitimized by parturition, and since this is inherently a temporary stage in the cycle, it is mutually exclusive with the ranking principle of a hierarchy.

It is conceivable that there would be selection for female hierarchies if they created a superior milieu for infant or childcare. This would certainly be the case if these activities lent themselves to specialization. Would it be, for example, most efficient if one mother did all the grooming of infants, another did the watching during play hours, another bedded them all down, and so forth? If we can answer in the affirmative, then this is a basis for hierarchy: specialization not only requires organization, but it also invites the ranking of tasks in order of their importance or difficulty, and the assumption by specialists of rank assigned to their work.

However, specialization flourishes under conditions of mass production. For it to be applied to childcare, all infants should be the same age, because one mother cannot easily watch clingers, creepers, and climbers, for instance. Moreover, there is the problem of nursing. So long as mothers are the food source for the infant, a one-to-one task orientation is nearly unavoidable: that particular infant is that particular mother's job.

When the young become juveniles and are weaned, there is more flexibility in maternal arrangements. In fact, chimpanzee females have been observed with a cluster of several young, obviously a situation of temporarily caring for other mothers' babies. Whether or not this service is usually reciprocated is not known. Nor has the kinship relationship of absent mothers and the caretaker been reported, to my knowledge.

This chimpanzee behavior has a correlate in the baby-sitting pools formed by suburban mothers in the United States. In passing it may be noted that tight social networks are most successful in operating such pools, probably because their children share values and expectations about appropriate behavior and controls. Under these circumstances, caring for someone else's child does not degenerate into the chaos either of constant policing or else allowing the visiting child to exert a corrupting influence on the established standards of the hostess's menage.

But trading baby-sitting time does not create a hierarchy. Although there may be an organized redistribution of time so that mothers are not continuously responsible for their children, the services performed are identical. There is little basis for grading or ranking. Mothering has always been and continues to be essentially the same work. Women may relieve each other, but there is no apparent gain from instituting specialization or levels of organization within which higher levels can orchestrate the behavior of successively lower levels.

These observations and speculations suggest that over evolutionary time there has been little functional advantage associated with the formation of female hierarchies. Insofar as the female usually has assumed responsibility for childrearing, and noting that there is little advantage to hierarchical organization when this is the task, a logical conclusion is that hierarchical behavior has never been a focus of selective pressure and that genetic predisposition toward the creation of hierarchy is not a major determinant of female behavior.

One may now ask how these conclusions tally with observations on female hierarchies. First let us admit that female hierarchies are hard to find, and when found a suspicion lingers that they are imitative of male archetypes: sororities and religious orders have this quality. There is no doubt that the monasteries and fraternities existed prior to their female counterparts. So, to posit independent invention of the later groups is unnecessarily complicated. Imitation remains the most parsimonious explanation of their origins. Yet more clearly, other hierarchically organized female groups openly describe themselves as satellites or auxiliaries of male organizations: observe, for example, the relationship of Rebekka's Daughters to DeMolay and Masons.

If formal organizations seem to be so easily disposed of, what can still be said of informal hierarchies (for instance those based on school performance, skill as a hostess, or popularity)?

A female colleague with whom I discussed this problem suggests that, although competition may be intense, it is unacknowledged, unspoken, and subject to denial. A corollary, or perhaps the cause of this, is the pervasive sense that the competition and also the resulting ranking is not legitimate. For some performance goals, this lack of legitimacy in the competition appears intuitively to be a correct appraisal. That is, for a girl to admit that she is working for popularity would diminish her; similarly with the hostess. The effect is less clear to me, however, when the objective is academic grades, but here we enter a realm that clearly is task-oriented and where standards apply equally to men and women.

I suspect that, for a woman, the legitimacy of a hierarchy depends largely upon its being task-oriented. Professions that are traditionally female, such as nursing, are hierarchically organized to some extent, and competition for achievement within them is open and approved. It appears that when work is most effectively organized within the pyramidal structure, women can work in this way with other women. Florence Nightingale's organization of nursing services during the Crimean War and subsequently in England is an example. Another is the outstanding achievement of the Frontier Nursing Service in depressed areas of Kentucky and Tennessee. And although women have not usually been in the higher levels of the work force, it seems reasonable to suppose that this capability to give or take orders within a goal-oriented hierarchy extends to participation in heterosexual realms.

All of this *is* consistent with the position that there is a difference between male and female, although naturally any differences refer to modal behavior and do not imply that distributions of male and female potentialities do not overlap. Some women appear to perform well in a hierarchy that is goal-oriented, but this is also a realm in which many men are obviously effective. I do not need to be the one to propose that the male is the political animal, who invents, works well in, and manipulates power structures of which hierarchy is the purest type.

Here, I wish to inject a cautionary note. The obverse side of the coin is that not uncommonly, in many realms of behavior, pathology appears in a few individuals in whom special talents or virtue become overdeveloped: for example, the musclebound athlete; the actor who compulsively continues to act off stage so that he or she becomes confused about his/her real identity; or to take a possibly controversial example, medicine's life prolonging technology, which sometimes threatens to overwhelm considerations of what is most comfortable for the patient.

Applied to hierarchical organizations, this development, past the point of maximally effective functioning, occurs when hierarchies rigidify so that there are delays either in the collection and processing of information or in the use of information to coordinate activity. Studies in business administration suggest that information is translated into action more slowly where there are strict hierarchies; that is, when information must go all the way to the top before directives begin to flow down the chain of command. Where there is a high level, central control point where all information is collected and all action coordinated, decision making is time consuming, and thus it appears that this form of organization functions best where the environment is stable. Where the environment is changing rapidly so that new information must be processed and acted upon quickly, the optimal point for decision making is the point where all information can first be made available. This usually creates what is known as a lattice structure; it by-passes many hierarchical levels and is capable of more effective adaptation to a changing environment; but it takes considerably greater interpersonal skills to operate in a lattice-type organization (Lawrence and Lorsch 1967).

In business, the profit motive is a constant source of pressure for adaption of the organization to the exigencies of the environment. In concrete terms, the container industry, where standardization of a product is the primary objective, functions well with a rigid hierarchy. However, the prepared food industry, which must adjust to volatile consumer tastes, is most profitable when organized along lattice work lines (so, for example, that basic and applied research are directly coordinated with the sales department).

However, in the many bureaucratic organizations where profit is *not* the accepted measure of performance, tendencies toward nonadaptive rigidification of a hierarchy may go uncorrected. In this case the nonfunctional dimensions of hierarchy could come to be powerful determinants of procedure, perhaps to the detriment of the organization's goals.

In my view, dimensions of hierarchy that are most likely to be elaborated beyond the point where they are functional are all aspects of status and rank, preserving an image, or saving face. Secrecy is a technique often used in the service of enhancing status. When secrecy becomes an important element of procedure, it seems often to be true that status and rank have come to be of importance for their own sake, rather than to facilitate action. An ultimate example is the ritual hierarchy of a fraternal organization. I suggest that the very persons who invent hierarchies, which have little purpose other than to legitimize control of some men by their fellows, are the ones who savor the structure, the pomp and ceremony, the exclusiveness, and the further trappings and perquisites of power.

Hierarchy focuses power for action. But it can become an end in itself, where self-perpetuation by the organization and self-aggrandizement by the individual displace goals.

This returns to the subject of this symposium: I wish to propose that, because females are not innately disposed to organize into hierarchies and because, as others have said, primate males appear to be the archetypal "political animal," the male is more susceptible than the female to the pathological exaggeration implicit in hierarchical structure. That is, the male more often than the female is emotionally fulfilled by the hierarchy per se.

A corollary is that hierarchical structures and lines of authority are more likely to be used by a woman exclusively in pursuit of a goal, so that the status aspects of hierarchy, including secrecy and strict protocol, are less likely to be elaborated by a woman than by a man. All of this has been conjecture, although potentially framable as testable hypotheses focusing on the executive styles of men and women who have risen to equivalent positions of power. The ideal research design would include controls for sex of interviewer or other research personnel as well as a double-blind condition, but Hennig and Jardim's recently published *The Managerial Woman* (1977) is a valuable approach to many of the issues under discussion.

Overall, this essay leads one to the tentative suggestions that, although the woman's reflexive skills in the consolidation and management of power may be less acute than those of a male counterpart, there should be a measure of compensation in the absence of her need for rigid procedures and reassurance of rank. If the hypothesis on women's use of hierarchy is correct, the woman is likely to be accessible and informal, willing to risk the image of infallibility, and theoretically, information should flow more easily up to a woman.

Clearly, one or two instances do not make a case. Systematic research is in order. Thus, my objective here is limited to framing a hypothesis, i.e., that women in the higher levels of a hierarchy will be found to be more informal and able to dispense with the ceremonial attributes of power than men at comparable levels. The hypothesized female style could have weakness with respect to focusing attention and eliciting superior performance from subordinates, but this also is unknown. On the basis of the small amount of evidence available, therefore, I wish only to suggest that femaleness apparently does not preclude possession of administrative ability. And the willingness to risk an image by dispensing with the nonfunctional attributes of hierarchy can be viewed as a positive asset.

REFERENCES CITED

ABERNETHY, VIRGINIA
    1973—Social Network and Response to the Maternal Role. *International Journal of Sociology and the Family* 3(1):86-92.
BOTT, ELIZABETH
    1957—*Family and Social Network: Roles, Norms and External Relationships in Ordinary Urban Families*. London:Tavistock.
DeVORE, IRVEN, ed.
    1965—*Primate Behavior*. New York:Holt, Rinehart and Winston.
GOODALL, JANE (VAN LAWICK)
    1965—Chimpanzees of the Gombe Stream Reserve. In *Primate Behavior*, I. DeVore, ed. New York:Holt, Rinehart and Winston.

HENNIG, MARGARET and ANNE JARDIM
  1977—*The Managerial Woman*. New York:Doubleday.
LAWRENCE, P. and J. LORSCH
  1967—*Organization and Environment*. Boston:Division of Research, Graduate School of Business Administration, Harvard University.
WHITING, BEATRICE
  1965—*Mothers of Six Cultures*. New York:Holt, Rinehart and Winston.

5

Sex Differences in the Structure of Attention

M.R.A. CHANCE

"One more man-made construction, an abstraction placed over the mystery of things"—is what we need and seek. We must want to get closer to the things themselves, particularly to things that are not of man so that we can discover our lost kinship with them and a cosmos can be born for man again.

We have to learn to live again in the presence of mystery that forever baffles the understanding but renews us even as it goes on baffling us.

William Barrett, *Time of need*

The information in the behavioral sciences is still very meager and, as a consequence, science as a whole is heavily biased towards the physical sciences. The scientific information we have on ourselves is, therefore, itself biased, so much so that the way we discuss our behavior is still largely the outcome of traditional ways of thinking. This means that we are not really aware of the potential for understanding what lies ahead of us when a single behavioral science has been established. Ethology, together with social anthropology, should be concerned with establishing such a basis for human understanding. The reader should therefore welcome and appreciate the fact that ethological dis-

135

coveries already challenge behavioral scientists to realign their thinking. At the beginning of this article I shall present a framework which, for the first time, makes it possible to discuss primate behavior, both human and nonhuman.

If you will allow yourself to judge the claim by the consistency of the presentation you will, I think, agree that we have all the essentials of a comprehensive paradigm for a biosocial science. This does not mean that we reduce humankind's status to that of the ape or monkey, nor that we elevate features discernible in subhuman primates to overriding importance in the explanatory scheme. We simply have achieved a congruency in the way we are thinking about the structure of behavior, and can therefore discern a structure common to both humans and subhuman primates. This enables us (despite the small amount of material that so far exists) to determine for our present purposes how sex differences could be responsible for a deep-seated bias in the development of an individual's behavior.

Two recent discoveries not only clarify the data on subhuman primate behavior, but also have profound implications for understanding human behavior. They are: 1) the existence of two mutually exclusive and antithetical modes in which behavior is organized; and 2) the concept of a social referent. I will define these two concepts in this paper and discuss them with reference to the way they operate in controlling the growth of behavior in the young. By comparing and contrasting the features of subhuman primate societies of those Old World species closest in phylogeny to ourselves, we can discuss features that are prominent in one and absent in another. In this way we are able to unravel some of the complexity of the underlying structure of human social behavior.

CLASSIFICATORY FEATURES OF PRIMATE SOCIETIES

I have defined attention structure and shown that it consists of an analysis of forms of predominant attention (Chance 1967; Chance and Jolly 1970). Predominant attention occurs when subordinate members of the rank order, cohort, or band focus persistent or repeated attention toward more dominant members, especially a social referent. In these situations, a predominant amount of the individual's attention is involved in maintaining social cohesion.

Using predominant attention as the criterion for classifying subhuman primate societies, we can see that agonistic species can be both centric, if predominant attention of all individuals is directed toward a focal individual, usually the dominant male; or acentric, if it is directed toward the environment. As demonstrated in the lattice in Figure 1, subhuman primates can be divided into two types with humans being predominantly centric, but possessing the characteristics of both the agonistic and hedonic modes.

C E N T R I C	Man	
	Baboon $\diagdown$ Gelada — Hamadryas $\diagdown$ Savannah	Chimp
	Macaque $\diagdown$ Rhesus — Japanese $\diagdown$ Barbary ape	Gorilla Bonnet macaque
A C E N T R I C	Patas Drills Mandrills	Orangutan
	AGONISTIC	HEDONIC

FIGURE 1. *Attentional classification of primate societies*

The organization of attention into agonistic and hedonic modes has already been discussed (Chance 1973, 1975). In the agonistic mode, an individual's behavior is rigid. In other words, the individual organizes elements of flight and aggression (or ritual elements arising from a balance between the two) around a predominant focus of attention by acting out attentional "cut-offs," displacement acts, and submission postures—all of which circumscribe behavior and make it rigid. Contact between individuals also takes place in fixed, ritualized ways, e.g., grooming or behavior of a sexual type. In the hedonic mode, however, the behavior structure is flexible. There is no predominant focus of attention, so that exploration can be made, possibly by attention to the object explored; then curiosity (alertness to novelty) and interest (direction of attention by awareness of particular environmental features) come into play. Contact behavior between individuals, also organized by exploration, is polymorphous and flexible.

Features of human societies arise from the fact that these two basic modalities (agonistic and hedonic) are combined in different ways with the centric tendencies. Lomax's (1972) multifactorial analysis of dance forms has revealed a classification of societies that illustrates the operation of the agonistic and hedonic features of human societies. They are his manipulative and sensuous aspects, respectively.

The predominance of the hedonic mode arises in any simple human society through favorable environmental circumstances in the past and/or the present. The situation is reversed for the prominence of the agonistic mode. In more complex and powerful societies, these two modes interact in the way discovered by Lomax and by the degree to which internal differentiation provides enclaves within which the hedonic mode can be developed by individuals of a predominantly agonistic society. In our own society, it is potentially within the capabilities of individual men and women to determine their mode of behavior. But we must consider the extent to which inherent hedonic and agonistic tendencies are influenced during ontogeny by sex of the individual and whether or not this then affects gender role.

FORMS OF SOCIAL ATTENTION AND COHESION

Every species of subhuman primate has its own unique pattern of social relations which results in a set of subgroupings within the society as a whole. However, as pointed out in Chance and

Jolly (1970), three types can be identified in the majority of groups studied thus far. They are: 1) the assemblies of adult females and their juveniles; 2) adult cohorts of males; and 3) clusters of juveniles, consisting of young that are no longer dependent on their mothers but have not yet joined either of the adult groups (Chance and Jolly 1970).

All these subgroups are simply modalities in a structure of attention that functions to hold individuals together and serves as the base on which social behavior is built. The infrastructure operates in two distinct modes to bring the society as a whole together. In both modes, group members cohere on the basis of the common attention to a focal individual.

To argue that a society of a particular species is constructed on one of these modes is to suggest that for the greater part of their lives individuals are related to each other in one of these ways. Chimpanzee and gorilla societies, for instance, are constructed primarily in the hedonic mode, recently found to be based on display as a means of getting attention. Chimpanzees, moving through the trees, are often separated except that they are able to call to one another; mutual display is used to reunite the group after they have come together again. Gorillas, on the other hand, move on the ground through forest and keep in touch by a chain of attention ending up with the focal male.

Macaque and baboon societies, by contrast, are constructed in the agonistic mode, based on conflict and avoidance of attack from the dominant male. The open terrain inhabited by these species makes it possible for individuals to be constantly aware of the predominant focus. Monkeys foraging in open country are potentially under attack by predators and always keep sight of the dominant males for the protection afforded by coordinated defense.

We shall now consider the features typical of these two modalities as shown by chimpanzees, on the one hand, and macaques and baboons, on the other. Then we shall show that these two systems by which behavior is organized exist in the behavior structure of two species of macaque. The great apes are exceptional in that they appear not to be able to cohere by agonistic means.

Hedonic Cohesion

First let us consider how the cohesion of the whole group is achieved in a hedonic society through display. Schaller (1963) in his study of the wild gorilla, was the first to point out that when the dominant male was ready to move off again after a rest period, he stood in a prominent position and in a characteristic posture: legs fully extended, vertical and rigid, looking ahead of him. After he had held this posture for some time, the rest of the group gathered round him, and he then moved off. Schaller also pointed out that when an adult male beats his chest and advances toward an intruder (such as Schaller himself), he not only acts out an intimidating display toward the intruder but also indicates his whereabouts to the rest of the group. Reynolds and Reynolds (1965) in their study of the Budango forest chimpanzees early on witnessed the so-called "carnivals" in which all the chimpanzees hoot, jump about, beat the resonant bases of trees, and wave sticks in the air, displaying toward each other in this manner. They noticed that this display took place particularly when two groups of chimpanzees met in the forest and that it was followed by much contact behavior including kissing, touching, and some pseudosexual behavior.

Reynolds and Luscombe (1969) found that it was much easier to understand the nature of this mutual display when they studied chimpanzees in a thirty-acre enclosure in New Mexico where an American Air Force research unit was stationed. On my own visit there, I noticed that in the early morning chimpanzees would wander over the enclosure and explore in various directions, often separated by 200 yards. Then perhaps, as a group, they would clamber into the old trees where they would see another group. Immediately, they would move toward them and make contact, showing some excitement when they met. On one occasion, this led to some old sacking and sticks being thrown into the air.

Briefly, what Reynolds and Luscombe found was that at times when fruit was provided early in the morning the chimpanzees gathered into a group and a lot of mutual displaying took place. They also found that the amount of attention paid to any particular chimpanzee depended on his displaying ability and did not correlate in any way with the amount of aggressive behavior shown by any individual. Moreover, an individual's ability to become the focus of attention through displays led him to be the center of a group when fruit-sharing took place. In this way a successful displayer was also successful in getting a large share of the fruit. Subsequently, the group broke up into twos and threes and moved off in pursuit of different activities.

As I pointed out earlier, the great apes are peculiar in that they do not show any persistent agonism. This means that, apart from the coherence of small groups, the whole group is brought together only through mutual display, binding the individual's attention from time to time onto one another.

Agonistic Cohesion

The mechanism that holds agonistic societies together is of a different kind. As pointed out earlier, the fact that baboons and macaques live largely in open country means that it is possible for them to be aware of the dominant male at all times and for him thereby to be the focus of the group's attention. Although they may be largely preoccupied with foraging and thereby be spread over quite a large area, they are nevertheless ready at any moment to coordinate their own behavior with that of the dominant male in defense of the group as a whole. As individuals, they do not move out of sight of the center, so we must assume that they are always attentive to it. This has been demonstrated in the way the hamadryas baboon and the rhesus macaque behave as the troops move away from their sleeping sites in the morning. Here, the direction of the movement of the troop as a whole results from the initiative of subadult males moving out in different directions, and from the eventual coordination of their initiative with the direction ultimately taken by the dominant male.

Kummer and Kurt's study (1963) of the one-male groups of the hamadryas baboon, moreover, makes it clear that this unit is the result of the confinement of the individual's attention within his own group, focused on the male. In this way, hamadryas baboons move about as a very tightly packed group. Here their attention is coordinated through neck bites inflicted by the male on harem members that remain any distance away.

From time to time in semi-captive colonies and during fairly prolonged episodes in the wild, threatening, chasing, fleeing, and various forms of submission are shown in vigorous agonistic encounters between adults of the group, mainly the males. At all times the individual in an agonistic community must be ready to defend his status or avoid being the object of severe attack, and this can only be done by persistent awareness of the dominant focus. The dominant males, having a superfluity of aggressiveness, may be provoked either accidentally or because certain spatial and behavioral regularities have been transgressed. It is not surprising, therefore, that spacing out and status are persistent preoccupations of the individuals of such a group. Most interactions within the group (e.g., submission, flight) are designed to terminate the conflict inherent in the situation. In this respect, therefore, agonistic behavior contrasts markedly with hedonic behavior as it tends to terminate active interactions, whereas hedonic behavior tends to promote social intercourse.

COMPARISON OF HEDONIC AND AGONISTIC BEHAVIOR

In order to make a comparison between the agonistic and hedonic modes, it is easier to describe one of them to contrast this description with the corresponding features of the other. In doing so I shall attempt to abstract from the information available the characteristic features of the hedonic mode. I shall do this by contrasting the behavior of the chimpanzee, which exhibits the hedonic mode in its most characteristic form, with the agonistic behavior shown by baboons and macaques. Until we have as clear an idea as possible about the characteristics of the modes of behavior in the subhuman primates, we cannot hope to interpret human behavior.

Undoubtedly the feature that affects most aspects of behavior is its flexibility in the hedonic mode. This leads to an increase in the range of behavior and the readiness with which a switch in behavior can take place. In the chimpanzee, the range is extended by the variety of behavior that it exhibits in the wild and also by its readiness, in semi-captive conditions, to acquire entirely new behavioral forms. This may well reflect an enhanced ability to receive rewards for acquiring a new skill. This in turn undoubtedly reflects a greater flexibility in the control of attention and excitement.

One of the outstanding features of chimpanzee society is the prominence of contact behavior, as illustrated by Reynolds (1973). In the first place, greetings involve contact behavior in a number of ways; for example, touching hands, touching another's body, kissing and various forms of hugging, and frequently, when greatly excited, some form of sexual behavior. This is often followed by the group's breaking up into pairs which move off with their arms around each other. These actions lead to the separation of the various subgroups of the society and provide the opportunity for a later reunion.

From the work of Mason (1965) it is possible to infer that contact in all these instances is a form of reassurance. Undoubtedly, the widespread occurrence of contact in chimpanzee behavior reduces tension and enables the individual rapidly to control his excitement.

By contrast, members of an agonistic society are constantly aware of each other and in each other's presence. Thus the opportunity for meeting in the way chimpanzees do does not arise. Unlike chimpanzees, which can be seen moving in an exploratory fashion over fairly large areas in pairs or even threes with their arms around each other, subadult macaques or baboons have no contact except that the younger ones may jump on elder males' backs in periods of social excitement.

The meeting of two individuals in an agonistic society always involves a heightening of the latent conflict, met with postural and facial appeasement gestures, such as presentation, lip-smacking, and "appeasement face." If physical contact is established, it is in the form of very stereotyped ritual grooming. One individual usually grooms another, although mutual grooming occasionally takes place. The action consists of a sharp downward and sideways combing movement of the fingers of one hand, while the other hand is used for examining and picking at the exposed skin.

Another contrast between the types is in their use of tools. Chimpanzees in the wild use sticks as tools in a great variety of ways. They use sticks and branches to hit the ground or to throw at potential predators. They also use them for extracting termites from their hills; in these circumstances awkward projections are broken off. Suitable twigs may be found by discarding many until a usable one is found, or until one is fashioned in the way described.

Tool use is not a behavioral feature of macaques and baboons in the wild, a fact that is almost certainly due to their preoccupation with rank order. This preoccupation is responsible for maintaining a persistent, raised level of arousal that has, in their evolutionary past, led to a limited expressive repertoire. Most important, it has imposed upon them a form of social attention that precludes the visual awareness essential for the development of tool use.

Awareness of external features is yet another criterion by which we can contrast the two types. It is particularly well illustrated by a mother's awareness of the situation of her young. Both gorilla and chimpanzee mothers are able to anticipate and protect their infants from potentially dangerous situations (Chance and Jolly 1970). A macaque or baboon mother protects her infant from potential danger only by restricting its activities or responding to its calls.

A notable feature of the expansion of awareness is the switch of attention from social to nonsocial aspects of the environment, clearly seen in the mutual inspection of an object by two chimpanzees. They will sit next to each other. One will trace the line of a crack in the floor with his finger or a stick; the other will watch and momentarily indicate the shared attention between them by running his finger along the crack. A startling recent discovery by Menzel (1972) reveals the significance of the control of attention by awareness of physical features. He has shown that a group of young chimpanzees who had grown up in semi-captivity were able to develop and jointly exploit a new method of using a pole as a ladder.

A critical component of the chimpanzees' attention involved the successful use of a pole as a ladder. The "stupid" chimp lifted the pole in one hand, looking at its far end as he placed it against the tree. He then allowed the end he was holding to rest on the ground. In the more impetuous instances, he dropped it to the ground and immediately tried to climb it, whereupon, the base, not being securely placed, fell over. Then the stupid chimp had a tantrum!

A successful user of the pole as a ladder withdrew his attention from the far (distal) end of the pole to the base while he placed it firmly in a secure position; if necessary, he readjusted the placement of the distal end before climbing onto it. Hence, only by paying attention to the pole in its new relationship to the environment was the potential of the pole seen as a ladder utilized. The attention of the chimps literally flows up and down the pole. Parker (1974) describes the attention of a chimp flowing out from its hand along a pole or stick towards an object that it may often reach out to touch with the distal end. Attention, free to be guided by and flow out over objects, is therefore an integral, even crucial, part of the intelligent use of tools.

In these studies, the ability of the chimpanzee to adjust the use of an instrument to the situation—not only to reach a set objective but to use an invented skill for more than one purpose —indicates clearly that the chimpanzee is capable of extending its repertoire much closer to that of man than any other sub-human primate. *Groups* of chimpanzees can expand their repertoire by invention, because the social binding of attention seen in agonistic societies is absent in the social relations of the hedonic apes.

Many rudimentary elements of problem-solving and inventiveness can be found in some species of basically agonistic societies, as in groups of long-tailed macaques (Angst 1974). These societies fall between the two modes. Their problem-solving capacities are less extensive than those of hedonic societies. However, there is more flexibility of attention than in predominantly agonistic ones, where mechanisms designed to reduce conflict place rigid limitations on individual behavior.

Agonistic societies contain a very large element of conflict, both in the relationships between individuals and the state of the individual's motivation. As a result, spacing out is a way of reducing the impact between two individuals. So also is a "cut-off" act (Chance 1962). This is a "cut-off," in the simplest instance, of the visual awareness of another individual by deflecting the gaze. Very often, this means paying attention to something else and not simply closing the eyes, for example. "Cut-off" brings about a continual interruption of attention, preventing ongoing attention to a single environmental feature or the joint inspection of the same object by two individuals, so typical of the hedonic mode.

In the agonistic mode, displacement of behavior may take the form of scratching in the ground, for example. If so, it is of a rigid and repetitive kind, not controlled by an environmental awareness, as it is when a chimpanzee moves its fingers along a crack in the ground. The fixity and rigidity of these displacement activities and deflections of attention originate more from the value of these actions in curtailing the conflict between individuals than from an intrinsic interest in the alternative object towards which attention is directed.

Moreover, attention is frequently deflected to another individual of lower status. This may then be used to displace aggression by threats or actual chasing, as in the following example.

On April 10th, 1962, for no apparent reason, 1956-Male-1 attacked an unrelated adult female while she was drinking. Immediately, the dominant male of the group, Old-Male-A, attacked 1956-Male-1, who fled. Old-Male-A chased him round for about half a minute or more; from a bush, up a palm tree and down the other side, round a building and down a trail. Suddenly, out from under another bush 1956-Male-1's parent, Old-Female-1 came running on hind legs carrying her five day old infant. She ran to stand at her son's side, and together they made violent threat gestures and vocalisations at a part of the area empty of all monkeys and observers and away from the dominant male. Old-Male-A stopped chasing to look at what they seemed to be threatening, then chased

1956-Male-1 again, who again threatened loudly away from Old-Male-A. Old-Male-A sat down three feet away peering again in the direction in which 1956-Male-1 was threatening. Old-Female-1 climbed to sit between them and her son immediately sidled up to her, sat touching her and groomed her. She walked away and 1956-Male-1 followed her closely, grooming her whenever she stopped, leaving Old-Male-A peering at nothing (Chance 1977).

BIMODAL POTENTIAL IN THE MACAQUE REPERTOIRE

So far, we have described the difference between the hedonic and the agonistic modes in terms of the behavior of species organized predominantly in one or other of these two different modes, and we have abstracted the characteristics of each mode. Following the publication of my paper (Chance 1967) putting forward the hypothesis that rank-ordered behavior was best understood in terms of the structure of attention, Virgo and Waterhouse (1969) found from their study of the Bristol Zoo macaque colony that there were two structures of attention, each focused on a different individual in the colony. They showed that the structure of attention based on agonistic behavior was focused on an adult female, and the other, based on grooming and affiliative relations (sitting next, etc.) was focused on an adult male. This immediately drew attention to earlier observations of my own at Bristol Zoo, in which changes of the leadership of the colony followed a period of display by the future dominant male. Hence, it became clear that the features of both modalities are present and employed by members of a single species (the rhesus macaque). And therefore the propensities for these two behavioral features were present in the individual rhesus macaque. Current studies under way with Tom Pitcairn (n.d., 1978) are providing evidence of the same potentials in the behavior structure of the long-tailed macaque.

We are nearing the point, therefore, when we will be able to say of the subhuman primates that an individual possesses potential for developing these two modes. Since the hedonic mode is alone capable of enabling behavior to be constructed entirely on the basis of extetrnal information, and the stereotype of the agonistic mode is in such marked contrast to it, we are forced to conclude that the agonistic mode is constructed from fixed-action patterns and is therefore programmed from internal sources. This distinction is illustrated by the fact that a chimpanzee smokes a cigarette just as we do, by imitation, but throws objects using a stereotyped underhand and rocking from fore to hind feet, a type of behavior programmed from an inherited pattern.

Switch between Modalities

What then is the nature of the structure of behavior that controls or determines the emergence of one or other modality? We can see quite clearly that whether or not a flexible attention to surroundings can develop in an individual's repertoire is dependent upon the type of social relations with which the individual grows up. These social relations determine the type of attention he is either compelled to adopt (agonistic condition) or is free to employ (hedonic condition). How then, we may ask, do these two modalities coexist in one society and how is the change from one to the other modality brought about?

A Division in the Social Repertoire of the Long-Tailed Macaque

Tom Pitcairn (n.d.) has discovered in a recent study of the Basel colony of long-tailed macaques that the social repertoire is organized around two distinct modes of visual attention. The first is "looking at," which takes place from one individual who is spatially separated from others in society and can be divided into "look," "look at," and "stare."

The other modality is "looking around," which is mainly used when sitting next to another individual, an activity that frequently continues for a period of time. "Looking around" consists of scanning the environment, both physical and social, and may lead to a specific interest in the activity of another animal or a feature of the environment.

"Looking at," as we shall now see, is less flexible than "looking around," and consists of persistent attention to specific individuals, usually high in rank. In the long-tailed macaque, "looking around" is associated with "sitting next to," "grooming," and "sitting with," i.e., next to and not in contact with—the stylized forms of contact macaques employ to get close to each other and to reassure one another.

PLAY GROUPS

In the chimpanzee, body contact takes many and varied forms as illustrated by Reynolds (1973) and Goodall (1971).

Now, while "looking around" is flexible, and therefore basically hedonic, and associated with the static contact of sitting next to, etc., the flexibility of attention provided by contact can also be combined with flexibility of movement in play. Here, the arousal is controlled by the contact component. Attention can be focused both on the physical and social elements of the environment, as we see when play—swinging, climbing, rolling, etc.—is used to exploit the potential of the physical environment, often in combination with mutual interaction with another youngster. In contrast, a chimp may be forced off its mother when it is obliged to rely on an agonistic "look at" technique.

THE REFERENTS OF THE BASEL COLONY OF MACAQUES

The attention structure theory postulate that any individual in a community of nonhuman primates pays attention for a significant proportion of time to particular other members of the community has proved to be so. Pitcairn (n.d.) discovered in the Basel colony, which varies from 60 to 90 individuals, that certain individuals receive a significantly large amount of attention from others. Pitcairn calls these individuals "referents." They are the dominant male, the dominant female, the consort of the dominant male at any particular time, and for those in the middle rank of the society, the monkey next in rank above that individual. For the society as a whole, referents are important because of the amount of attention paid to them.

They are significant also because, to a large extent, they control the behavior of those who pay so much attention to them. The movement of the dependent individuals is often arranged so as to keep them in view, despite the fact that they may be obliged to move aside should they be approached by the more dominant referent.

DEVELOPMENT OF SIGNIFICANT SOCIAL RELATIONS

Therefore, let us look at the situation of the developing young in a centric type of society where male rank orders are established. The infant macaque, for example, starts its life clinging to its mother by all four limbs and, hence, is pressed close to the body, with its mouth holding the nipple. During the first few weeks of its life the mother holds the infant except when she is walking from place to place, when the infant relies on its grip and mouth hold on the nipple. More and more, however, the infant is rejected in certain instances by the mother. This might be in response to rough handling by the infant, when the mother is otherwise occupied, or when the tension is high in the colony and she is obliged to approach a source of potential danger, such as an unfamiliar attendant offering food. In these circumstances the rejection leads to a protracted startle reaction in the infant, the form of which is very instructive (Chance and Jones 1974). On a look from her, it instantly releases the nipple, falls off, and gives a violent kick with its hind legs. This action often takes it away from her into the cage, where it adopts a posture ("gecko") of maximum leap potential, while oscillating rapidly to and fro in circular figures and figure-eight movements, or what has been collectively termed distance equilibratory movements. When this behavior first appears (at a month old), its attention is at all times on its mother, assessing the moment when she is likely to welcome it back to her. All this time it is "looking at" her, for how else could it achieve a successful retreat from the potential hazards of the outside world, about which it does not yet know enough to organize its own escape?

This is what it eventually has to do when it has established contact with older juveniles or the various refuges available to it in the environment. At the start of its life, this fixed attention on mother is the single escape mechanism available. By contrast, when it is on its mother and on the nipple, at the end of a long and flaccid breast, it is able, and frequently does, look around, even in times of excitement in the colony. When conditions are relaxed, it will look around without the nipple in its mouth and may drop off her to explore, returning at intervals to sit next to her.

Social equilibration, being based on "looking at" is a strategy for the conflict engendered by rejection from the only source of safety hitherto experienced by the young. The mother is primarily significant as providing a refuge of the only type known to the youngster. *Rejection, therefore, forces on the young infant a strategy totally dependent on "looking at."* To the extent that this happens earlier in the young males than females, so the male may be forced to rely on such simple equilibratory responses to a more dominant and potentially threatening individual, who is nevertheless a source of protection.

This simple response to danger is later transferred to other individuals who may be invested with the same significance and are, thereby, referents for the developing young. These are older juveniles, and, as we shall see, other dominant individuals of the group, especially for male infants, the overlord male.

Mother/Infant Relationships of the Two Sexes

Evidence that male infants suffer separation from the mother earlier than the females in the four species *Macaca fuscata*, *Macaca nemestrina*, *Macaca mulatta*, and *Macaca radiata* is provided by a number of authors.

In *Macaca fuscata* Itani (1959) has reported that male infants in the field leave their mothers sooner than female infants. Jensen, *et al.* (1968) show that in *Macaca nemestrina*, female infants from four to fourteen weeks old are less frequently and for shorter times separated from their mothers than are male infants. The converse—being in mother's lap—is also true.

According to Chance and Jones (1974), "the data on relative positions show that male monkeys and their mothers change from greater dependence to greater independence in the first two months of the infant's life. This finding substantiates our original hypothesis that sex differences develop early in life, and that males become more *independent* [italics added], earlier than females. This comes about by mothers leaving the infant and not vice versa."

Our observations of mother/infant relations in *Macaca fascicularis* do not suggest that if the infant leaves the mother it is "more independent" of her (an unwarranted assumption), but that the dependence is of a different type; the infant keeps her in view, even though at a distance, and the mother forces on the baby the strategy based on "look at."

This amounts to active rejection, as "mothers of male infants were punitive towards the infants during early weeks, hitting, shoving, pushing, tossing, throwing and otherwise handling them violently" (Jensen, *et al.* 1968:9). The male infants are rejected in this way for a maximum of six weeks, and after this, mothers of females increase punishment. In this way, male infants acquire more "looking at," being off the mother earlier than the female infants. Mothers still carry female infants when male infants are predominantly free of their mothers, up to 14 weeks.

Although species differences exist in the behavior of the mothers to their male and female offspring, the same difference exists for the rhesus, as studied by Mitchell (1968). He writes:

If protection can be defined as close non-primitive physical contact, the mothers protected the female infants more than the males. The frequencies of maternal restraint observed also supported this notion. The female infants both received and reciprocated more positive physical contact than did the males. The mothers of males did not differ significantly from the mothers of females in the amount of punishment administered to the infants, but they promoted independence in their male offspring by not restraining them and by withdrawing from them (1968:616).

Mitchell comments: "Generally speaking in the rhesus monkeys, and probably in all primates, the mother's relations with the male and female infant are very much alike. However, the differences that do exist may be crucial to the long-term development of the primate" (1968:619) and "Differences in mother/infant interaction apparently *engender* differential long-term effects along a male-female continuum of behaviour" (1968:619).

The Cohort Forming Behavior of the Subadult Male

What clearly emerges is that the male infant, by being separated from its mother to a significantly greater extent over a period of about three months, is forced to exercise and rely on "looking at" its mother for security, rather than achieving early reduction of alarm through contact. During this period, maturational changes almost inevitably leave their impact on fixing this mechanism, thus evoking its basic form later in life, even if this interval does not span or constitute a critical learning period. So, the young male learns to rely on constantly attending to the whereabouts of possible protective individuals other than its mother. These include, in the early stages, juveniles of its own clan; later the dominant male becomes the most significant in its life.

How does this come about? In the Uffculme colony of long-tailed macaques, the young are always attending to the adult male, glancing at him repeatedly whenever there is excitement within the colony, even though they may carry on with what they are doing. But Arlo, the first-born of Ann, shows another form of attentive relation to Percy, the adult male. Percy spends most of his time on sentinel duty and so is only infrequently aggressive within the colony in a threatening manner to specific individuals. Between 18 months and two years old, Arlo began to threaten Percy, which surprised us because Percy threatened back. Then Arlo would mime (the signal for approach) from a vantage point high up in the cage, where Percy rarely followed, and might then come down to where Percy was on the floor or a shelf, and run round him "miming," leaping to and fro in and out of Percy's grasp range. When Arlo was a little older, he would signal to Percy in a different way, by looking towards him and beating downwards with his outstretched arm with open palm. In this way he could draw Percy's attention without much counterthreat, and then the same equilibratory game would start, this time more vigorously and with the added dimension of Arlo leaping wildly over Percy just out of arm's reach, then circling Percy, and leaping to and fro toward him. At this stage the game might end with Arlo rushing into Percy's arms, both of them hugging and mock biting each other. So to the original agonistic and repeated glances is now added a game which provides evidence of a hedonic attraction between them, the game providing the means whereby the agonistic components can be reduced to a point where they are able to hug each other. Here we see, displayed in dramatic form, the mechanisms which Mason (1964) deduced as early as 1964 could be responsible for the apparently attractive property of threat.

Mason writes: "One of the most difficult problems is to reconcile the finding that dominance is based on fear-agression with the observation that the dominant animal is often sought or followed by other members of the group." Chance (1955) hypothesized "attraction towards the aggressor" would account for this paradoxical situation. The difficulty, however, is that the most common reaction to direct aggression is flight. Nevertheless, it may be possible to explain the attraction to the dominant animal by placing Chance's hypothesis within a somewhat broader conceptual framework. Investigation with inanimate objects has shown that whether a primate ignores, approaches, or avoids a given stimulus depends on its physical properties (size, complexity, movement characteristics) and on the amount of previous exposure to the stimulus or to similar objects (Menzel 1964; Welker 1961). Objects that produce avoidance in the beginning may, after a series of exposures, elicit strong approach. It is important to note that the moderately novel stimulus is generally more attractive than the familiar one. Thus, on a continuum of emotional arousal there appears to be an intermediate range between "fear" and "disinterest" when attraction is maximal (Hebb 1955).

Applying this line of reasoning to social stimuli, one would expect that the animal that generates mild fear for whatever reason—because of its size or its general comportment, e.g., chest thumping, branch shaking, loud vocalizations, rushing, chasing, all of which are characteristic of dominant males in various species—will become the object of ambivalent reactions. According to this view, a dominant animal that is frequently and openly aggressive will be less attractive than one that merely threatens aggression. It is true that serious, full-fledged attacks by dominant animals appear to be infrequent, whereas threats and aggressive "displays" are a fairly common occurrence. Chance's (1955) observation that attraction to an aggressor appeared after a delay is consistent with the present hypothesis, since approach would not be expected until the initially high level of emotional arousal had dissipated somewhat.

The present thesis also explains the attraction to a dominant animal in the absence of overt aggression, as apparently occurs in the young male langur. According to Jay:

> The male infant has no contact with adult males until he is approximately ten months old. At this time, the infant first approaches the adult in a highly specialized manner. The infant runs, squealing tensely, to the moving adult and veers away just before it touches him. Gradually the infant appears to gain confidence and touches the male's hindquarters. Within a week after this, the infant approaches and mounts by pulling himself up over the adult's hindquarters. . . . In a few weeks another element is added and the infant runs around to face and embrace the adult (Jay 1965:220).

Although this is a highly specialized pattern seen only in the young male langur, the basic sequence is remarkably similar to that described by Menzel (1964) for the reaction of rhesus monkeys and chimpanzees to novel inanimate objectives.

All this bears on the question of whether major differences exist in males and females in their ability to set up rank orders. Because of maternal withdrawal at an early age, the young male is on his own. Differentiation between the sexes starts here in that the male is forced at an earlier age than females to begin visually attending to his mother and, thereby, does not receive contact reassurance as often as his sister. This immediately raises the level of his general arousal as well as turning his attention to others in the community for refuge. But, as we have seen, this also raises the level of his hedonic desires for attachment and forces strategies on him to satisfy this need as well. He is therefore doubly attached to the male to whom his attention is perforce transferred, whereas the female, more secure in her relation to her mother, does not force clasping contact. Instead she is content with sitting next to and grooming her mother and others of the female group to which she has become so attached through familiarity and constant proximity.

Rank order for males is born out of maternal rejection, threat and avoidance, persistent attention, and hedonic attraction. Among females rank order is acquired from kinship, the rank of their consorts, and the maintenance of an even state of arousal, usually at a low level. This is probably the reason why individual females frequently possess rank, but do not depend for it on their ability to bond into a rank order. It is also the reason why they assemble in groups rather than form cohorts.

Macaca radiata, the bonnet macaque, contrasts with the three species discussed earlier, as it is noticeably more hedonic in its adult relations (Chance and Jolly 1970), adult males often playing with younger individuals of the group. Young males develop their adult relations mainly through play in the juvenile groups at a time when the female young depend on grooming and remain closely associated with their mothers. Simonds (1974) reports: "The females of the bonnet macaque remain close to the adult female and spend more time grooming and being groomed than infants or juvenile males, who often move with the play group rather than linking with their mothers."

In this predominantly hedonic species of macaque, the cohort bonding is of the type demonstrated by Arlo towards Percy, dependent on the exploratory and contact generating activation of play. So this species provides evidence of a different kind of an early differentiation between the sexes, but without the "looking at" bonding component. Nevertheless, it is consistent with the scheme presented in Figure 1.

Pitcairn's study (n.d.) of the adult macaques of the Basel colony shows that adults who "look at" females do so as part of "looking around," without subsequent "cut off." But, when males are "looked at" by an other adult, that individual will then "cut off" by looking "down," "up," or "away." Hence an essentially agonistic relationship is evident in the attention paid to the males, but hedonic attention is paid to females. When adult males look at adult males they are continuing the habits of their youth or infancy, but adult females are not. The ability of males to form cohorts may come from this early experience.

The only other species to provide evidence of sex differentiation early on is the hamadryas baboon (Kummer 1968). Here, it is the adult female that becomes bonded to her overlord male as part of a one-male harem consisting of two to five females. The male, on the other hand, after passing through a play group like the bonnet, does not form male bonds and, hence, no persistent male cohorts. This early experience allows for the separate existence of the adult male with his following of females to operate over the desert terrain in search of food. The bonding of the female to him has two components. It starts when the adolescent male captures a prospective juvenile female and, while hugging her for long periods of time, teaches her by delivering neck bites not to stray too far. This is a learned response, as Kummer has shown and has been referred to at this symposium by Dr. Zihlman as evidence of female flexibility. If what we are witnessing is evidence of the operation of a state of flexible attention in the female as opposed to the male such as I have attempted to define, then I am in agreement. But in this species the males do not form rank orders, so Kummer's observations are, without further elaboration, not evidence of flexibility. All we can say is that an initial bias leads by genetically programmed behavior to a distinct adult differentiation of the sexes. This condition differs from that of the adult macaque, and its cause is not known.

What Lionel Tiger has called the infrastructure of human behavior has been here displayed in terms of the way attention is organized, either in a fixed agonistic form, displayed in its simplest manner in the "looking at" from a distance, or in a more flexible hedonic form that has "looking around" as the basis of the awareness infrastructure. Evidence does exist to show that male young, macaques especially, are forced to adopt the first strategy for self-protection while their sisters are still gaining reassurance from their mothers. A model exists, therefore, in the social infrastructure of a closely related primate group which indicates how similar differences could arise in man's ontogeny.

THE HUMAN POSITION

Omark and Edelman (1975) have recently studied the mental capabilities of children in relation to the social attention structure of the class. They write:

> The results indicate that the structure of attention among children may be similar to the attention structure among primates as described by Chance and Jolly [1970]. Although boys have more agreement on "toughest" among themselves than do girls, there is no sex difference in how well children can accurately perceive the dominance relations in the class. Hence, irrespective of one's own dominance relations, attention is still paid to other's dominance relations. For many classes, the Chance and Jolly [1970] hypothesis that attention is directly upward in the hierarchy was confirmed in that the children had more agreement on the ranks of the two toughest children than on the two bottom children (1976:146).

The sex differences not only involved the ability to discriminate the rank of high ranking individuals, but "coupled with this are apparently differences in the emotional involvement of each sex in the formation of some kinds of hierarchies" (Omark and Edelman 1976:146). Emotional involvement appears to interfere with boys' responses to the cognitive questions more than it does for girls. The play patterns of each are also different so that they experience different amounts of information from these interactions.

Sex differences do therefore develop in young children out of their different attentional relations, mainly cognitive, and through different involvement and differences in experience from play.

From the evidence presented, it seems that early in life sex differences influencing personality do exist and that they do arise from initial sex differences in social attention. These differences will tend to be exaggerated by some features of the patterns of upbringing to which men and women are exposed. But, at present, individual psychological characteristics are examined against a background wholly idiosyncratic to the psychologist's profession. Logical deduction, which will enable us to predict the psychological characteristics likely to arise out of the peculiarities of the sex differences described, is not possible.

Silverman (1970:110) summarizes the differences between what he is happy to describe as Logos, the adult male genotype, and Eros, the adult female genotype, which he says are "integrally associated with differences in physiological responsiveness and sensitivity to stimulation." The male type he characterizes by: "a) a relative lack of sensitivity to subtle social and non-social cues; b) minimal distractability; c) a counteracting analytic, restructuring perceptual attitude; d) an inhibition of responses to emotional and non-rational inner stimuli; e) a disposition to augment the experienced intensity of strong stimulation" (Silverman 1970), with the converse for females. Probably, a, b, and d arise in the way we have seen in young children.

The reader will now be aware that states of behavior are rigid in the agonistic mode. What may have happened in evolution is that these physiological sex differences reported by Silverman are residual psychophysiological elements built into the constitution of men in support of an essentially rank-ordered adult life for males, whereas females do not require these rigid elements. If so, these differences will not necessarily appear in present-day human behavior without social circumstances calling forth the distinction in the ontogeny of the individuals living today. If they do, who can gainsay the possibility that early experience will not perpetuate hormonal biases that may, in later life, be at variance with a civilized life, create unsuspected biases of behavior and perception, and thus lead men and women to become so divergent as not to get on with one another. What is abundantly clear is that, without a logical paradigm capable of integrating behavior at all levels, no amount of psychological investigation will make any sense or get us nearer to understanding how sex differences of behavior will or will not appear in present-day human beings.

The paradigm presented here does clearly suggest that if agonistic components are prominent in a society and do, at the same time, influence the ontogeny of the young, then sex differences will be a prominent feature of that society. The reverse is not necessarily so, since the hedonic mode is a flexible state and learning is then free to play a major role. In predominantly hedonic societies, therefore, whether or not sex differences of behavior and personality will appear will depend on whether or not the initial differences are enhanced or suppressed by cultural factors.

REFERENCES CITED

ANGST, W.
    1974—Das Ausdraucksverhalten Des Javaneraffen. Macaca Fascicularis Raffles. *Advances in Ethology* 15. (Supplement to *Journal of Comparative Ethology.*)

BOLWIG, N.
    1963—Observations on the Mental and Manipulative Abilities of a Captive Baboon (*Papio droguera*). *Behaviour* 22(1):24-40.

CHANCE, M.R.A.
    1955—Sociability of Monkeys. *Man* 55:162-165.

    1962—An Interpretation of Some Agonistic Postures: The Role of "Cut-Off" Acts and Postures. *Symposium of the Zoological Society,* volume eight. London:London Zoological Society.

    1967—Attention Structure as the Basis of Primate Rank Orders. *Man* 2(4):503-518.

    1973—Structure of Our Social Behaviour. In *Limits of Human Nature,* J. Benthall, ed. London:Longmans/New York:Dutton.

    1975—Social Cohesion and the Structure of Attention. In *Biosocial Anthropology,* Robin Fox, ed. American Sociological Association Series 1. London:Malaby.

    1977—The Organization of Attention in Groups. In *Methods of Inference from Animal to Human Behaviour,* Mario von Cranach, ed. The Hague:Mouton/Chicago:Aldine.

CHANCE, M.R.A. and C.J. JOLLY
    1970—*Social Groups of Monkeys, Apes and Men.* London:Jonathan Cape.

CHANCE, M.R.A. and E. JONES
    1974—Protracted Startle Response to Maternal Rejection in Infants of *Macaca fascicularis*. *Folia Primatologica* 21(3):167-182.

GOODALL, J. (VAN LAWICK)
    1971—*In the Shadow of Man.* London/Glasgow:Collins Fontana.

HEBB, D.O.
1955—Drives and the CNS. *Psychological Review* 62:243-254.

ITANI, J.
1959—Paternal Care in the Wild Japanese Monkey *Macaca fuscata fuscata*. *Primates* 2:61-93.

JAY, P.C.
1965—The Common Langur of North India. In *Primate Behavior: Field Studies of Monkeys and Apes*, I. DeVore, ed. New York:Holt, Rinehart and Winston.

JENSEN, G.D., R.A. BOBBITT, and B.N. GORDON
1968—Sex Differences in the Development of Independence of Infant Monkeys. *Behaviour* 30:1-14.

KOHLER, W.
1927—*Mentality of Apes*. London:Methuen. (Translated by E. Winter.)

KUMMER, H.
1968—Social Organization of Hamadryas Baboons: A Field Study. *Bibliotheca Primatologica,* volume 6. Basel:S. Karger.

KUMMER, H. and F. KURT
1963—Social Units of a Free-Living Population of Hamadryas Baboons. *Folia Primatologica* 1:14-19.

LOMAX, A.
1972—An Evolutionary Taxonomy of Culture. *Science* 177:172-178.

MASON, W.A.
1964—Primate Sociability and Social Organization. In *Advances in Experimental Social Psychology*, volume 1, Leonard Berkowitz, ed. New York:Academic.

1965—Determinants of Social Behavior in Young Chimpanzees. In *Behavior of Non-Human Primates*, volume 2, A.M. Schrier, et al., eds. New York:Academic.

MENZEL, E.W.
1964—Patterns of Responsiveness in Chimpanzees Reared through Infancy under Conditions of Environmental Restriction. *Psychologische Forschung* 27:337-365.

1972—Spontaneous Invention of Ladders in a Group of Young Chimpanzees. *Folia Primatologica* 17:87-106.

MITCHELL, G.D.
1968—Attachment Differences in Male and Female Infant Monkeys (Rhesus). *Child Development* 39:611-620.

OMARK, D.R. and M.S. EDELMAN
1976—The Development of Attention Structures in Young Children. In *The Social Structure of Attention*, M.R.A. Chance and R.R. Larsen, eds. New York:Wiley.

PARKER, C.
  1974—The Antecedents of Man the Manipulator. *Journal of Human Evolution* 3:493-500.

PITCAIRN, T.K.
  1976—Attention and Social Structure in *Macaca fascicularis*. In *The Social Structure of Attention*, M.R.A. Chance and R.R. Larsen, eds. New York:Wiley.

  1978—*The Structure of Attention and Social Behaviour in Two Groups of* Macaca fascicularis. Ph.D. thesis, University of Birmingham. (Forthcoming.)

REYNOLDS, V.
  1973—Man Also Behaves. In *Limits of Human Nature*. London: Longmans/New York:Dutton.

REYNOLDS, V. and G. LUSCOMBE
  1969—Chimpanzee Rank Order and the Function of Display. *Second Conference of the International Primatological Society of Behaviour* 1, C.R. Carpenter, ed. Basel:S. Karger.

REYNOLDS, V. and F. REYNOLDS
  1965—Chimpanzees of the Budongo Forest. In *Primate Behavior*, I. DeVore, ed. New York:Holt, Rinehart and Winston.

SCHALLER, G.B.
  1963—*The Mountain Gorilla: Ecology and Behavior*. Chicago:University of Chicago Press.

SILVERMAN, J.
  1970—Attention Styles and the Study of Sex Differences. In *Attention: Contemporary Theory and Analysis*, D. Mostovsky, ed. New York:Appleton-Century-Crofts.

SIMONDS, P.E.
  1974—Sex Differences in Bonnet Macaque Networks and Social Structure. *Archives of Sexual Behavior* 3:151-165.

VIRGO, H.B. and M.J. WATERHOUSE
  1969—The Emergence of Attention Structure among Rhesus Macaques. *Man* n.s. 4(1):85-93.

WELKER, W.I.
  1961—*Functions of Varied Experience*, D.W. Fiske and S.R. Maddi, eds. Dorsey Series in Psychology. Dorsey, Ill.:Dorsey.

6

Gathering and the Hominid Adaptation

ADRIENNE ZIHLMAN AND
NANCY TANNER

INTRODUCTION

For most of human history, until the advent of domesticated plants and animals, a gathering-hunting way of life provided the economic base for human existence. Did gathering and hunting arise simultaneously, or one much earlier than the other? How have they been interrelated during various stages of hominid evolution, and what have been the implications for social life?

We believe that the divergence of early hominids from the apes was based on gathering plant foods on the African savannas: a new feeding pattern in a new environment that led to the invention of tools for obtaining, transporting, and preparing a range of foods that could potentially be shared with more than one individual. This adaptation combined two behavioral elements—bipedal locomotion and tool use—that made possible the

We are indebted to S.L. Washburn for his introduction and approach to the study of human evolution and to Karl Butzer for his continuing encouragement. We are grateful to Jerold Lowenstein, Karen Wcislo, and Susan Nordmark for valuable comments. For financial support we thank the Wenner-Gren Foundation for Anthropological Research for grants given to Adrienne Zihlman; the Ford Foundation under Grant #739-0003-200 (given to Nancy Tanner); and the Faculty Research Committee, University of California, Santa Cruz for grants given to us both. And last, our thanks to Lionel Tiger and the Harry Frank Guggenheim Foundation for the opportunity to participate in the symposium.

search, collection, and transport of food over considerable distances for sharing. This pattern contrasts with that of apes in forest habitats, where each individual forages for food and eats it on the spot. Plant foods formed the bulk of early hominid diet and predatory behavior provided some meat. Hunting with tools, we believe, did not fully develop until the later part of the Pleistocene, perhaps as late as *Homo sapiens* (see Table 1).

The social life of early hominids was necessarily interrelated with their subsistence pattern. If it is assumed that they were primarily hunters, and that meat procured by males made up a large portion of their caloric intake, there are different deductions to be made about mating patterns, social relations, economics, and sex roles (Washburn and Lancaster 1968; Isaac 1976), than if it is hypothesized that plants formed the primary food source and were gathered and shared mostly by females.

This paper presents a reconstruction of the way of life of *Australopithecus*,[1] based on interpretations of new evidence and reinterpretation of the old. We challenge the assumption that hunting arose early in human evolution and that meat was a primary food source. In its stead, we propose that gathering of plant foods was the basic adaptation, and we interpret social organization, parental investment, and mating patterns within this framework.

QUESTIONING THE HUNTING HYPOTHESIS

The assumption that hunting was invented early pervades the literature on human evolution (Tiger 1969; Tiger and Fox 1971; Pfeiffer 1972; Washburn and Moore 1974; Cachel 1975; Suzuki 1975). Because the difference between hunting and predation is often glossed over when discussing early hominids, we define hunting as the catching, killing, and butchering of large and small animals with the help of tools, in contrast to simple predation, which is the capturing and killing by hand of relatively small animals.

It is usually further assumed that a male-female pair bond or nuclear family was essential to reduce competition among males for females and to insure that females and young were fed.

TABLE 1. *Major events in human evolution*

Time Scale (Years before present)	Events	Interpretation
10,000	Domestication of plants and animals in the Old World	Major changes in family and sex roles? Food concentrated; Permanent settlements
100,000	Spread of *Homo sapiens* throughout Old World	Gathering-hunting well developed
	Humans in Europe and northern Asia	Beginning of hunting in temperate regions?
1,000,000	Human populations expand to Southeast Asia	Gathering successful in habitats outside Africa
2,000,000	Earliest stone tools; some in association with animal bones	Butchering large animals for meat; predation continues
3,000,000	Abundant hominid fossils in East and South Africa	Sharing food among kin; gathering and predation of small animals
4,000,000	Fossil evidence for human line in Africa	Moving into savanna; collecting dispersed food bipedally with organic tools; mothers sharing food with young
6,000,000	Chimpanzee-gorilla-human divergence??	

While females, burdened with young, cared for them at the home base, man the hunter, tool-maker, and tool-user hunted in cooperative male groups and defended the helpless females and young.

Is hunting the inevitable interpretation? New data present a basis for challenging the presumption of an early hunting adaptation with meat the major food source. This information is derived from several sources: studies of gathering-hunting peoples, the fossil and archeological records, primate behavior, and concepts in evolutionary biology.

The significance of gathering first became apparent at a conference on "hunting-gathering" peoples, organized by Richard Lee and Irven DeVore in 1966. There it was revealed that the majority of such groups in Africa, Asia, Australia, and North America subsists mainly on plant foods gathered by women, or on fish, and much less on hunting per se. In actuality, most such groups are "gatherer-hunters" (Lee and DeVore 1968a). Fluidity and flexibility appear as the most characteristic social structural features of modern gathering-hunting groups. Lee and DeVore (1968b) propose that vegetable foods were probably always available and that early women likely played an active role in subsistence. Linton (1971) further emphasized the role of women in gathering during evolution and reexamined the assumptions underlying the hunting hypothesis.

Recent studies of early hominid dentition reveal extensive wear and chipping, and suggest a diet that required a great deal of chewing or was quite gritty (Wallace 1972; Wolpoff 1973). These are not the teeth of a predominantly meat eating species. The masticatory apparatus itself of both ancient and modern humans is specialized for grinding tough foods, a parallel to conventional herbivores (Crompton and Hiiemäe 1969).

Recent studies on bone accumulations from hominid sites (Behrensmeyer 1975; Brain 1976) are beginning to distinguish among several possibilities: whether the animal bones are residues from hominid meals, tools used by hominids, or natural death assemblages. The studies indicate that bone breakage and concentration may be due more to carnivore activity and transportation by water before burial, and less to hominid activities, than previously supposed.

In primate field studies, predatory behavior and meat eating have been well documented in chimpanzees and baboons (Teleki 1973a; Harding 1973; Strum 1975; Hausfater 1976). Chimpanzees eat mostly fruit but occasionally kill small animals with their hands, consume the meat at leisure, and share with others. Contrary to previous assumptions, neither upright walking, weapons, nor possibly even the need for food are necessary for predation by baboons and chimpanzees, or by extension, for early hominid predation (Kitahara-Frisch 1975). This reduces the likelihood that predatory behavior and meat eating were the new elements in hominid origins; on the contrary, the omnivorous diet of humans probably represents the continuation of an ancient primate pattern (Harding 1975).

New theoretical concepts have been developed that focus on the evolution of social behavior and broaden out from a simply descriptive ethology. They have provided an impetus for looking at kinship and mating systems of primates and humans. These approaches combine genetic-evolutionary theory with observed social patterns and examine the selective advantages of various behaviors in terms of reproductive success. From this, models have been proposed to explain the evolution of altruistic behaviors through kin selection and of mating systems through parental investment and sexual selection (Hamilton 1964; Trivers 1972; Eberhard 1975; Wilson 1975).

The fossil and anatomical data, observations of living primates and information on contemporary gatherer-hunters, all lead us to question the view that early humans were hunters and primarily meat eaters from their first appearance on the savanna. These new data and sociobiological concepts provide a basis for proposing a different interpretation of early hominid behavior.

WHY CHIMPANZEES AS A MODEL FOR HOMINID ORIGINS?

Chimpanzees fascinate zoo-goers and behaviorists alike because of their "humanlike" intelligence, gestures, facial expressions, and ability to communicate. Their anatomical similarity to humans was noted a hundred years ago by Huxley and Darwin and detailed more recently by numerous others. On the assumption of phylogenetic continuity, chimpanzees are compared frequently with early human fossils to assess evolutionary change.

The biochemical evidence from studies on protein, DNA, and chromosomal similarity has demonstrated an even closer relationship than was previously suspected. Virtual identity of many human and chimpanzee proteins (Wilson and Sarich 1969; Cronin 1975; King and Wilson 1975) suggests that the two species are as close as sibling species with an evolutionary divergence about five or six million years ago (Sarich and Cronin 1976). Molecular studies provide a valuable perspective on phylogeny, especially because of the skimpy fossil record for hominids and African apes during the crucial period of divergence between five and ten million years ago.

Behavioral continuity between humans and chimpanzees is documented from observations in the field and laboratory (Goodall 1976). Particularly applicable to the study of human evolution are the findings that chimpanzees prepare and use tools, prey upon small mammals, occasionally walk bipedally, share plant and animal food (Teleki 1974, 1975), and communicate social and environmental information (Menzel 1973a; Menzel and Halperin 1975). Since similarities in behavior, anatomy, and genes in the two species are so extensive, it becomes extremely unlikely that all these shared traits are due to evolutionary convergence. In fact, all the elements appear to be present in chimpanzees that one might postulate necessary in an ancestral population giving rise to the australopithecines and, ultimately, modern humans.

The omnivorous and diverse chimpanzee diet includes a preponderance of fruits, supplemented by buds, insects, and animals weighing five to ten pounds. Plant and animal foods are occasionally shared among associated chimpanzees. Both females and males modify and use materials in a variety of ways—as sponges, probes, hammers, and levers (Goodall 1968a); they also wave objects during displays and sometimes throw stones or branches at other animals (Kortlandt 1967; Albrecht and Dunnett 1971).

Chimpanzee social organization is flexible and suited to ranging over many square miles in search of food. There is a stable regional population or "community" of 30 to 80 chimpanzees which occupies a similar home range; the smaller units, "bands," or subgroups change frequently in number and composition, depending on varying food supply, encounters with other subgroups, or personal choice (Itani and Suzuki 1967; Izawa 1970). There are enduring relationships between mothers and offspring, siblings, and friends of the same or opposite sex (Goodall 1971). Their extensive communicative repertoire permits varied and complex responses to different social situations (Goodall 1968b).

Chimpanzees have been found in a variety of habitats—humid tropical forests, gallery and montane rain forests, savanna woodlands with wet and dry seasons, and dry, sparsely wooded areas —over a broad geographical range covering much of equatorial Africa from Guinea in the west to Tanzania in the east (Jones and Sabater Pi 1971; Kano 1971). Size of home range varies with the habitat and presumably food availability, from only a few square miles in the Budongo Forest in Uganda, to about 80 square miles in the drier areas of Tanzania (Reynolds 1965; Suzuki 1969), to as much as 200 square miles in the Ugalla areas of Tanzania (Itani 1978). Certainly no greater flexibility and adaptability in ecological range than this is needed to serve as a useful model of early hominids venturing into the African savanna.

EVALUATING OTHER SPECIES AS MODELS

Because the savanna is the setting for hominid origins and early evolution, and because baboons and social carnivores number among savanna inhabitants, these species have often been proposed as models for hominid social behavior. (Washburn and DeVore 1961; Schaller and Lowther 1969; Kummer 1971). The assumption here is that similar selective pressures operated on all three. We will briefly evaluate these models vis-à-vis the chimpanzee model.

Savanna and hamadryas baboons feed on the ground in open grasslands in eastern and southern Africa. Savanna baboons live in troops consisting of many males and females, with a central hierarchy formed by a few males. Males are twice the size of females, strong, and have large canine teeth; their fighting ability gives pause even to such predators as cheetahs and leopards. Since predator pressure is great, the troop always moves as a unit (Hall and DeVore 1965). There are no lone baboons, in contrast to occasional lone chimpanzees or lions. The closely related hamadryas baboons inhabit arid parts of Ethiopia, where food is scarce but predator pressure less. They forage on the sparse and scattered food resources during the day in one-male, multi-female units, and come together in the evening in large groups at the few available sleeping cliffs (Kummer 1968).

By analogy then, it is proposed that the early hominids, as they moved onto the savanna, adopted a social structure like that of baboons. A major difficulty with the baboon model, but paradoxically one reason it has been so favored, is the rigid social organization and male hierarchy. Their inflexibility makes it difficult to imagine how hominid gathering and later hunting could develop, with the essential frequent changes in group size and composition that are apparent in most gathering-hunting peoples today.

The carnivore model seems to originate primarily from that view of human evolution which focuses on the "hunting way of life." Carnivores and living gathering-hunting peoples at first glance seem similar in these features: they hunt cooperatively, share meat, and have a division of labor. These traits are assumed to have been equally characteristic of early hominids. But on closer examination, the analogy does not hold up.

Much has been made of meat sharing; however, this is highly variable among carnivores. Their young have a relatively long period of development and cannot provide for themselves. African hunting dogs and wolves, for example, regurgitate meat for the young and their male or female caretaker (Kühme 1965); lions, hyenas, and leopards lead the young to the kill, but lion cubs eat last and often die of starvation (Schaller 1972). Adult carnivores, such as hyenas, do not share meat, but merely tolerate other adults feeding alongside (Kruuk 1972). Sharing among chimpanzees and humans is a more give-and-take process. In contrast to the usual assumption about early humans, there is no division of labor among carnivores except for adults staying with the young while the others go after prey, and females do much of the killing and providing for the young.

Certain characteristics of predatory mammals—persistence, strategy, cognitive mapping, cooperation—have been described as forming "a behavioral substrate that fostered the evolution of human intelligence" (Peters and Mech 1975:280). But these behaviors are neither unique to predators nor equivalent to those of human groups. Chimpanzees map resources cognitively (Menzel 1973b) and demonstrate persistence and strategy in going after prey (Teleki 1973b), as do baboons (Harding and Strum 1976). "Cooperation" during the hunt in lions, hunting dogs, and hyenas involves several individuals engaging in the same activity at the same time; this behavior has been selected because it increases the success of capturing and killing prey. However, cooperation in this sense seems qualitatively different from human cooperation, which implies conscious choice and self-identification as a group member. In any case, several chimpanzees may also participate in a common activity, such as searching for food and going after small prey.

We are not minimizing the insights gained from other species in understanding human origins. But a species' adaptation is the result of interaction between potentialities inherent in its genetic makeup and the challenges of the environment. Ecological factors can influence but not determine social structure (Eisenberg, Muckenhirn, and Rudran 1972; Gartlan 1973; Altmann 1974). Models based on particular adaptations, such as living in a savanna habitat, cannot replace a more comprehensive model that includes not only ecological and behavioral factors, but a common, recent evolutionary history—as the chimpanzee model does.

AUSTRALOPITHECUS: DIRECT EVIDENCE OF THE PAST

Fossil hominids become abundant at the period referred to as the Plio-Pleistocene (about 3.5 million years ago), and by two million years ago there was a radiation of two or more species. The existing fossil record is not inconsistent with an estimated divergence of apes and humans some five or six million years ago. The earliest possible evidence of hominids consists of a fragmentary jaw from Lothagam and a piece of arm bone from Kanapoi, sites located west and southwest of Lake Turkana (formerly Lake Rudolf), Kenya. These fragments are about five million years old (Coppens, *et al.* 1976). After this time, hominid remains are found in several areas: East Africa in the Omo Basin and Afar lowlands of Ethiopia, at Koobi Fora east of Lake Turkana, and in Tanzania at Olduvai Gorge and Laetolil; and South Africa at the cave sites Swartkrans, Sterkfontein, and Makapan. There is as yet no fossil record for chimpanzees and gorillas, presumably because their forested environment did not favor fossilization.

How might we reconstruct the adaptation of early hominids, given the fossil and archeological evidence and a behavioral model of a chimpanzeelike ancestor? The data which provide a basis for interpretation include: 1) location and environmental setting of the hominid sites; 2) the bones and teeth of the hominids for clues on functional anatomy and conditions of transport and deposition; 3) and the context and association of animal bones and stones, which give some indication of hominid activities, possible predators, food sources, and animals co-existing with the hominids.

Hominid fossils are found at sites near water sources—streams, lakeshores, or karstic sinkholes—in the eastern and southern savannas, away from the tropical rainforests of central Africa which most monkeys and apes inhabit (Butzer 1977). The vegetation today in savannas varies from wooded areas along water courses to low shrub, woodlands, and open grassland areas; and, as is characteristic of tropical savannas, the plant life is dominated by the alternation of wet and dry seasons (Bourlière and Hadley 1970). There is evidence suggesting that this patchy character also existed during the Plio-Pleistocene. In the Omo Basin, for example, studies on fossil pollens confirm the mosaic nature of the vegetation between 2.5 and 2 million years ago (Bonnefille 1976); and the overlap of fossil pollen taxa with present day flora suggests that plant community types of closed and/or open woodland, grassland, tree-shrub grassland, shrub thicket, and shrub steppe characterized this area during the Plio-Pleistocene (Carr 1976).

Volcanic activity in eastern Africa left materials for absolute dating by potassium-argon, and ages of several sites have been calculated with the dates falling between five and one million years ago (Bishop and Miller 1972). Unfortunately, dating the South African sites has proved difficult, because there was no volcanic activity there during the last five million years. Animal associations, however, have been used to estimate relative ages.

Overall, the anatomy of *Australopithecus* is quite well known. Remains of all parts of the skeleton exist: teeth; skulls and faces; and arm, hand, pelvic, leg, and foot bones (Tobias 1972). Teeth are the most numerous. The large molar and premolar teeth show extensive wear, and skull and jaw features indicate well-developed chewing muscles. The canine teeth in all specimens are small; in contrast with most other primates, hominid canine size does not differ markedly by sex. Skeletal remains suggest that the australopithecines were within the body weight range of chimpanzees, but with body mass proportioned differently. Anatomical features of the pelvic, leg, and foot bones indicate that effective bipedalism had already developed (Le Gros Clark 1967). The foot had a large nonopposable great toe for stability and support of body weight, and the pelvis was shaped for extensive attachment of muscles critical for bipedalism (Zihlman and Cramer 1976). Arm bones were very much like our own, and hand bones indicate a well-muscled thumb capable of power and hand skills. The brain was comparatively small by human standards, averaging about 500 cubic centimeters with a range of 435-650 cubic centimeters (Tobias 1975); but with its expanded cortex it was significantly larger than brains of living chimpanzees, when considered relative to body weight (Holloway 1972).

Hominid bones are often found in association with stones and animal bones; in East Africa this occurs in areas called "living floors"—sites undisturbed by water action where occupation remains (both stones and bones) were found *in situ* and were sealed by subsequent deposits. Shaped stones identifiable as worked tools have been found in both East and South African sites from two million years on (M.D. Leakey 1970a, 1970b, 1971; Merrick, *et al.* 1973; Tobias 1965). Shaped cores (called choppers), flake tools, and material remaining from tool manufacture, as well as stone piles possibly used as bases for crude shelters—all provide evidence of hominid activity. In addition to tools, there are at these sites stone materials, not modified, shaped, or worn with use, that originate from sources some distance away. At this stage, tools were simply and crudely made and primarily multi-purpose.

The animal bones at the hominid sites include a variety of species and sizes: reptiles; fish; small animals; medium-sized mammals such as pigs, antelopes, baboons, and carnivores; and large ungulates such as giraffes, hippos, and elephants. Predators, such as hyenas, leopards, lions, and sabre-toothed cats were numerous at this time and posed a formidable danger to hominids (Cooke 1963). In the South African cave at Swartkrans, for example, there is convincing evidence that leopards killed and ate australopithecines (Brain 1970).

Early hominid sites have primary associations of animal bones, stone tools, rock debris, and foreign stones. The pattern of the animal bone concentrations varies from site to site and the association of the bones with stone tools may or may not be fortuitous. Although some of the animal bones may represent the remains of hominid meal taking and possibly butchering, natural processes other than hominid activity might have been significant factors in these depositions. Scavenging by carnivores, bone collecting by porcupines and hyenas, and sorting of bones by moving water may also have accounted for the associated animal bones at the hominid sites (Behrensmeyer 1976; Brain 1977). Plants do not fossilize as bones may under optimal circumstances, and information on ancient plant life through the study of fossil pollens is only beginning to accumulate at these early sites. So, although the paleontological and archeological records provide some information on australopithecine economic activities, this evidence alone cannot be taken to represent the entire picture; biases of preservation in overrepresenting animal bones and underrepresenting plant remains must be taken into account.

Organic tools, such as wooden digging implements; containers made of skin, bark, bamboo, or vines; and vegetation used in constructing shelters are important to the way of life of many living peoples. In addition, plants and insects are often used as food. Yet campsite residues composed of only organic debris, such as that left by many modern gatherer-hunters, would leave little or no trace in an archeological record (Lee 1968a). By analogy, the available record of early hominid activity has biases built in by the procedures used to locate and identify sites and in the differential preservation of animal bones contrasted with plant remains and in stone artifacts as opposed to organic implements. In interpreting early hominid behavior, we must account for the available fossil and archeological material and also recognize that extremely important evidence may not have been preserved.

GATHERING AS THE ECONOMIC BASE OF
EARLY HOMINID LIFE

We propose that the new pattern in hominid behavior and the basis of divergence from the ancestral apes was the bipedal gathering of plant food. The early hominids moved from the forest into the savanna, a mosaic of mixed and patchy vegetation. Potential plant as well as animal food was abundant, but so were predators. Sticks may have been used for digging up roots and knocking down nuts and fruits; crude containers would have made it possible to collect in quantity and return to a shaded, safe, and social place for eating and sharing with others. Gathering enough for more than one individual would have been especially important for females with dependent offspring (Tanner and Zihlman 1976).

Meat was likely not a major dietary component, although it was occasionally obtained in the manner of chimpanzees—by catching and killing small animals and pulling them apart with their bare hands. Predatory behavior no doubt occurred more frequently in the early forest-dwelling hominids because of the greater availability of young and small animals on the savanna.[2] Scavenging and the consumption of large dead animals found by chance were probably infrequent activities early in the hominid divergence, but after tools for cutting were invented, butchering large animal finds might have become fairly common. More regular protein sources probably included eggs, insects and other invertebrates, and small vertebrates. Gathering techniques could encompass these foods as well as seeds, fruits, roots, and other plants.

Gathering and Hominid Anatomy

The gathering hypothesis must be evaluated in terms of australopithecine anatomy: bipedal locomotion, large posterior teeth, small canines, skull morphology, and body size. We think that bipedal locomotion developed for covering long distances while carrying gathered food for sharing, digging sticks, objects for defense, and offspring. It has been proposed that this loco-motor pattern developed to track animals and to carry tools for hunting and the meat back to camp. But endurance for long distance walking does not differ by sex. The large home range needed for obtaining widely dispersed resources on the savanna suggests both females and males travelled frequently and far. With hands and arms freed from locomotor functions, the effec-tiveness of capturing small prey with the hands might also in-crease.

The large, worn and chipped teeth suggest that gritty plant foods were a significant part of diet (Wallace 1975), and the markings on the skull and jaw indicate prominent attachments for large chewing muscles (Wolpoff 1974). Gritty and tough foods may have included fibrous vegetation, seeds, roots, and other food from the ground. Indeed, the molars and premolars provided a larger grinding surface, relative to body size, in all species of these early hominids than is present in either apes or later hominids (Pilbeam and Gould 1974). The reduced canines are incorporated into the incisor row and function as part of the overall biting and grinding mechanism (Pilbeam 1972).

Bipedalism, body size, and canines have implications for anti-predator behavior too. Canine and body size must have differed only slightly in australopithecines by sex (Zihlman 1976). When there are marked differences between the sexes, as in baboons, large male canine and body size may function as part of a species' defense (Leutenegger and Kelly 1977); but this kind of anatomical adaptation was not available to the early hominids. The scattered trees on the savanna could not have been a practical retreat for hominids with nongrasping feet, burdened with food, tools, and infants. Upright posture probably enhanced alternative defenses: an expanded field of vision for avoiding predators, and increased effectiveness of arm-waving displays, threats, and hurling objects.

With bipedalism came the loss of a grasping foot for young to cling to mothers, and a long time for walking skills to develop in the young. Hominid mothers, then, had to carry and care for their offspring for an extended period; even after the young could walk, they could not go far without occasionally being carried. Among Kalahari !Kung gatherer-hunters, children lack endurance to keep up with a gathering group and ask to be carried when tired (Draper and Cashdan n.d.).

The minimal sexual dimorphism in body and canine size in *Australopithecus* has social implications. In primates, large canines are a visible threat, and larger-bodied individuals can dominate smaller ones. The small canines and not more than moderate body size differences in *Australopithecus* may reflect increased sociability among all group members—with minimal dominance of one sex over the other and alternatives for communicating other than physical appearance.

Gathering and Tools

Tool use as an essential part of hominid evolution interrelates with diet, bipedalism, and social behavior. The earliest human technological inventions were probably in the realm of gathering—pointed sticks and stones for digging, large leaves and nut shells as crude containers, and rocks to crack open nuts and scrape dirt from roots and tubers. They were often organic, perhaps reminiscent of some chimpanzee tools; or if stone, they were not used in a context or sufficiently modified to be recognizable to archeologists. A sling-container invented early would have been an enormous advantage for mothers supporting infants who could no longer cling.

Worked stone tools appear in the archeological record about two million years ago,[3] almost two million years after the first fossil hominids. The functions of stone tools are not well known. But at three sites at Olduvai Gorge and Koobi Fora, Lake Turkana, flake tools occur in association with a dismembered elephant or hippo (M.D. Leakey 1971; Isaac, Leakey, and Behrensmeyer 1971) and presumably were used for butchering the large animals. Stone artifacts called "choppers" might be interpreted as digging tools or may have been used for making organic tools; others called "spheroids" perhaps were utilized to pound tough plant food prior to eating.

Tools have important implications for social behavior. When tool using and making are an integral part of food getting, a long period is necessary for the young to master the appropriate skills. For example, chimpanzees require four to five years before they are proficient at "termiting" (McGrew 1978). With tool using, as with bipedalism, the young must be cared for while learning. Containers are a means for the adults, especially mothers, to provide food for the younger members less able to gather effectively. The invention of cutting tools, such as those for butchering large animals, enhances the ease of sharing food. As with gathering, females were probably very involved in butchering to provide meat to share with offspring. The way of life of these early hominids thus relied upon tools made and used by both sexes.

Gathering and Social Behavior

How did australopithecine social behavior, especially mating patterns and the care and socialization of the young, interrelate with gathering? What was the role of males? This subject is further removed from economics and therefore more in the realm of speculation, but concepts of kin and parental investment provide a framework for our interpretations.

Among chimpanzees and other primates, maternal investment is high, and the young have strong ties which persist throughout life with their mothers and siblings. Hominid mothers probably carried and nursed their young for almost four years—the average time for chimpanzees and mothers in many gathering-hunting societies (Goodall 1967; Lee 1972). Even after weaning, it was several years before hominid young were independent in locomotion and in using tools to get food. Maternal investment increased in early hominids as the period of dependency lengthened. Hominid mothers probably gathered food frequently and intensively, because the survival of their offspring depended on it.

Because so much energy went into the care of the offspring to ensure survival to adulthood and because the period of development and dependency was long, selection would have also favored a social group where several individuals besides the mother assisted in the care, protection, and feeding of the young. The mother-offspring unit was the most likely core unit within the larger group structure, as it is in many monkeys and apes (Lancaster 1975). Strong sibling ties were probably the basis for extending this core. These small kin groups, perhaps three to eight individuals, shared food and helped protect each other and, particularly, the immature members. Such care not only would have increased the chances that young born in the group would reach adulthood and reproduce, but would have increased a mother's reproductive rate by allowing her to have another offspring before the first was entirely independent. Sisters and brothers of the mother or her older offspring well might have assisted in providing such nurturing. This type of behavior would have evolved through kin selection, an aspect of natural selection where an individual, by contributing to the survival of kin with whom he or she shares genes, passes on those common genes to the next generation (Hamilton 1964; Eberhard 1975). We suggest that australopithecine kin ties, especially among siblings, were increased over those of their primate ancestors. The relatively strong bond we envision between mothers and sons and between male and female siblings would serve to integrate male hominids into the kin group, where they contributed to the survival of their shared genes through kin investment.

Parental investment involves energy expenditure and caring for one offspring at the expense of investing in future offspring. Mating patterns in many vertebrate species have been shown to correlate with the relative amount of parental investment: the sex which invests most in each offspring selects mates from among several potential partners while the other sex "competes" for the limited partners (Trivers 1972). This process of sexual selection is one aspect of natural selection. The necessarily high maternal investment of early hominids suggests that females, rather than males, chose their mates.

What kinds of males might these females choose and how were the males competing? It seems plausible that females might have preferred the more sociable males, and that males therefore were "competing" in being sociable not only by their involvement in their own kin groups where they were sharing food, protecting, and carrying their siblings or sister's offspring, but also in friendly interaction with females and males at the camp-sites where members of several subgroups met and slept. Specific studies of mating patterns in monkeys and apes are few, but female choice of sexual partners has been observed in several species including chimpanzees, baboons, and macaques (Nishida 1968; Sugiyama 1969; McGinnis 1973; Lindburg 1975; Saayman 1975). There is evidence that females may avoid aggressive males as sexual partners and may choose sociable ones. Mc-Ginnis reports that chimpanzee females may run from males that approach to mate in a threatening manner. In a baboon troop, the male most preferred as a sexual partner was the least aggressive; he spent the most time near females and their offspring, frequently intervened on their behalf during agonistic encounters, and was often groomed by females in all stages of the reproductive cycle (Saayman 1975).

The small australopithecine canines may be an anatomical expression of increased sociability among all group members.[4] Selection pressure for large canines was reduced, due to their integration into the changing masticatory apparatus and their replacement by tools in protective functions. But there may also have existed a positive selection pressure for small canines as a result of reduced intragroup aggression and dominance displays (Holloway 1967). Such behaviors, we believe, would have been highly advantageous to the australopithecine way of life.

The settings for early mating and social interactions were campsites along water sources, for which evidence exists as long ago as two million years (M.D. Leakey 1976). We do not know the length of time these sites were used nor the number of individuals who associated there, but these wooded areas may have provided protected places for eating, sleeping, and social interactions. The size of campsite groupings was probably variable. Within a regional community, subgroups or "bands," consisting primarily of kin groupings, may have been the smaller units. Two or more such small groups, perhaps somewhat related genetically, might have associated frequently, with still larger groups congregating anywhere food, water, and trees were abundant.

These larger groups would have made possible a wide choice of sexual partners. As with chimpanzees, the sexual act did not automatically imply aggression between males or long-term bonds between males and females (Sugiyama 1973). We hypothesize female choice operating among hominids, but with considerable variability and flexibility in mating patterns, especially in the length of time a mating pair stayed together. At this stage in evolution, we propose relatively distinct economic and sexual units; the economic units were the smaller kin groups that shared food and cared for young, whereas the sexual or reproductive units were the larger associations at campsites and abundant food sources.

Social behavior is a major part of subsistence and survival. We propose for the australopithecines a cooperative kin group where both sexes engaged in gathering, butchering, and defense, and where food was shared among close kin. Several adults in the group, particularly males unencumbered by infants, were advantageous for defense against predators; but several females, without a male present, could defend themselves and young adequately when necessary. We do not envision a rigid division of labor by sex, but doubtless the frequency of certain activities varied both by sex and age. Females carrying young could not travel as far in search of food and would likely concentrate on reliable sources, whereas males might gather less consistently and more frequently chase small animals and bring back meat to share.

Natural selection would have enhanced those processes adaptive for the gathering way of life: greater intelligence for cognitive mapping of food sources, for communicating this information to others, and for participating in complex social relations.

Hominids needed to conceptualize, find, or make digging tools and containers, apply their use to widely scattered food resources, and pass on the techniques to subsequent generations. Selection would have favored young who readily learned the techniques and technology of gathering by observing and imitating the adults. Effective communication, still nonverbal, along with reduction of the threatening large canines, would have increased sociability.

Flexibility in behavior, organizational fluidity, and sociability were vital ingredients in hominid survival and success. They were essential for effectively exploiting savanna resources, for diminishing death by predation, and for increasing the chances of survival of the young. It is difficult to begin with a baboon social model or a pair bond model and end up with the flexibility that is characteristic of gathering-hunting peoples today (Bicchieri 1972), as well as the cultural variability in social organizations and ecological adaptations of peoples around the world, historically and at present. In *Australopithecus*, flexibility in behavior and social structure, plus the ability to learn and communicate effectively, were as much a part of the hominid potential as the ability to walk upright and to make and use tools: they provided the type of biological base from which later, culture-bearing humans evolved.

THE ORIGIN OF HUNTING

Hunting, as pointed out earlier, is rarely precisely defined; it may mean predation, scavenging, butchering, or taking prey— large or small, solitary or in herds. It may mean killing with teeth, bare hands, or tools. Not only is there no simple extension from chimpanzee predation to hunting, in the sense of killing with tools, but also the social implications of these modes of obtaining meat are very different. The comparison of carnivore with human hunting confuses rather than clarifies, because it is a mixture of behavioral, technical, and dietary analogies with no consistent evolutionary or genetic framework. Not to distinguish each factor involved in "hunting" is to ignore differences in technique that may have taken several million years to evolve.

Plants were almost certainly a major food source for early hominids (Bartholomew and Birdsell 1953; Washburn and Avis 1958; Isaac 1971). Meat consumption likely increased, first, by more frequent predation of small animals. Sharp implements began to be used to dress scavenged meat and butcher large animals trapped in swamps. Eventually, hominids developed to the point of killing animals at close range with various artifacts and, only much later, pursuing and killing them with specialized tools.

Hunting with tools is a high risk, low return activity that, to be reasonably effective, requires precise skills and refined tools. It seems logical to us that it could only have become common in this form after gathering was fully developed. Gathering then could have provided a secure nutritional and social base from which a few hunters could go forth and expend energy for uncertain success. Hunting perhaps had its technological base in the system of tool-aided gathering and its social base in the gathering kin group, where some individuals engaged in predatory activity, and both plant and animal food were regularly shared (Zihlman n.d.).

In support of this hypothesis, the small flake tools apparently used to butcher the elephant and hippo at Olduvai and Koobi Fora may well have developed from artifacts originally used to divide, scrape, or otherwise process plant foods and to prepare organic tools. The three butchering sites are located along ancient lakeshores, probably swampy areas. There, big animals could have been trapped and killed, rather than being tracked and hunted down—a much more advanced social and technical development.

We believe that this style of hunting did not emerge until about half a million years ago. Meat may have become a critical food source when hominids expanded out of Africa into the temperate zones where plant availability is seasonal (Butzer 1971; Campbell 1972). Hominids entered Southeast Asia about a million years ago, but there were no large herd animals there, and no suggestive collections of tools and animal bones have been found from this period (Luchterhand 1974). There is evidence that hominids were in Europe by half a million years ago (Butzer and Isaac 1975), and there are associations of tools and dismembered elephant bones from the Middle Pleistocene in Spain, in what were ancient swamps.

Possibly the earliest undisputed evidence for hunting with weapons is found at Lehringen, northwestern Germany, a site from the Third Interglacial (about 0.1 million). Here was uncovered a fossil elephant with a wooden spear nearly eight feet long between its ribs (Movius 1950). The spear point had been sharpened with stone knives and hardened by fire. This was probably after the first appearance of *Homo sapiens*.

We have stressed gathering plant foods as the critical innovation in human evolution, one that logically emerged from ape behaviors, such as tool using and food sharing. The omnivorous diet of chimpanzees, with 98 percent of foods being plants, finds a parallel among living gatherer-hunters where gathered plant foods may account for 50 to 90 percent of their diet (Lee 1965, 1968b; Gale 1970). We believe that the picture of hunting emerging from the very beginning of human origins with meat as a major food source is no longer supported by the evidence.

It is all too easy to make generalizations about "human nature" based on contemporary societies, particularly our own culture, or look to animal behavior for "evidence" of these conceptions and project them back in time to human origins. It is more sound, we believe, to start with the primates genetically most closely related to our species and consider how, consistent with evolutionary principles, human society may have developed in stages of increasing technical and social complexity from the hominid divergence five or six million years ago to the modern age.

NOTES

[1] We have chosen to use the term *Australopithecus* to delineate the earliest hominids, undoubtedly more than one species, dated between about two and four million years ago. Taxonomically, two or more lines have been identified, and R. Leakey and others have given them two generic names (*Homo* and *Australopithecus*). However, we refer to them collectively as the genus *Australopithecus* because:

1) they shared a number of anatomical and behavioral characteristics as part of their adaptation to the African savanna during the Plio-Pleistocene; and 2) they are differentiated as a group from apes by bipedalism, large grinding teeth, small canines, and larger brains.

[2] The frequency and sophistication of predatory activity in one troop of baboons at Gilgil, Kenya increased rapidly as the antelope population increased (Harding and Strum 1976).

[3] Redating of the KBS tuff from 2.6 to 1.8-1.6 million years ago (Curtis, *et al.* 1975) apparently changes the age of the archeological sites at Koobi Fora, Lake Turkana (Isaac, Harris, and Crader 1976) to less than two million years old.

[4] Among nonhuman primates, minimal canine dimorphism indicates minimal social role differentiation between the sexes and less competition between males than in species where canines are dimorphic (Leutenegger and Kelly 1977).

REFERENCES CITED

ALBRECHT, H. and S.C. DUNNETT
1971—*Chimpanzees in Western Africa*. Munich:R. Piper.

ALTMANN, S.A.
1974—Baboons, Space, Time and Energy. *American Zoologist* 14: 221-248.

BARTHOLOMEW, G. and J. BIRDSELL
1953—Ecology and the Protohominds. *American Anthropologist* 55:481-498.

BEHRENSMEYER, A.K.
1975—The Taphonomy and Paleoecology of Plio-Pleistocene Vertebrate Assemblages East of Lake Rudolf, Kenya. *Museum of Comparative Zoology Bulletin* 146(10):473-578.

1976—Fossil Assemblages in Relation to Sedimentary Environments in the East Rudolf Succession. In *Earliest Man and Environments in the Lake Rudolf Basin: Stratigraphy, Paleoecology, and Evolution*, Y. Coppens, F.C. Howell, G.L. Isaac, and R.E.F. Leakey, eds. Chicago:University of Chicago Press.

BICCHIERI, M.G., ed.
1972—*Hunters and Gatherers Today: A Socioeconomic Study of Eleven Such Cultures in the Twentieth Century*. New York: Holt, Rinehart and Winston.

BISHOP, W.W. and J.A. MILLER, eds.
1972—*Calibration of Hominoid Evolution*. Toronto:University of Toronto Press.

BONNEFILLE, R.
   1976—Palynological Evidence for an Important Change in the Vege-
        tation of the Omo Basin between 2.5 and 2 Million Years.
        In *Earliest Man and Environments in the Lake Rudolf Basin:
        Stratigraphy, Paleoecology and Evolution.* Y. Coppens, F.C.
        Howell, G.L. Isaac, and R.E.F. Leakey, eds. Chicago:Uni-
        versity of Chicago Press.

BOURLIÈRE, F. and M. HADLEY
   1970—The Ecology of Tropical Savannas. *Annual Review of Ecol-
        ogy and Systematics* 1:125-152.

BRAIN, C.K.
   1970—New Finds at the Swartkrans Australopithecine Site. *Nature*
        225:1112-1119.

   1976—Some Principles in the Interpretation of Bone Accumulations
        Associated with Man. In *Human Origins: Louis Leakey and
        the East African Evidence,* G.L. Isaac and E.R. McCown,
        eds. Menlo Park, Ca.:W.A. Benjamin.

   1977—Some Aspects of the South African Australopithecine Sites
        and their Bone Accumulations. In *Hominidae of the African
        Plio-Pleistocene,* C.J. Jolly, ed. London:Duckworth. (Forth-
        coming.)

BUTZER, K.
   1971—*Environment and Archaeology: An Ecological Approach to
        Prehistory.* Chicago:Aldine.

   1977—Geo-Ecological Perspectives on Early Hominid Evolution.
        In *Hominidae of the African Plio-Pleistocene,* C.J. Jolly, ed.
        London:Duckworth. (Forthcoming.)

BUTZER, K. and G. ISAAC, eds.
   1975—*After the Austrapolithecines: Stratigraphy, Ecology and
        Culture Change in the Middle Pleistocene.* World Anthro-
        pology Series. The Hague:Mouton.

CACHEL, S.
   1975—A New View of Speciation in *Australopithecus.* In *Socio-
        ecology and Psychology of Primates,* R.H. Tuttle, ed. World
        Anthropology Series. The Hague:Mouton.

CAMPBELL, B.
   1972—Man for All Seasons. In *Sexual Selection and Descent of
        Man 1871-1971,* B. Campbell, ed. Chicago:Aldine.

CARR, C.J.
   1976—Plant Ecological Variation and Pattern in the Lower Omo
        Basin. In *Earliest Man and Environments in the Lake Ru-
        dolf Basin: Stratigraphy, Paleoecology, and Evolution,* Y.

Coppens, F.C. Howell, G.L. Isaac, and R.E.F. Leakey, eds. Chicago:University of Chicago Press.

COOKE, H.B.S.
1963–Pleistocene Mammal Faunas of Africa, with Particular Reference to Southern Africa. In *African Ecology and Human Evolution,* F.C. Howell and F. Bourlière, eds. Chicago: Aldine.

COPPENS, Y., F.C. HOWELL, G.L. ISAAC, and R.E.F. LEAKEY, eds.
1976–*Earliest Man and Environments in the Lake Rudolf Basin: Stratigraphy, Paleoecology, and Evolution.* Chicago:University of Chicago Press.

CROMPTON, A.W. and K. HIIEMÄE
1969–How Mammalian Molar Teeth Work. *Discovery* 5(1):23-34.

CRONIN, J.E.
1975–*Molecular Systematics of the Order Primates.* Ph.D. dissertation in Genetics-Anthropology, University of California, Berkeley.

CURTIS, G.H., *et al.*
1975–Age of KBS Tuff in Koobi Fora Formation, East Rudolf, Kenya. *Nature* 258:395-398.

DRAPER, P. and E. CASHDAN
n.d.–*The Impact of Sedentism on !Kung Socialization.* Paper presented at the American Anthropological Association Meeting, 1974, Mexico City.

EBERHARD, M.J.W.
1975–The Evolution of Social Behavior by Kin Selection. *Quarterly Review of Biology* 50(1):1-33.

EISENBERG, J.F., N.A. MUCKENHIRN, and R. RUDRAN
1972–The Relation Between Ecology and Social Structure in Primates. *Science* 176:863-874.

GALE, F., ed.
1970–*Woman's Role in Aboriginal Society.* Australian Aboriginal Studies, number 36. Social Anthropology Series 6. Canberra: Australian Institute of Aboriginal Studies.

GARTLAN, J.S.
1973–Influences of Phylogeny and Ecology on Variations in the Group Organization of Primates. In *Precultural Primate Behavior. Symposia of the Fourth Congress of Primatology,* volume 1, E.W. Menzel, Jr., ed. Basel:S. Karger.

GOODALL, J. (VAN LAWICK)
1967–Mother-Offspring Relationships in Free-Ranging Chimpan-

zees. In *Primate Ethology*, D. Morris, ed. London:Weiden-feld and Nicolson.

1968a-The Behavior of Free-Living Chimpanzees in the Gombe Stream Reserve. *Animal Behavior Monographs* 1:165-311.

1968b-Expressive Movements and Communication. In *Primates: Studies in Adaptation and Variability*, P. Jay, ed. New York: Holt, Rinehart and Winston.

1971—*In the Shadow of Man*. Boston:Houghton Mifflin.

1976—Continuities between Chimpanzee and Human Behavior. In *Human Origins: Louis Leakey and the East African Evidence*, G.L. Isaac and E.R. McCown, eds. Menlo Park, Ca.: W.A. Benjamin.

HALL, K.R.L. and I. DeVORE
1965—Baboon Social Behavior. In *Primate Behavior: Studies of Monkeys and Apes*, I. DeVore, ed. New York:Holt, Rinehart and Winston.

HAMILTON, W.D.
1964—The Genetical Evolution of Social Behavior. *Journal of Theoretical Biology* 7:1-52.

HARDING, R.S.O.
1973—Predation by a Troop of Olive Baboons (*Papio anubis*). *American Journal of Physical Anthropology* 38:587-591.

1975—Meat-Eating and Hunting in Baboons. In *Socioecology and Psychology of Primates*, R.H. Tuttle, ed. World Anthropology Series. The Hague:Mouton.

HARDING, R.S.O. and S.C. STRUM
1976—Predatory Baboons of Kekopey. *Natural History* 85(3):46-53.

HAUSFATER, G.
1976—Predatory Behavior of Yellow Baboons. *Behaviour* 56(1-2): 45-68.

HOLLOWAY, R.L., Jr.
1967—Tools and Teeth: Some Speculations Regarding Canine Reduction. *American Anthropologist* 69:63-67.

1972—Australopithecine Endocasts, Brain Evolution in the Hominoidea and a Model of Hominid Evolution. In *The Functional and Evolutionary Biology of Primates*, R.H. Tuttle, ed. World Anthropology Series. The Hague:Mouton.

ISAAC, G.L.
1971—The Diet of Early Man: Aspects of Archaeological Evidence from Lower and Middle Pleistocene Sites in Africa. *World Archaeology* 2:277-299.

1976–The Activities of Early African Hominids: Review of Archaeological Evidence from the Time Span Two and a Half to One Million Years Ago. In *Human Origins: Louis Leakey and the East African Evidence*, G.L. Isaac and E.R. McCown, eds. Menlo Park, Ca.:W.A. Benjamin.

ISAAC, G.L., J.W.K. HARRIS, and D. CRADER
1976–Archeological Evidence from the Koobi Fora Formation. In *Earliest Man and Environments in the Lake Rudolf Basin: Stratigraphy, Paleoecology, and Evolution*, Y. Coppens, F.C. Howell, G.L. Isaac, and R.E.F. Leakey, eds. Chicago:University of Chicago Press.

ISAAC, G.L., R.E.F. LEAKEY, and A.K. BEHRENSMEYER
1971–Archaeological Traces of Early Hominid Activities, East of Lake Rudolf, Kenya. *Science* 1973:1129-1134.

ITANI, J.
1978–Distribution and Adaptation of Chimpanzees in an Arid Area (Ugalla Area, Western Tanzania). In *The Great Apes: Perspectives on Human Evolution* 5, D. Hamburg and E. McCown, eds. Menlo Park, Ca.:W.A. Benjamin. (Forthcoming.)

ITANI, J. and A. SUZUKI
1967–The Social Unit of Chimpanzees. *Primates* 8:355-381.

IZAWA, K.
1970–Unit Groups of Chimpanzees and Their Nomadism in the Savanna Woodland. *Primates* 11:1-46.

JONES, C. and J. SABATER PI
1971–Comparative Ecology of *Gorilla gorilla* (Savage and Wyman) and *Pan troglodytes* (Blumenbach) in Rio Muni, West Africa. *Bibliotheca Primatologica*, number 13. Basel:S. Karger.

KANO, T.
1971–The Chimpanzee of Filabanga, Western Tanzania. *Primates* 12(3-4):229-246.

KING, M. and A. WILSON
1975–Evolution at Two Levels in Humans and Chimpanzees. *Science* 188:107-116.

KITAHARA-FRISCH, J.
1975–Book review of G. Teleki's *The Predatory Behavior of Wild Chimpanzees*. *Primates* 16(1):103-106.

KORTLANDT, A.
1967–Experimentation with Chimpanzees in the Wild. In *Progress in Primatology*, D. Starck, R. Schneider, and H.J. Kuhn, eds. Stuttgart:Gustav Fischer.

KRUUK, H.
1972—*The Spotted Hyena: A Study of Predation and Social Behavior.* Wildlife, Behavior and Ecology Series. Chicago: University of Chicago Press.

KÜHME, W.
1965—Communal Food Distribution and Division of Labor in African Hunting Dogs. *Nature* 205:443-444.

KUMMER, H.
1968—*Social Organization of Hamadryas Baboons.* Chicago:University of Chicago Press.
1971—*Primate Societies: Group Techniques of Ecological Adaptation.* Chicago:Aldine.

LANCASTER, J.
1975—*Primate Behavior and the Emergence of Human Culture.* New York:Holt, Rinehart and Winston.

LEAKEY, M.D.
1970a-Early Artefacts from the Koobi Fora Area. *Nature* 226:228-230.
1970b-Stone Artefacts from Swartkrans. *Nature* 225:1222-1225.
1971—*Olduvai Gorge,* volume 3. Excavations in Beds I and II, 1960-1963. Cambridge:Cambridge University Press.
1976—A Summary and Discussion of the Archaeological Evidence from Bed I and Bed II, Olduvai Gorge, Tanzania. In *Human Origins: Louis Leakey and the East African Evidence,* G.L. Isaac and E.R. McCown, eds. Menlo Park, Ca.:W.A. Benjamin.

LEE, R.B.
1965—*Subsistence Ecology of !Kung Bushmen.* Ph.D. dissertation, University of California, Berkeley.
1968a-Comments. In *New Perspectives in Archeology,* S.R. Binford and L.R. Binford, eds. Chicago:Aldine.
1968b-What Hunters Do for a Living, or How to Make Out on Scarce Resources. In *Man the Hunter,* R.B. Lee and I. DeVore, eds. Chicago:Aldine.
1972—Population Growth and the Beginning of Sedentary Life among the !Kung Bushmen. In *Population Growth: Anthropological Implications,* B. Spooner, ed. Cambridge, Ma.:MIT Press.

LEE, R.B. and I. DeVORE, eds.
1968a-*Man the Hunter.* Chicago:Aldine.
1968b-Problems in the Study of Hunters and Gatherers. In *Man the Hunter,* R.B. Lee and I. DeVore, eds. Chicago:Aldine.

LE GROS CLARK, W.E.
1967—*Man-Apes or Ape-Men?* *The Story of Discoveries in Africa.*
New York:Holt, Rinehart and Winston.

LEUTENEGGER, W. and J.T. KELLY
1977—Relationship of Sexual Dimorphism in Canine Size and Body
Size to Social, Behavioral and Ecological Correlates in
Anthropoid Primates. *Primates* 18(1):117-136.

LINDBURG, D.
1975—Mate Selection in the Rhesus Monkey, *Macaca mulatta.*
American Journal of Physical Anthropology 42:315.

LINTON, S.
1971—Woman the Gatherer: Male Bias in Anthropology. In *Women
in Perspective: A Guide for Cross-Cultural Studies,* S.E.
Jacobs, ed. Urbana:University of Illinois of Illinois Press.
Reprinted under Sally Slocum in *Toward an Anthropology
of Women,* R.R. Reiter, ed. New York:Monthly Review.

LUCHTERHAND, K.
1974—*Mid-Pleistocene Hominid Distribution and Adaptation in
Eastern Asia.* Ph.D. dissertation, University of Chicago.

McGINNIS, P.R.
1973—*Patterns of Sexual Behaviour in a Community of Free-living
Chimpanzees.* Ph.D. dissertation, Cambridge University,
Cambridge, England.

McGREW, W.C.
1978—Evolutionary Implications of Sex Differences in Chimpanzee
Predation and Tool Use. In *The Great Apes: Perspectives
on Human Evolution* 5, D. Hamburg and E. McCown, eds.
Menlo Park, Ca.:W.A. Benjamin. (Forthcoming.)

MENZEL, E.W.
1973a-Leadership and Communication in Young Chimpanzees. In
Precultural Primate Behavior, E.W. Menzel, ed. Basel:S.
Karger.

1973b-Chimpanzee Spatial Memory Organization. *Science* 182:
943-945.

MENZEL, E.W. and S. HALPERIN
1975—Purposive Behavior as a Basis for Objective Communication
between Chimpanzees. *Science* 189:652-654.

MERRICK, H.V., J. DEHEINZELIN, P. HALSAERTS, and
F.C. HOWELL
1973—Archaeological Occurrences of Early Pleistocene Age from
the Shungura Formation, Lower Omo Valley, Ethiopia.
Nature 242:572-575.

MOVIUS, H.L., Jr.
  1950–A Wooden Spear of Third Interglacial Age from Lower
    Saxony. *Southwestern Journal of Anthropology* 6:139-142.
NISHIDA, T.
  1968–The Social Group of Wild Chimpanzees in the Mahali
    Mountains. *Primates* 9:167-224.
PETERS, R. and L.D. MECH
  1975–Behavioral and Intellectual Adaptations of Selected Mam-
    malian Predators to the Problem of Hunting Large Animals.
    In *Sociobiology and Psychology of Primates*, R.H. Tuttle,
    ed. World Anthropology Series. The Hague:Mouton.
PFEIFFER, J.
  1972–*The Emergence of Man* (second edition). New York:Harper
    and Row.
PILBEAM, D.
  1972–Evolutionary Changes in Hominoid Dentition Through Geo-
    logical Time. In *Calibration of Hominoid Evolution*, W.W.
    Bishop and J.A. Miller, eds. Edinburgh:Scottish Academic.
PILBEAM, D. and S.J. GOULD
  1974–Size and Scaling in Human Evolution. *Science* 186:892-901.
REYNOLDS, V.
  1965–Some Behavioral Comparisons Between the Chimpanzee and
    the Mountain Gorilla in the Wild. *American Anthropologist*
    67:691-706.
SAAYMAN, G.S.
  1975–The Influence of Hormonal and Ecological Factors upon
    Sexual Behavior and Social Organization in Old World
    Primates. In *Socioecology and Psychology of Primates*, R.H.
    Tuttle, ed. World Anthropology Series. The Hague:Mouton.
SARICH, V.M. and J.E. CRONIN
  1976–Molecular Systematics of the Primates. In *Molecular Anthro-
    pology*, M. Goodman and R.E. Tashian, eds. New York:
    Plenum.
SCHALLER, G.
  1972–*The Serengeti Lion*. Chicago:University of Chicago Press.
SCHALLER, G. and G. LOWTHER
  1969–The Relevance of Carnivore Behavior to the Study of Early
    Hominids. *Southwestern Journal of Anthropology* 25(4):
    307-341.
STRUM, S.C.
  1975–Primate Predation: Interim Report on the Development of a
    Tradition in a Troop of Olive Baboons. *Science* 187:255-
    257.

SUGIYAMA, Y.
1969–Social Behavior of Chimpanzees in the Budongo Forest, Uganda. *Primates* 10:197-225.
1973–The Social Structure of Wild Chimpanzees: A Review of Field Studies. In *Comparative Ecology and Behaviour of Primates*, R. Michael and J. Crook, eds. New York:Academic.

SUZUKI, A.
1969–An Ecological Study of Chimpanzees in a Savanna Woodland. *Primates* 10:103-148.
1975–The Origin of Hominid Hunting: A Primatological Perspective. In *Socioecology and Psychology of Primates*, R.H. Tuttle, ed. World Anthropology Series. The Hague:Mouton.

TANNER, N. and A. ZIHLMAN
1976–Women in Evolution. Part I: Innovation and Selection in Human Origins. *Signs: Journal of Women in Culture and Society* 1(3, Part 1):585-608.

TELEKI, G.
1973a-*The Predatory Behavior of Wild Chimpanzees*. Lewisburg, Pa.:Bucknell University Press.
1973b-The Omnivorous Chimpanzee. *Scientific American* 228(1): 33-42.
1974–Chimpanzee Subsistence Technology: Materials and Skills. *Journal of Human Evolution* 3:575-594.
1975–Primate Subsistence Patterns: Collector-Predators and Gatherer-Hunters. *Journal of Human Evolution* 4:125-184.

TIGER, L.
1969–*Men in Groups*. New York:Random House.

TIGER, L. and R. FOX
1971–*The Imperial Animal*. New York:Holt, Rinehart and Winston.

TOBIAS, P.V.
1965–*Australopithecus, Homo habilis*, Tool-Using and Tool-Making. *South African Archaeological Bulletin* 20(80):167-192.
1972–Progress and Problems in the Study of Early Man in Sub-Saharan Africa. In *Functional and Evolutionary Biology of Primates*, R.H. Tuttle ed. World Anthropology Series. Chicago:Aldine.
1975–Brain Evolution in the Hominoidea. In *Primate Functional Morphology and Evolution*, R.H. Tuttle, ed. World Anthropology Series. The Hague:Mouton.

TRIVERS, R.L.
1972–Parental Investment and Sexual Selection. In *Sexual Selection and the Descent of Man 1871-1971*, B. Campbell, ed. Chicago: Aldine.

WALLACE, J.A.
1972–Tooth Chipping in the Australopithecines. *Nature* 244:117-118.
1975–Dietary Adaptations of *Australopithecus* and Early *Homo*. In *Paleoanthropology, Morphology and Paleoecology*, R.H. Tuttle, ed. World Anthropology Series. The Hague:Mouton.

WASHBURN, S.L. and V. AVIS
1958–Evolution of Human Behavior. In *Behavior and Evolution*, A. Roe and G.G. Simpson, eds. New Haven:Yale University Press.

WASHBURN, S.L. and I. DeVORE
1961–Social Behavior of Baboons and Early Man. In *Social Life of Early Man*, S.L. Washburn, ed. Chicago:Aldine.

WASHBURN, S.L. and C.S. LANCASTER
1968–The Evolution of Hunting. In *Man the Hunter*, R.B. Lee and I. DeVore, eds. Chicago:Aldine.

WASHBURN, S.L. and R. MOORE
1974–*Ape into Man: A Study of Human Evolution*. Boston:Little, Brown.

WILSON, A.C. and V.M. SARICH
1969–A Molecular Time Scale for Human Evolution. *Proceedings of the National Academy of Sciences* 63:1088-1093.

WILSON, E.O.
1975–*Sociobiology: The New Synthesis*. Cambridge, Ma.:Harvard University Press.

WOLPOFF, M.H.
1973–Posterior Tooth Size, Body Size and Diet in South African Gracile Australopithecines. *American Journal of Physical Anthropology* 39:375-394.
1974–Sagittal Cresting in the South African Australopithecines. *American Journal of Physical Anthropology* 40(3):397-408.

ZIHLMAN, A.L.
1976–Sexual Dimorphism and its Behavioral Implications in Early Hominids. Prepared for Colloque VI "Les plus anciens hominides." *Neuvième Congrès International des Sciences Préhistoriques et Protohistoriques*. September 13-18, Nice, France.
n.d.–Women in Evolution, Part II: Subsistence and Social Organization in Early Hominids. *Signs: Journal of Women in Culture and Society*. (Forthcoming.)

ZIHLMAN, A.L. and D. CRAMER
1976–Human Locomotion. *Natural History* 85(1):64-69.

7

Women in Politics

WILLIAM L. O'NEILL

In a brief paper one cannot do more than discuss a few episodes in the political history of women during the past two centuries. The task is made all the more difficult because professional historians have largely neglected women until very recently. All the same, the evidence that exists does permit a few tentative generalizations. One is that, except under special circumstances, women have never participated in politics on an equal basis with men, whatever their legal status. Another is that women did not participate in politics as women at all until the French Revolution. Of course, women were politically active as individuals long before that. Numerous wives, mothers, courtesans, and queens made their mark on history before the age of revolution, but indirectly as a rule and never as members of female political movements.[1]

Even as late as the American War of Independence, to the success of which many women contributed, their labors were seldom well organized and only marginally political. And for the most part, their work was consistent with prevailing doctrines as to women's role and capacity (Clinton and Green 1912). During the early troubles women pledged to boycott British goods. In New England and elsewhere, groups calling themselves Daughters of Liberty met to make homespun substitutes for British textiles. In North Carolina young ladies agreed not to marry anyone who had failed to serve in the army. At

195

least one large charitable and patriotic society was organized in the middle states and raised money to help clothe soldiers. These scattered contributions did not alter their status. Neither in theory nor in practice did the War of Independence have much effect on the position of American women in the eighteenth century (Benson 1935).

WOMEN IN REVOLUTIONARY MOVEMENTS

Thus, the world was little prepared for the significant role women played in the French Revolution. A handful of women are still associated by name with it. For example, Marie-Jeanne Phlipon, a well-read young woman who married a civil servant named Jeane-Marie Roland in 1780. Roland was an inspector of manufactures who wrote extensively on trade and manufacturing in hopes of reforming French practices. When the Revolution broke out, the Rolands supported it for ideological reasons—because Roland's career had been frustrated by the incompetence and corruption of the old regime, and because it offered an opportunity to put his ideas into practice. They moved to Paris, where they joined the moderate Gironde faction. Madame Roland operated a salon, and through her influence with leading Girondins, Roland was made Minister of the Interior. After the Jacobin seizure of power, Roland went into hiding and Madame Roland and her lover, a Girondin deputy, were imprisoned. While confined Madame Roland wrote her memoirs, which are entitled *Appeal to Impartial Posterity*. The appeal did not save her head; but because of it, Madame Roland continues to be one of the few women whose revolutionary experiences are well-known. Madame Roland is also remembered for her last words, provoked by a statue dedicated to liberty she saw just before ascending the scaffold: "O liberty, what crimes are committed in thy name" (May 1970).

Madame de Staël, even more than Madame Roland, achieved fame not so much for her contributions to the Revolution as for her political writings. The daughter of a Swiss banker and philanthropist who held several high offices in France, she supported the Revolution for feminist reasons, unlike most women involved in politics at the time. Her actual contribution to the Revolution was not great, although she conducted a political salon and thus had some influence in the traditional manner of intelligent, upper class Parisian women. A moderate, she was obliged to flee Paris to escape the terror and afterward was exiled by Napoleon. Most of her life from 1791 until her death in 1817 at the age of 51 was spent outside of France.

Madame de Staël expressed her feminist convictions in two ways. In her personal life she was independent, daring, a ruthless guardian of her right to happiness, and a woman who was more than equal to her husband and lovers. Professionally, she became famous through her books and essays on politics, morality, and history. She was a notably effective critic of the social order that kept women from being themselves, believing that it was her sex alone which kept her from rising, as she put it, "to a man's reputation." In her novel *Delphine* one of her characters says: "I was, and I still am, convinced that women, being the victims of all social institutions, are destined to misery if they make the least concession to their feelings, and if, in any way whatever, they lose control of themselves" (Christopher 1958).

In the past, historians, if they dealt with women in the Revolution at all, concentrated on famous individuals like Madame Roland and Madame de Staël (Wilson 1936). Recent scholarship makes clear, however, that the great majority of largely unknown female revolutionaries had a greater effect on events. Most of these were working class women, of whom more later, but several hundred were organized in a specifically feminine body allied with a political tendency and called by historians the Enragés. This was the left-wing faction closest to the working class. A woman leader associated with the Enragés was Pauline Léon, who managed a chocolate business left by her father. She helped throw up barricades in the street actions of 1789 and participated in other violent demonstrations. She attended meetings of several revolutionary clubs and in 1791 asked the Constituent Assembly to authorize her to raise and arm a body of women for military purposes. Although turned down, she responded two years later by organizing the Society of Revolutionary Republican Women. She led a band of women to a meeting of the Jacobin club where she announced the formation of a body of female volunteers for service against the Vendée insurgents.

The Society was not a club but a group of militant women, uniformed and armed with pistols and daggers, who used force against people they considered enemies of the Revolution. According to their historian, they played a serious part in gaining control of the streets for the Jacobins, denying the public galleries to all but ultrarevolutionaries, rioting in the Palais Royal, spurring on the Jacobins, and demonstrating against the Girondins (Rose 1965). They also favored massacring the Convention and volunteered to do the job themselves. Although numbering only a few hundred, they were important not only for their real service to the Revolution, but because they were the only organized body of militant women produced by it. They were not feminists yet they did demand the right to participate in the Revolution on much the same terms as men.

Their end came after August, 1793, when they moved their headquarters to a crypt near the great central Paris markets, where thousands of tough, working-class women labored as stall-keepers, vendors, fishwives, and the like. There was friction between the market women and the Revolutionary Republican Women on several points. The Society compelled others by force to wear the cockade, symbol of the Revolution. It also supported a price ceiling known as "the maximum," which outraged market women both because it froze the price of their goods during an inflationary period, and because house-to-house searches were used to enforce it. Instigated to some extent by the Jacobins, market women physically broke up a meeting of the Revolutionary Republican Women on October 28, 1793. A decree by the Convention abolishing all women's clubs followed. The Jacobins were tired of being nagged by the Society, which was in any case aligned with the Enragé faction which the Jacobins later suppressed as well. So ended women's role as an organized force in the Revolution.

Though interesting as a symptom of a rising feminine, if not feminist, consciousness, the Revolutionary Republican Women were of less significance than the thousands of working-class women who played key parts in many of the Revolution's great moments. This was because street actions were crucial to the revolutionary cause, and rioting was a traditional feminine tactic, indeed almost the only sanctioned public activity allowed women. Though illegal, it had become customary in England, France, and elsewhere for women to riot when the price of bread reached dangerously high levels. One English observer said of food rioters: "Women are disposed to be mutinous; they stand less in fear of law, partly from ignorance, partly because they presume upon the privilege of their sex, and therefore in all public tumults they are foremost in violence and ferocity" (Thompson 1971:116). Bread accounted for a large part of lower class expenditures. In Paris as much as half of a wage earner's income would be spent on it. The importance of bread and the relation of women to it thus made feminine violence a socially sanctioned act during periods of inflation. As a rule, French women were subsequently punished by the law only if they seized property other than bread or injured someone.

It was not suprising, then, that as conditions in Paris deteriorated, women became involved in street actions. After the "Réveillon riots" of April, 1789, four rioters were sentenced to death, two of them women. (One was later found to be pregnant and reprieved, a tradition many women in similar circumstances found helpful.) At least one survivor of the storming of the Bastille was a woman. The most important single action taken by women during the Revolution began with a bread riot on October 5, 1789, after which the women, mostly from the central markets, were joined by armed men. A mixed crowd of some six or seven thousand people then marched to Versailles, where a deputation of six women saw the king and demanded bread. On the next day the royal family was brought back to Paris, escorted by National Guardsmen and what Burke in his *Reflections on the Revolution in France* (1976) called "all the unutterable abominations of the furies of hell, in the abased shape of the vilest of women" (Rudé 1959:2). Women were active later in the Revolution, but removing the king from Versailles was their most important accomplishment.

As it turned out, those women who did the most to advance the Revolution were most injured by it. The working women of Paris suffered in many ways from conditions brought on by the Revolution. Many were employed as seamstresses, glove makers, etc. in the fashion industry, which almost collapsed thanks to the emigration of nobles, hard times, and the Revolution's emphasis on plain dress. Poor people generally were harmed by the complete failure of the Revolution to provide relief to the poor. The revolutionary government took over the church-supported hospices that cared for the old, sick, and orphaned. It abolished almsgiving and charity bureaus, creating instead work projects to employ able-bodied males, and made cash grants to the fathers of large families. Working women were discriminated against by these measures.

Even worse, the measures were based on false assumptions. To a large extent, poverty was a function of substandard wages rather than unemployment, upon which the acts concentrated. The wealth of the hospices was greatly overestimated. As the government discovered how extensive poverty was (at least a fifth of the population was destitute), it became aware that most of the poor could not be helped much. Moreover, the government took over the hospices just when war expenses rendered it incapable of maintaining them. Thus, the old relief system was destroyed but not replaced at a time when inflation and scarcity made the condition of the poor more desperate than ever.

Even so, women remained enthusiastic supporters of the Revolution for a time. In Chalons alone, 20,000 pounds of sheets for bandages were donated, although linen was normally a working woman's only important possession. At the peak of their enthusiasm in 1792, women sent innumerable addresses and petitions to the Assembly affirming their patriotism and hatred of the enemy. In 1793, when the war went badly, women searched out suspected traitors and friends of the old regime. Their historian says: "When Pourvoyeru, a police official, spoke in the Year II of the bestialization of women and compared them to tigresses and vultures anxious for blood, the language seems rather strong, but the evidence to support it is not lacking" (Hufton 1971:101).

This enthusiasm was short-lived. In 1793 the female political clubs were ordered dissolved on the grounds that the working man had a right to expect his woman to stay home and look after the family while he was at his club. Women cannot have had much enthusiasm for a system under which the men were constantly out attending political meetings and getting drunk, while they were obliged to stay home and avoid politics. As food supplies dwindled, irritation with the government began to rise among women. Price ceilings, the maximum, worked to some extent in Paris but not in the provinces where they led, as always, to black markets. In late 1794 the wheat harvest failed in Northern France and the wheat belt. The maximum was lifted in December and food prices soared. As early as May the women of Masannay were demanding the extermination of everyone over the age of sixty in order to conserve food for their young. In 1795 starvation took place, since working class families had by then sold everything they owned to buy food. The infant death rate increased, as did the number of miscarriages and still-births and the maternal mortality rate. In places, many more women died than men. Thus, women turned against the Revolution in growing numbers. They staged bread riots against the government in Germinal and Prairial of the Year III (April and May of 1795). Suicides increased. There was a great revival of popular Catholicism following these harrowing times. The Revolution had brought women, especially those of the working class, nothing but misery, starvation, and death. The final irony of women's situation was that the Revolution to which they contributed so much not only did them great harm, but left them worse off legally than before. The Civil Code enacted under Napoleon allowed them fewer property and personal rights than they had enjoyed during the old regime (Paulson 1973:43-54).

Frenchwomen were not involved in great events again until the liberal revolution of 1848. But their greatest notoriety was attained in the Paris Commune, during whose brief life they were once more swept into affairs of state. During the siege of Paris in the Franco-Prussian war women served as ambulance nurses, canteen workers, and the like. A few fought alongside the National Guard. More participated in neighborhood vigilance committees. These women, most of them working class, shared the general dismay of Parisians after the new Republican government of France surrendered to Prussia. On March 18, 1871, when the government moved to reoccupy Paris following the German evacuation, the city rebelled. French Army units were kept by crowds of women from firing on rebellious National Guardsmen, and some went over to the insurgents, who on March 26 elected a new government called the Commune. (Its followers were called Communards, as against the Capitulards of the national government.)

During the next several months women associated with the newly organized First International formed the Union of Women for the Defense of Paris. Composed mostly of working class women, it did relief work, made sand bags, gave the wounded first aid, and so on. When the Commune decided to give women piecework to do in their homes and provide outlets for selling it so as to relieve unemployment, the Union was put in charge. Other women also did relief work, organized neighborhood vigilance committees, formed political clubs, and even assumed some police functions. When national troops attacked the city on May 21, women fought on the barricades and allegedly helped burn down some of the buildings destroyed by Communards. Hundreds of suspected women incendiaries were thought to have been killed by government troops in the savage fighting that put an end to the Commune. Afterwards, some 200 women were convicted of crimes during the Commune period, and many of these were among the 7,500 persons deported by the Third Republic (Thomas 1966).

Although thousands of professional revolutionaries, a few of them women like Elizabeth Dmitrieff of the First International, were involved in the Commune, it was not Marxist, but rather the last in the line of great popular uprisings (Thompson 1957). Thereafter, radical political activity would take two quiet different directions. In the more developed states, radicals (anarchists being a notable exception) generally turned to parliamentary politics and organized social democratic movements, such as the German Social Democratic party and the British Labour party. Prominent individuals—Klara Zetkin, Rosa Luxumbourg, Beatrice Webb—notwithstanding, most women occupied distinctly inferior roles in these groups.

In underdeveloped countries radical politics was clandestine, underground, even terroristic. The supreme example of the latter was the Russian revolutionary movement, in which women were unusually conspicuous. Indeed, there appears to be no other revolutionary movement in recent history in which women played such a significant part. Unlike in the West, where social democratic movements subordinated women, in Russia women were encouraged to be active in radical movements. Not surprisingly, there was little feminism in Russia, the energies that would otherwise have gone into it being fully absorbed by radical politics. There was already a tradition of feminine insurgents in Russia before the modern era. Of 7,000 serfs exiled to Siberia in the reign of Nicholas I, more than a third were women. After the Sevastopol revolt of 1830, 375 women were condemned to death (Halle 1933). Sustained revolutionary activity began in the 1870s with the narodnik movement, which was devoted to working among the peasantry.

Robert H. McNeal suggests that the eagerness displayed by male narodniks in recruiting women might have been related to their larger failure (McNeal 1971). Having made little headway among the peasants, narodniks found some success with another great exploited group, women, especially women of their own class. McNeal's study of hundreds of biographies indicates that from the 1860s to the 1880s, the narodnik years, about 60 percent of radical women were drawn from the noble and merchant classes, from which male narodniks also came. Women were especially conspicuous in terrorist groups. Among the five people condemned for assassinating Alexander II were two women. A third, Vera Figner, could have been added, as she helped arrange the murder. Of 43 sentences to hard labor (nearly always given for terrorism) handed down between 1880 and 1890, 21 were to women. Women were particularly welcome in terrorist organizations because it was thought they had more opportunities to commit violence. Several women terrorists used their fur muffs to conceal revolvers with which they attacked public officials. Another stuffed her bodice with 13 pounds of dynamite before shooting the director of prison administration in St. Petersburg. However, "she did not detonate her bust and died on the gallows" (McNeal 1971:154).

Even among the narodniks, however, women did not participate in ideological discussions. Despite their high level of education (perhaps a third of all female narodniks had been to college); no Russian woman ever made a significant ideological contribution. And in the Social Democratic party, the Marxist organization of Lenin and Trotsky, women played a smaller part than among the narodniks or the Social Revolutionary movement that succeeded them. Only about a quarter of Social Democratic women seemed to have come from the privileged classes, which might account for their lesser position by comparison with narodnik women. Another reason for their inferior place was that the Social Democrats put more emphasis upon ideology than other Russian radical movements. Leadership in the Social Democratic party was largely a function of ideological competence, and it seems to be a general rule that the more emphasis on theory in radical movements the less room there is for women at the top. Marxism may explain why women in Soviet Russia, despite their prominence in many fields elsewhere dominated by men, do not in practice have the status achieved by Russian women in the old terrorist groups.

Chinese women appear to have been far less active than Russian women in revolutionary movements. In her scrappy, impressionistic book, *Women in Modern China* (1967), Helen Snow says that the first execution of a revolutionary woman did not take place in imperial China until 1907, when the Empire had but a few years left. The first woman member of Sun Yatsen's Kuomintang party was not recruited until 1904. There was no real women's organization in China before 1919. The first congress of the reorganized Kuomintang in 1924 had only three women delegates. After Chiang Kai-shek expelled the left in 1927, women had virtually no influence in the party. They were more active in the Communist party.

For example, Chu Teh, who began life as a slave girl, led Communist troops in battle, as did Chen Shao-min, a guerilla leader in World War II and afterwards a member of the Communist Central Committee. Their contribution to the revolution in China does not, however, seem to have been as great as women's contributions in Russia. This is almost certainly because Chinese women were even more poorly educated than Russian women, and Chinese domestic practices more oppressive than Russian. As late as 1950, when the new Chinese Marriage Law forbade them, footbinding (which crippled Chinese girls), child slavery, concubinage, and female infanticide were commonplace. Snow asserts that these horrible practices led Chinese women to support the Communist revolution in larger numbers than men—an interesting point if true, since women are nearly always more conservative than men politically.

FEMINISM AND THE FRANCHISE

Organized feminism began in the United States and not in the more highly developed countries of Europe (Flexner 1959; O'Neill 1969). There was a long European tradition of individuals speaking out for women's rights, of whom Mary Wollstonecraft is the best known, but almost no precedent for women organizing on their own behalf (Flexner 1972). The obvious reason for American initiative in the field of women's rights is that the United States was then the only country in the world with an officially sanctioned egalitarian ethic. A less obvious one is that women frequently make the greatest gains in new or underdeveloped countries, where their contributions are more highly valued. In America the birth of feminism was associated with reform movements. Frances Wright, a radical Scotswoman, spoke and wrote on behalf of women's rights among other subjects in the 1820s (Lane 1972). The Grimke sisters of South Carolina began as abolitionists and became feminists when told that being women they had no right to speak in public (Lerner 1971). Susan B. Anthony was a temperance worker before she turned to feminism for much the same reason. Reform movements inspired women to defy convention. When doing so was held against them, conversion to feminism often followed.

So also in England, where many women became feminists as a result of campaigns to repeal the Contagious Diseases Acts (which discriminated against prostitutes and women suspected of prostitution in certain towns).[2] Feminism seemed more radical in England than in America, where women could point to the

Declaration of Independence and claim to be mere reformers, seeking only to make practice conform to theory. In fact, although nearly always viewed as a radical step in the nineteenth century, woman suffrage was often granted for conservative reasons. The Territory of Wyoming appears to have been the first political unit in the modern world to enfranchise women on the same terms as men. It did so in 1869 to attract women settlers to a territory where they were outnumbered by men six to one. Utah granted women equal suffrage because the dominant Mormon community was being challenged by non-Mormon immigrants who were mostly male. Woman suffrage gave the Mormons an advantage in their struggle to preserve the status quo.[3] These gains were accomplished virtually without effort on the part of women.

Equal suffrage came almost as easily to New Zealand—like the American territories, a new and underpopulated society (Grimshaw 1972). New Zealand women almost got the vote in 1879 when manhood suffrage became universal. In 1890 the Women's Christian Temperance Union began enlisting the support of working class women for equal suffrage. Women's Franchise Leagues were formed in 1892. The next year, when voters overturned a conservative government, women got the vote. Compared with the United States, where it took almost three-quarters of a century to enfranchise women, the suffrage campaign in New Zealand was astonishingly easy. This has been attributed to the pioneer character of New Zealand society, its freedom from tradition, and the greater liberalism of New Zealanders which led them to enact more advanced social legislation than any other Western country at the turn of the century. In Australia women gained the vote in several colonies in the 1890s, and then, when a federal government was established in 1901, it was decided to give all Australian women the federal vote to avoid partial disenfranchisement of women who already had the local vote.[4]

However, enfranchisement did not have quite the same meaning in both countries. New Zealand women already enjoyed many rights before they got the vote, having been admitted to the university and to the practices of law and medicine. Hence, as later in the United States and some other countries, gaining suffrage did not so much emancipate women as signify that they had already made important gains. In Australia, on the other hand, getting the vote meant comparatively little. The first woman was not elected to Parliament until 1922, not just because women were enfranchised at a time when the feminist movement was weak, but even more because Australian society was unusually masculine by Western standards. Because of its predominantly working class culture, Australia put great emphasis on security, equality, and "mateship," a peculiarly intense form of male bonding. Thus, Australian legislation enhanced the security of families, but maintained traditional role differences between men and women. This combination of economic radicalism and social conservatism produced a society, as one scholar has written, "in which woman's legal rights were secure, her economic subordination ensured, and her primary social role ideologically and operationally maintained" (Paulson 1973:131).

As in Australia, New Zealand, and the American West, so too in Europe. The first European country to give women equal voting rights with men was Finland, the frontier of Scandinavia. Finnish women were enfranchised in 1907 as part of the Finnish national struggle against Russification. In part, the vote was given them for having loyally supported a passive resistance campaign against Russia, partly also to unite the Finnish people in their struggle for independence. Sweden, the most developed Scandinavian country, lagged behind not only Finland but Norway as well, where women were partially enfranchised as soon as independence was achieved in 1905. Here Sweden resembled the more advanced Western states where the suffrage struggle was long and hard. But Sweden differed from them in that woman suffrage was less strongly argued than the endowment of motherhood. As proposed by Ellen Key and other spokeswomen, this issue involved state support for mothers whether they were married or not (Lloyd 1971).

Although most developed Western states had feminist movements, they varied greatly in strength and effectiveness. The largest was in the United States for numerous reasons. Organized feminism started early here. The women's rights convention in Seneca Falls, New York, in 1848 was apparently the first of its kind anywhere. Feminism, like most other kinds of political activity among women, is related to education, and there were many more women college graduates in the United States than elsewhere. American women were also far better organized than the women of other nations, having church and missionary societies, temperance bodies, social clubs, and hundreds of other voluntary associations. Indeed, many international women's organizations—the Young Women's Christian Association, the Women's Christian Temperance Union—originated in the United States. The feminist movement was thus part of a larger tendency on the part of American women to organize themselves for social and political purposes. Even so, organized feminists were few compared with the millions of women who belonged to religious, temperance, and purely social organizations. They only became numerous in the last stages of the woman suffrage campaign after 1913. The strength of woman suffrage in America, and to a lesser extent in England, was a reflection of women's greatly improved circumstances, not their cause.

After America, the largest feminist movement was in Great Britain. Feminism advanced more slowly than in the States, because there were fewer educated women and fewer women's organizations of any sort. Then too, as noted earlier, woman suffrage seemed more radical in England than in the United States with its formal commitment to equal rights. Moreover, the major British parties, the Tories especially, formed women's auxiliaries which drained off a certain amount of feminine political energy. A further complication in the early twentieth century was that while the dominant Liberal party was more sympathetic in theory to woman suffrage, Asquith, the party leader, was personally against it, fearing with good reason that women voters would favor Conservative candidates. Perhaps also the nonviolent character of the women's movement held back equal suffrage. Whereas in America universal manhood suffrage came early and easily, in England suffrage was extended gradually and in stages, sometimes, as in 1832 and 1867, after mob action. This led a cabinet minister to make the unwise observation that, because suffragists were not violent, they should not be enfranchised (Pankhurst 1914:213-214). Mrs. Emmeline Pankhurst seized on this remark to justify the tactics of the Women's Social and Political Union, which she had founded in 1903.

She believed the established woman suffrage groups (called suffragists or constitutionalists to distinguish them from Mrs. Pankhurst's followers, who were known as militants or suffragettes) were too cautious. Suffragettes demonstrated in public, disrupted political meetings, chained themselves to railings, and, when these public confrontations failed to get results, launched a secret campaign of destruction during which pictures were slashed, bombs set off, railway locomotives fired upon, and mail boxes infused with sticky substances. When the police arrested suffragettes for these acts they went on hunger strikes, forcing the government to either release or abuse them, as with forced feeding, a painful and often dangerous technique. If released, suffragettes went back into action; if force-fed, they became martyrs. These methods brought thousands of new recruits to the suffrage movement and enormously increased the WSPU's income. It reached a peak of 37,000 pounds in 1913-1914, considerably more money than was available to the British Labour party. Even so, women did not get the vote.

The government insisted that it could not give way in the face of violence. (This showed the double bind feminists were so often placed in. If they didn't use violence they were defying tradition and if they did were practicing blackmail. Either way they didn't get the vote.) When World War I began, Mrs. Pankhurst ordered her militants to devote all their energies to war work. The constitutionalists lobbied quietly, and at the end of the war women were enfranchised. Asquith was no longer Prime Minister, and the substantial contribution made by English women to the war effort allowed politicians to say they had been convinced by this demonstration of women's right to full citizenship.[5]

The story in America somewhat resembles England's. American militants imitated the suffragettes and began demonstrating for the vote in 1913. They did not practice arson and sabotage, but broke laws, got arrested, and went on hunger strikes. Their example revitalized the sagging movement and focused attention on the long neglected effort to get a Constitutional Amendment enfranchising women. The National American Woman Suffrage Association gained hundreds of thousands of new members and millions of dollars in contributions, stepped up its pressure in Washington, and, after the Nineteenth Amendment was passed by Congress, lobbied it through enough state legislatures to secure ratification in 1920. Here also political leaders, including President Woodrow Wilson, announced that their war work had shown women to be worthy of the vote and that they, the politicians, were not changing their minds as a result of outside pressure though, in fact, they were.

Feminist movements in other great nations were less significant. France never did develop a substantial women's movement, and French women were not enfranchised until the end of World War II.[6] German women did rather better despite the extreme conservatism of Imperial Germany on feminine questions. In 1866 the Association for Women's Education was founded and soon afterwards the National Association for German Women, stressing the right of women to work and the importance of removing the obstacles that stood in the way of this (Puckett 1930). By 1877 the Association had 11,000 members. It supported education for women, petitioned government to ease the constraints on working women, and was an early advocate of the view that women and the proletariat suffered from a common oppression. As a rule, however, the distance between middle class and working class women's organizations was even greater in Germany than in English speaking countries. This was demonstrated in 1894 when the German Federation of Women's Associations was formed to link up the existing women's groups, as the National Council of Women attempted to do in the United States. It grew rapidly to a body with over 800,000 affiliated members, but the Socialist women's organizations did not join it. Neither did they interest themselves in woman suffrage. Rosa Luxumbourg, like most socialist women, believed that the vote for women was inevitable under socialism, but that the woman suffrage campaign was purely bourgeois.

This view was commonly held by women associated with left

wing and labor movements outside Germany as well. Mother Jones of the American mineworkers said that woman suffrage and prohibition were capitalist tricks to divert women from serious matters such as those raised by trade unions (Parton 1925). Angelica Balabanoff, a Russian exile active in left wing movements in Western Europe, founded a newspaper to offset feminist propaganda. She and her friends "were hostile to any form of 'feminism.' To us the fight for the emancipation of women was only a single aspect of the struggle for the emancipation of humanity. It was because we wanted women, particularly working women to understand this, to learn that they had to fight not against men, but with them against the common enemy, capitalist society, that we felt the need of this paper" (Balabanoff 1938:49).

Woman suffrage was not a major concern of German feminists in any case because voting meant less in Imperial Germany than in the Western democracies, and women were prohibited from engaging in any kind of political activity, until 1908. Even in the Social Democratic party, which challenged this ban and made Klara Zetkin a member of the national committee in 1896, women played minor roles for the most part. Rosa Luxembourg notwithstanding, after the ban on women's political activities was lifted, women were not represented in most regular party organizations. And the various woman suffrage associations achieved a total peak membership of only 12,000. German women got the vote anyway when the Weimar Republic instituted numerous liberal reforms. They promptly gave the majority of their votes to the conservative, religious parties that had been most against woman suffrage. This pointed up one of the movement's central ironies. Woman suffrage almost everywhere was advocated and fought for by left wing and liberal people, and women, once enfranchised, almost everywhere voted for conservative parties.

Another irony is that whereas the strength of feminism varied from country to country, this had little to do with their getting the vote. Between 1917 and 1920 women were enfranchised in Great Britain, the United States, Canada, and Sweden where there were strong feminist movements, but also in Belgium,

Poland, Hungary, and other countries where there were not. The same uneven pattern can be seen in the Third World. Women obtained the vote in Turkey in 1933, though the first feminist organization was not established there until 1957 (Woodsmall 1960). They also got it in Pakistan, India, and Indonesia, where women had begun organizing during the colonial era. The way in which the vote was achieved varied greatly from country to country, but it seems clear that there has been very little correlation between woman suffrage and organized feminism. No doubt the long agitation in Europe and the English speaking nations influenced other nations as well. But the prime movers in most countries have been war, revolution, and nationalism. Many countries gave women the vote after World War I. Many others granted woman suffrage after achieving independence or experiencing a revolution. Had there been no feminist movement anywhere in the world this might not have happened. All the same, woman suffrage was more commonly an idea whose time had come than something wrested by determined women from the hands of obdurate men. The Anglo-American experience has been the exception, not the rule.

WOMEN IN PARTY POLITICS

Here again the experience of women in different countries has varied greatly, but there are certain generalizations which seem to hold nonetheless. For one thing, women do not vote in a bloc, as feminists had expected, but distribute their votes in much the same fashion as men. On some points women differ from men, but in America at least these are becoming less important. Thus, although American women are somewhat more likely than men not to vote at all, the gap is narrowing. From 1948 to 1960 women trailed men in voter participation by about 10 percent, but in the 1964 and 1968 elections the difference between them was only 3 percent. As noted earlier in the case of Germany, women tend to be somewhat more conservative voters than men. Lyndon Johnson was the first Democrat running for President to have gotten a majority of the female vote.[7] But in 1968 women voted in higher proportions than men for Hubert Humphrey, the most liberal candidate, and in lower proportions than men for George Wallace, the most conservative.

A rule of thumb that still applies everywhere is that women participate in government much less frequently than men. In many countries the proportion of women in the national legis-lature reached an early peak soon after the vote was won and then declined. In 1919, 41 German women were elected to the Reichstag, but within a few years their number declined by one-quarter and in municipal bodies by one-half. The first election in which they participated saw 35 Japanese women elected to the legislature, a figure that declined later to 11 (Duverger 1955; Patai 1967). In Britain and the United States, on the other hand, it took years for women to achieve their present legislative rep-resentation, minute though it is.

Nowhere, not even in the communist nations, have women achieved political parity with men. And in communist states they are still concentrated in the lower ranks. In the late 1950s only 17 percent of the Supreme Soviet, Russia's parliament, were women. Moreover, while women in communist countries are more likely to work and hold office, this does not mean that they are significantly better off than women in the West. A number of studies indicate that communist women hold jobs in larger proportions than Western women, but receive significantly less help from their husbands with housework. So, while communist women may have more opportunities, they also bear heavier burdens (Paulson 1973:198).

Women are invariably underrepresented in politics. They seldom hold more than 10 percent of the seats in national legis-latures, and in the United States the figure is closer to 2 percent. During their first 50 years in politics only 65 women sat in the House and only ten in the Senate (Gruberg 1968). In 1970 there were still only ten women in the House and one in the Senate. Now that Margaret Chase Smith has been defeated, there is no female Senator (Amundsen 1971). Even these puny figures exaggerate the role of women in Congress. Congressional power is mostly a function of seniority and women do not serve as long as men on the average. Of the 65 women who had been in Con-gress as of 1968, 24 served one term or less and only 22 had served four terms or more. Only one woman Senator, Margaret Chase Smith, has ever held an important position (Republican Conference Chairman) and only one Congresswoman, Martha Griffiths, has ever served on the powerful House Ways and Means Commitee. Many Congresswomen are not professional politicians but are elected from districts previously represented by their husbands. In terms of power, experience, and independence, they probably rank beneath men elected in their own right. In 1940 six out of the seven women in Congress had replaced their husbands.[8]

Even when women do serve in Congress this normally does not further the cause of women's rights. The great majority of women in politics owe their position not to other women, but to male politicians. Very few feminists have ever been elected to office, and the ability of feminists to influence legislation in America declined sharply once it became clear that women did not vote in a bloc and could not be delivered by feminist organizations. In 1924 the League of Women Voters claimed that 420 bills desired by organized women had been passed by state legislatures. In 1930 only 16 additional bills of the hundreds more proposed had gone on the books (Breckinridge 1933). Since that time few laws promoted by feminists have been enacted. Thus, neither votes for women nor women in office have done much to enhance women's rights in America.

The position of women politicians in Britain is much the same as in America. As of 1966, 83 women had served in Parliament. Forty-seven of these were Labour members and 31 Conservative. This fact reflects the general rule that, while women are more inclined to vote conservatively, it is liberal and left wing parties who do the most for them—ideology triumphing over interest so to speak.[9] As in America few of them have served for long periods and few have achieved high positions. A fair number, including Lady Astor, who won her husband's seat after he was raised to the peerage, replaced their spouses (Sykes 1972). Mostly, however, women enter Parliament by being asked to contest a newly created district or one held by the opposition. Fifty-two of the 83 women members won their seats in this way, which helps explain why so few have served in Parliament. In a majority of cases they are only asked to run when their party expects to lose a contest. Unlike American women politicians who are frequently elected on the first try, English women must be persistent. Jean Mann lost six municipal and parliamentary elections before winning her seat (Mann 1962). One hundred and twenty-six women ran for Parliament in 1950, but only 21 were elected. Once elected, English women politicians are in much the same position as their American counterparts. Although seniority is not vital as in America, they still seldom receive important positions. They are generally excluded from the male affinity groups, the "old boys" network through which many decisions are made. Although sometimes sympathetic to feminine issues, women members of Parliament are products of male-dominated political organizations and are not free to press feminist demands on their own.[10]

CONCLUSIONS

As we saw, women's rights were most likely to be upheld by liberal and left wing movements, although in practice, except for Russian terrorist groups, even these seldom placed women on an equal basis with men. History continues to repeat itself. Women's liberation movements in both the United States and Great Britain began in the late 1960s, when radical women found themselves being oppressed within the New Left (Rowbotham 1972; Firestone 1970).[11] This led not only to the formation of strictly feminist organizations, but also to efforts to transcend the conventional leftist anticapitalist and anti-imperialist strategies as well, on the ground that male supremacy preceded capitalism and has outlasted it in socialist countries. Thus, the generalization that women are always politically inferior to men still holds true even among radicals.

We saw also that the strength of woman suffrage movements was only dimly related to the gaining of woman suffrage. Women got the vote often for extraneous, and sometimes conservative, reasons. So, while women sometimes were enfranchised, as in Great Britain and America, because they demanded the vote, they frequently achieved equal suffrage without much

effort. Feminine enfranchisement was related to a high degree
of economic development, but also to frontier conditions. Frequently it was a by-product of nationalism and revolution in
underdeveloped countries. Thus, women sometimes were given
the vote for practical purposes, but even more often for abstract
or ideological reasons having little to do with the utility of
enfranchised womanhood.

Feminism as an organized movement was largely confined
to modern Western societies and their colonies. It did not exist
in most Moslem countries or in Russia and China except as part
of larger male-dominated revolutionary movements. Not surprisingly, the political significance of women after enfranchisement is related to the strength of feminism before it. Thus, in
countries like Australia, France, and Japan, where woman suffrage was not a major issue, women have not been very active
politically. They are most important in communist states as a
function of ideology, and in Western nations like Great Britain
and Scandinavia, where feminism was significant. The United
States, which had the most active and largest feminist movement
but where women are less political than in most advanced countries, is an exception to this rule. Within the United States,
however, there is some connection between suffragist strength
and subsequent electoral activity. As of 1968 the states that had
sent the most women to Congress were New York and Illinois
(seven each), both having had active state suffragist organizations. A number of Southern states like Alabama, where woman
suffrage was a weak movement, have never sent a woman to
Congress. And in those Southern states which have, a high proportion (all three of South Carolina's Congresswomen for example) succeeded their husbands (Gruberg 1968:118). A final
rule of thumb seems to be that once women gain the vote they
seldom lose it, though here too there are exceptions. The women
of Utah were deprived of their vote by act of Congress in 1887,
regaining it in 1894 when Utah achieved statehood (Grimes
1967). Yugoslavian women recently lost the right to vote in national elections through a new constitution that ties voting to
employment rather than residence (Browne 1974).

In general, once they got the vote women failed to perform as expected. The political process was not transformed; women did not vote in a bloc for peace and social justice as their liberal supporters had claimed they would. On the other hand, neither did woman suffrage mean an end to home and family and the decay of morals as conservatives had feared. Everyone remarked on women's tendency to vote in the same manner as men, though in smaller proportions, and their unwillingness to run for office or support those women who did. The fact that votes for women did not revolutionize politics drew attention from the real changes that took place. Women got the vote in Wyoming Territory partly in hopes that they would strengthen the efforts of local reformers to clean up the railroad boom towns, and so they did. As jurors, women cracked down on violations of Sunday closing laws and other moral regulations and abolished the lockerroom atmosphere that had prevailed in courtrooms. Their presence reduced violence and fraud at polling places as well.

Although most women did not gain the vote in such rough and ready circumstances, woman suffrage has generally raised the tone of political life. Americans often used to vote in saloons but now exercise the franchise in schools and other sober places. Politics thus became more gentle and even genteel. Moreover, while women do not vote in a bloc, they are more interested in moral issues than men. This has both positive and negative implications. It means that candidates for office must appear to be chaste. (Grover Cleveland, who admitted paternity of an illegitimate child, could never have been elected President had women voted.) But it also means an enlarged vote for peace and social welfare, about which women seem to be as liberal as they are conservative when it comes to economics and religion. In New Zealand newly enfranchised women helped get through the first old age pension plan (Grimshaw 1972). American women have consistently voted for the less warlike presidential candidate.

American suffragists defended the poor showing that women made after enfranchisement by saying it was the result of inexperience. It was believed that as women matured politically they would do better. Where voting is concerned, this seems to have come true. Women now vote in almost the same proportions as men. And they vote more discriminatingly than before. Where once a majority of women always voted for the more conservative presidential candidate, they now support candidates who are most responsive to the issues—peace and human welfare especially—that women consider most important. And that support matters, not only at the polls, but in local political organizations where the work of women volunteers is crucial. There seems litle doubt that in America, at least, and probably elsewhere as well, woman suffrage has improved the quality of political life. Woman suffrage was a disappointment in countries like England and the United States only because it had been oversold. If the claims for it had been more modest the results would seem more impressive. Women voters have not changed the world; they have made it a little better. Surely that is something.

As office holders, however, women have had little effect. It was not unreasonable to suppose that when half the adult population became full citizens, the male monopoly on offices would be broken. But, of course, it was only dented a little. Many reasons have been given for this—domestic responsibilities, early conditioning, lack of time and money, male discrimination—all of them true to some degree. But in politics, women are their own worst enemy. In a 1972 Harris poll, 63 percent of women respondents agreed that "most men are better suited emotionally for politics than most women" (Editorial Research Reports 1973:123). A journalist talking to women who were politically active was surprised to find that, though deeply involved as volunteers, they were prejudiced against women candidates for office, whom they considered to be exhibitionists motivated by inner frustrations (Lamson 1968). Women seldom run for office and don't like those who do.

The low degree of sex loyalty among women has always been a problem for feminists. In the United States and Britain the struggle for the ballot was largely a matter of getting women to demand it. Theodore Roosevelt said in 1912 that the reason why women didn't vote is that they didn't want to.[12] Judging by the small number of women in suffragist organizations, this was probably true. But the several thousand suffragists of 1912 became several million in 1917. After this fabulous growth, there could be no question but that middle class women at least wanted the vote, and they soon got it. However, this newly acquired sense of sisterhood was weak and limited. It did not extend beyond equal suffrage and soon faded away.

Women everywhere seem to identify more with their families than with their sex and join men in supporting role definitions that keep women out of politics. This lack of solidarity distinguishes women from the minorities with which they are often compared. Racial and ethnic groups vote in blocs and support their candidates, giving them a leverage that women politicians do not have. Thus, behind the question of why women seldom run for office lies the more far-reaching question of why they do not identify with, and are not loyal to, their own sex. Their recent voting record, in America at any rate, suggests that women would improve politics if they participated more directly in it. But the main obstacle to their doing so would seem to be not masculine but feminine prejudices. The women's liberation movement appears, therefore, to be right in suggesting that women must raise their own consciousnesses before attempting to elevate those of men.

NOTES

[1] There are many books on learned and/or pious women (Bainton 1971; Reynolds 1920). There are also many biographies of famous queens and courtesans. However, there are few good general works, an exception being Stenton (1957), which includes material on women in politics, women pamphleteers, and related subjects. A number of books not chiefly concerned with women contain interesting passages on them, for example, Stone (1965) and Beattie (1967). Though universal woman suffrage exists only in the modern era, women have voted in the past, usually in their capacity as property holders. On this subject, see Ostrogorski (1893).

[2] Still the only survey is Strachey (1928). On woman suffrage, see Fulford (1957). Some comparisons are offered in O'Neill (1971).

[3] Grimes (1967) is confined to events in Utah and Wyoming for the most part.

[4] Women got the vote in southern Australia because it resembled New Zealand, and in western Australia, as in Utah, to strengthen

the hand of established settlers against newcomers (Paulson 1973: 122-131).

[5] Because they did not become eligible to vote until age 30, they were not entirely equal to men. In 1928, however, the voting age for women was lowered to 21. This came about by accident when the Home Secretary mistakenly declared, under tough questioning in the House, that it was the government's intention to lower the voting age for women. Though it had no such plans, the government felt it would be easier to go ahead than to admit error (Brooks 1967).

[6] French Canada was almost as backward. In the province of Quebec, women were not enfranchised until 1940, at which time there were only 40 woman suffragists in the city of Montreal (Cleverdon 1950).

[7] The voting habits of American women are discussed at length in Editorial Research Reports (1973) and Gruberg (1968).

[8] Moreover, wealth appears to be more important for female legislators. Three-fourths of all women sent to Congress as of 1968 had independent means (Gruberg 1968).

[9] This is true also in the United States, where as of 1968, there had been 37 Democratic and 28 Republican women in the House and Senate (Brooks 1967).

[10] For example, Edith Summerskill (1967) was a feminist, but despite long service in Parliament and high rank (she was one of the few women to become a cabinet minister), she could claim credit for only one measure of exclusive interest to women—a bill enlarging women's property rights.

[11] Firestone (1970) includes a number of articles dealing with the origins of radical feminism.

[12] Quoted in Anonymous (1909:3).

REFERENCES CITED

AMUNDSEN, KIRSTEN
    1971—*The Silenced Majority: Women and American Democracy*. Englewood Cliffs, N.J.:Prentice-Hall.
ANONYMOUS
    1909—An Anti-Suffrage Meeting in New York. *Remonstrance* Jan.
BAINTON, ROLAND H.
    1971—*Women of the Reformation in Germany and Italy*. Minneapolis:Augsburg.
BALABANOFF, ANGELICA
    1938—*My Life as a Rebel*. London:Greenwood. (Reprinted in 1968.)

BEATTIE, JOHN M.
1967—*The English Court in the Reign of George I.* Cambridge, England:Cambridge University Press.

BENSON, MARY SUMNER
1935—*Women in Eighteenth-Century America: A Study of Opinion and Social Usage.* New York:AMS. (Reprinted in 1976.)

BRECKINRIDGE, SOPHONISBA P.
1933—*Women in the Twentieth Century: A Study of their Political, Social, and Economic Activities.* New York:Arno. (Reprinted in 1972.)

BROOKS, PAMELA
1967—*Women at Westminster: An Account of Women in the British Parliament, 1918-1966.* Willits, Ca.:British American Books.

BROWNE, MALCOLM W.
1974—Yugoslav Women Get Day Off and Some Bad News. *New York Times* Mar. 9.

BURKE, EDMUND
1976—*Reflections on the Revolution in France.* New York:Dutton.

CHRISTOPHER, HEROLD J.
1958—*Mistress to an Age: The Life of Madame de Staël.* Indianapolis:Bobbs-Merrill.

CLEVERDON, CATHERINE L.
1950—*The Woman Suffrage Movement in Canada: The Start of Liberation.* Social History of Canada Series. Toronto:University of Toronto Press.

CLINTON, HARRY and MARY WOLCOTT GREEN
1912—*The Pioneer Mothers of America.* New York:Putnam's.

DUVERGER, MAURICE
1955—*The Political Role of Women.* Paris:UNESCO.

EDITORIAL RESEARCH REPORTS
1973—*The Women's Movement.* Washington, D.C.:Congressional Quarterly.

FIRESTONE, SHULAMITH, ed.
1970—*Women's Liberation: Notes from the Second Year.*

FLEXNER, ELEANOR
1959—*Century of Struggle: The Women's Rights Movement in the United States.* Cambridge, Ma.:Harvard University Press.
1972—*Mary Wollstonecraft.* New York:Coward, McCann and Geoghegan.

FULFORD, ROGER
1957—*Votes for Women.* London:Faber and Faber.

GRIMES, ALAN P.
  1967—*The Puritan Ethic and Woman Suffrage*. New York:Oxford University Press.

GRIMSHAW, PATRICIA
  1972—*Women's Suffrage in New Zealand*. New York:Oxford University Press.

GRUBERG, MARTIN
  1968—*Women in American Politics: An Assessment and Sourcebook*. Oshkosh, Wis.:Academia.

HALLE, FANNINA W.
  1933—*Women in Soviet Russia*. New York:Viking.

HUFTON, OLWEN
  1971—Women in Revolution. *Past and Present* Nov.

JONES, MARY
  1925—*The Autobiography of Mother Jones*. Chicago:C.H. Kerr.

LAMSON, PEGGY
  1968—*Few Are Chosen: American Women in Political Life Today*. Boston:Houghton, Mifflin.

LANE, MARGARET
  1972—*Frances Wright and the Great Experiment*. Totowa, N.J.: Rowman and Littlefield.

LERNER, GERDA
  1971—*The Grimke Sisters from South Carolina: Pioneers for Women's Rights and Abolition*. Studies in the Life of Women. New York:Schocken Books.

LLOYD, TREVOR
  1971—*Suffragettes International: The World-Wide Campaign for Women's Rights*. New York:American Heritage.

MANN, JEAN
  1962—*Women in Parliament*. London:Odhams.

MAY, GITA
  1970—*Madame Roland and the Age of Revolution*. New York: Columbia University Press.

McNEAL, ROBERT H.
  1971—Women in the Russian Radical Movement. *Journal of Social History* Winter:143-163.

O'NEILL, WILLIAM L.
  1969—*Everyone Was Brave: The Rise and Fall of Feminism in America*. New York:Quadrangle.
  1971—*The Woman Movement: Feminism in the United States and England*. New York:Franklin Watts.

OSTROGORSKI, M.
1893—*The Rights of Women: A Comparative Study in History and Legislation.* New York:Samuel Ambaras. (Reprinted in 1973.)
PANKHURST, EMMELINE
1914—*My Own Story.* New York:Hearst's International Library. (Reprinted 1970 by Collector's Editions.)
PARTON, MARY FIELD, ed.
1925—*The autobiography of Mother Jones.* Chicago:C.H. Kerr.
PATAI, RAPHAEL, ed.
1967—*Women in the Modern World.* New York:Free Press.
PAULSON, ROSS EVANS
1973—*Women's Suffrage and Prohibition: A Comparative Study of Equality and Social Control.* Glenview, Ill.:Scott, Foresman.
PUCKETT, HUGH WILEY
1930—*Germany's Women Go Forward.* New York:AMS.
REYNOLDS, MYRA
1920—*The Learned Lady in England.* Magnolia, Ma.:Smith, Peter.
ROSE, R.B.
1965—*The Enragés: Socialists of the French Revolution?* Victoria, Australia:Melbourne University Press.
ROWBOTHAM, SHEILA
1972—The Beginnings of Women's Liberation in Britain. *The Body Politic,* Michelene Wandor, ed. London:Stage 1.
RUDÉ, GEORGE
1959—*The Crowd in the French Revolution.* New York:Oxford University Press.
SNOW, HELEN FOSTER
1967—*Women in Modern China.* The Hague:Mouton.
STENTON, DORIS MARY
1957—*The English Woman in History.* New York:Macmillan.
STONE, LAWRENCE
1965—*The Crisis of the Aristocracy, 1558-1641.* New York:Oxford University Press.
STRACHEY, RAY
1928—*The Cause: A History of the Women's Movement in Great Britain.* Port Washington, N.Y.:Kennikat. (Reprinted in 1969.)
SUMMERSKILL, EDITH
1967—*A Woman's World.* London:Heinemann.
SYKES, CHRISTOPHER
1972—*Nancy: The Life of Lady Astor.* New York:Harper and Row.

THOMAS, EDITH
   1966–*The Women Incendiaries*. New York:Braziller.
THOMPSON, DAVID
   1957–*Europe since Napolean*. New York:Knopf.
THOMPSON, E.P.
   1971–The Moral Economy of the English Crowd in the Eigh-
      teenth Century. *Past and Present* Feb.
WILSON, R. McNAIR
   1936–*Women of the French Revolution*. Port Washington, N.Y.:
      Kennikat. (Reprinted 1970.)
WOODSMALL, RUTH F.
   1960–*Women and the New East*. Washington, D.C.:Middle East
      Institute.

8

Female Hierarchies in a Kibbutz Community

JOSEPH SHEPHER AND
LIONEL TIGER

Female hierarchies have been described and analyzed mainly in primate groups. Attention to this topic in human societies usually was limited to simple societies in which sexual division of labor ultimately split the population into male and female working groups. As Evans-Pritchard pointed out in his Fawcett lecture: "In primitive societies the spheres of activities of the sexes are clearly demarcated; and if a woman does not enter into male activities, neither does her husband seek to compete with her in female activities or interfere with her in such domestic matters as come conventionally under her control" (Evans-Pritchard 1965:50). Where female activities are not completely atomized according to nuclear monogamous family units—and in primitive societies they usually are not—there must be a certain hierarchical order in joint female activities even with a minimal division of labor among participants. The framework of such a hierarchy may vary from the minimum of females of the polygynous family to a maximum of all the adult females of a tribal group.

The hierarchical order among the females may be specific to a certain task (work or ritual) or diffuse in the sense that it may be based on general status among the families and/or in the society as a whole. The question of whether a female's status in this generalized order of females is defined solely by other females or by females and males, jointly, is very important: in the former complete female seclusion is indicated, whereas in

225

the latter some integration of the two hierarchical systems is present.

In modern society, few conditions exist that make the emergence of female hierarchies feasible. Although the social structure is interwoven with hierarchical systems, as for instance, in bureaucracies, these are usually either all-male or mixed. All-female hierarchies are rare (female prisons or schools), and one cannot be sure whether the norms of conduct in these systems are due to their bureaucratic character or to the fact that they are exclusively female. A comparative study of all-male, mixed, and all-female bureaucracies might reveal essential differences. Unfortunately, no such comparative study is known to us.[1]

Moreover, the almost general pattern of neolocal monogamic nuclear family prevents the emergence of task-oriented, all-female groups in the framework of the family. The possible exception of English working class families, with their tight network of kinship and frequent interaction between mothers, daughters, and female in-laws has been analyzed (Young and Willmott 1957; Bott 1957). These studies examined interaction between female actors but paid no attention to hierarchy. Komarovsky (1962) in her book about American working class families emphasizes the separate worlds of the sexes and the tight interaction between females—kin and friends—but does not find hierarchical elements.

On first sight, kibbutz communities might not seem suitable for the study of female hierarchies. These communities are to be classified within the framework of modern society as having a highly developed technology and a secular Weltanschauung. They are, however, village communities within which the monogamous nuclear families are neither neolocal nor isolated; and especially in older kibbutzim, multigeneration quasi-extended families develop. Moreover, although kibbutz ideology requires complete equality between the sexes, this equality in actuality exists mainly on the formal level. In fact, both at work and in political activity, a polar division of labor exists to a considerable extent. No member of the kibbutz would deny that work in the kitchen, the dining room, the laundry, the communal clothing store, the health care facility, and especially the childcare center is done exclusively or mainly by females. In fact, in the kibbutz under investigation, a male was never observed in the last three work areas. However, males occasionally were observed in the first three. And in the kitchen, there is always a male who characteristically is called "the male of the kitchen" (*zachar hamitbach*), pointing to the fact that the kitchen is a female branch par excellence and that the status of the male in it is exceptional and precarious. In the dining room, the permanent personnel are always female; occasionally, however, males work there on a temporary basis, especially during the rainy season, when a shortage of females may coincide with a surplus of males unable to work in the field. In the laundry, which has only two workers, sometimes one is a male but only on a temporary basis for several weeks. These characteristics are summarized in Table 1.

TABLE 1. *Female-dominated work branches in kibbutz Ofer*

Name of Branch	Usual Number of Females	Usual Number of Males
Kitchen	9	1
Dining room	3	occasionally several
Laundry	2	occasionally several
Communal store	15	none
Health care facility	2	none
Childcare center	17	none
TOTAL	48	1-3

All these posts refer to the population of kibbutz members. Nonmembers, who may be parents, training group members, and volunteers, work mainly in the kitchen, the dining room, and in the children's houses. Nonmembers may add one or two males or females to the team of the kitchen, one girl to the dining room, and several girls to childcare, but they do not change the sex constitution of the branch.

The political system is based on a General Assembly, wherein every member has a vote, and a series of elected committees in charge of different spheres of life. Committees hardly ever consist of single sex groups, but some of them are preponderantly male or female. Thus, for instance, in the Economic Committee the usual combination is eight males to one female, but there were years when there were no females at all. Moreover, a female member has never been chairman. On the other side, in the Committee on Education, there are usually seven females to two males; and one of the men is apt to be the chairman.

Another possible framework of female hierarchies is the quasi-extended family. In the kibbutz under investigation at least three such families can be described. The genealogies of these families follow:

In family A, eleven females are in the age of adulthood and adolescence; in family B, five, and in family C, also five.

FEMALE HIERARCHIES IN WORK BRANCHES

Among the work branches, we find explicit hierarchical systems in the kitchen, the communal store, and the childcare center.

In the kitchen, the dominant female is the branch manager (*ekonomith*). She is the decision maker in both matters of distribution of goods and work assignment organization.

As to the first, she in a sense dominates the whole kibbutz: she controls the distribution of food for the communal meals as well as the food every individual and/or family unit receives for afternoon tea, baking cakes for Shabbat, or other festive occasions. Since formal statutes do not govern the apportioning of materials for such purposes, the amount and quality given, as well as their accessibility, are highly dependent on the decision of the *ekonomith*. She usually gives a free hand to senior workers (the two cooks who, like herself, are older women of about 50), but in the case of a dispute her decision is final.

In her second capacity, the *ekonomith* deals more with work allocation of auxiliary workers. She stands in the center of the attention system. Everyone who comes to the kitchen looks for her and if she is not present, people must wait until she arrives. In disputes among the workers, she is called upon to decide.[2]

Family A

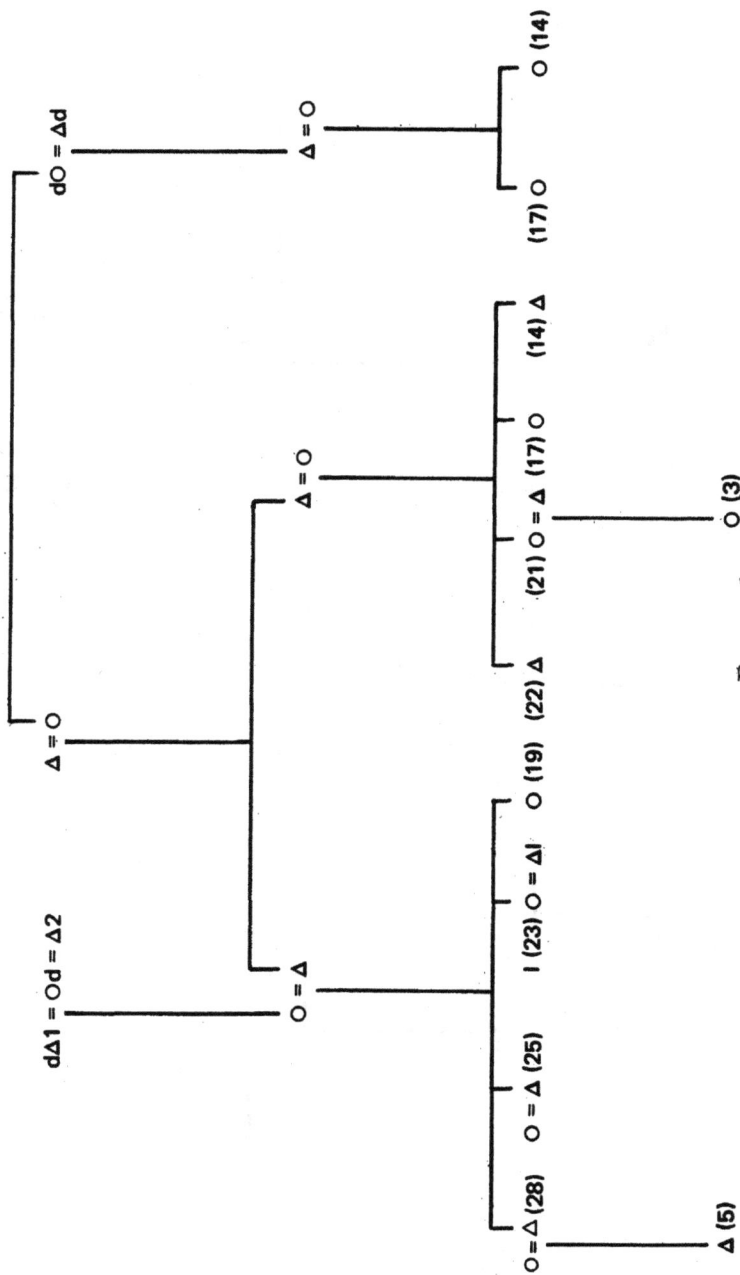

FIGURE 1.

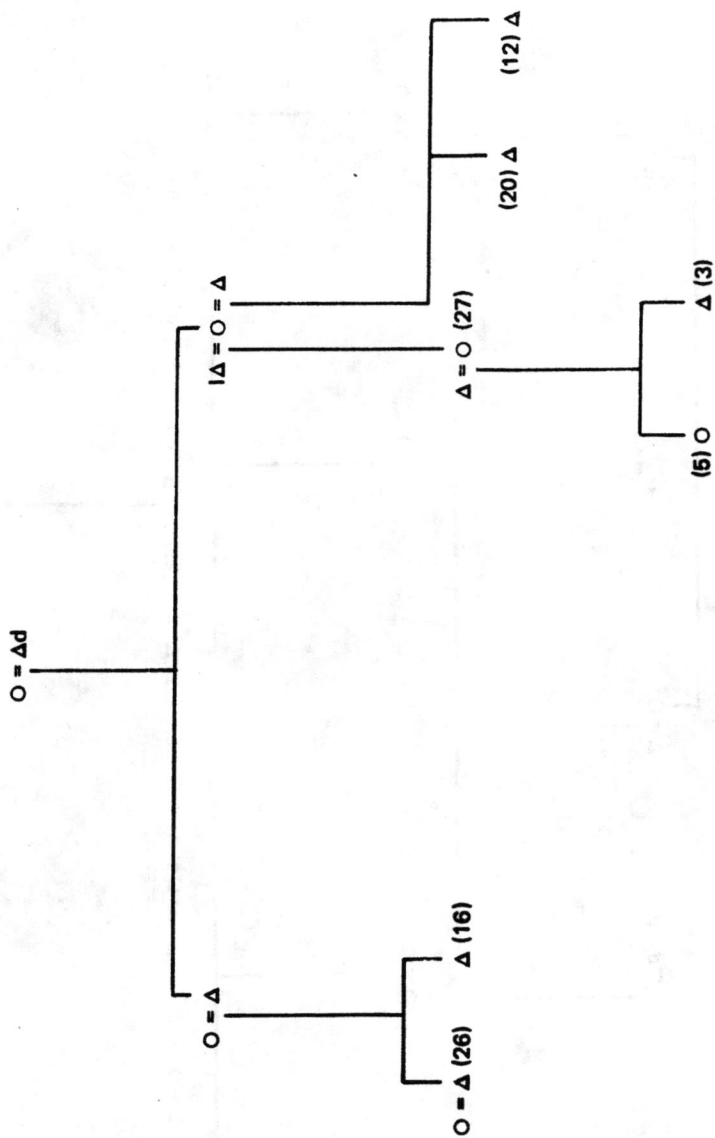

Family B

FIGURE 2.

Family C

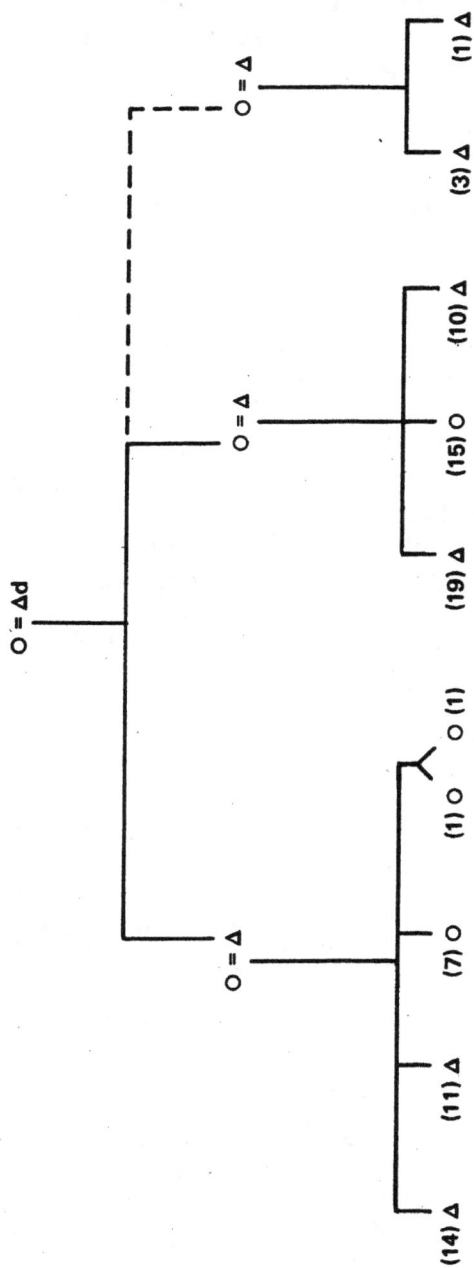

FIGURE 3.

d = deceased
l = left the kibbutz
— = adoption
number in parentheses = age of third and fourth generation
∧ = twins

Second in the kitchen's hierarchical order are the two permanent cooks. Once the *ekonomith* has decided upon the menu,
they are quite free to determine the form and the tempo of
performance. They give orders to the preparation room (*kilufim*)
and to a girl who, though she works separately preparing breakfast, assists the cooks after 9:30 a.m., doing cleaning and other
nonprofessional work. The two cooks are partly in command of
the dishwashers, especially with regard to larger utensils necessary for cooking.

The preparation room itself is somewhat hierarchically organized. An older woman is in charge of this work, assisted by 3 or
4 women, some of them older parents and others temporary
workers.

One other woman works separately and is subordinate only
to the *ekonomith:* she works in the children's kitchen, a separate
room. She prepares baby food, cakes, and sweets for festive
occasions. She works only half a day. The organizational structure of the kitchen may be presented graphically as is shown
in Figure 4.

What is especially female in this hierarchy? It is certainly not
the usual bureaucratic structure. First of all, no organizational
structures in the kibbutz are really bureaucratic, since they are
informal and have no statutory definitions of range of discretion
and authority. But beyond this, in the kitchen the hierarchy is
unusual: at all levels, authority is accepted somewhat reluc-
tantly; there is a constant worry about personal independence;
personal relations are usually strained; and the only male in the
kitchen is to a certain extent subordinate to almost everyone.
(On the other hand, there is a constant longing for male leadership.)[3] However, since permanent jobs for older females are very
valuable, the women desire to see the system maintained, whatever their opinions about the performances of their co-workers.[4]

Not only do almost all the permanent workers criticize each
other frequently, but they together are criticized by the public—
the customers. This criticism from outside contributes to the
maintenance of the system by motivating the permanent workers
to defend each other publicly—again, regardless of their fairly
low opinions of each other. This creates an uneasy balance ex-

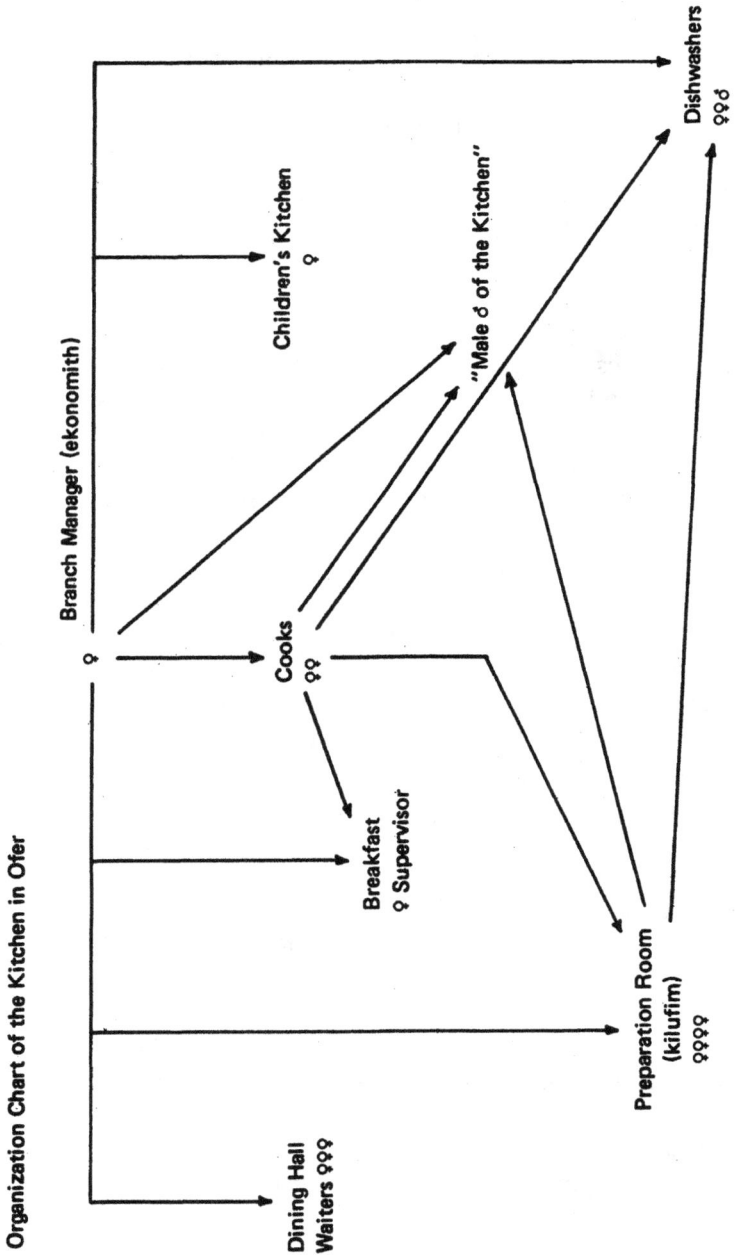

Organization Chart of the Kitchen in Ofer

FIGURE 4.

pressed in the absence of primary relations among the permanent workers beyond working hours.

Comparing this system with an all-male branch of approximately the same size, one can hardly escape the realization that acceptance of authority is much easier, personal relations are better, mutual criticism is more open, and personal independence is not a concern. If there are some females in the branch, the relationship to them is not domineering but secluding, one of courtesy and even gallantry. Such a situation exists in the dry farming (*phalcha*).

Etzioni (1957) would attribute the difference to the fact that female branches are service-oriented, whereas male branches are engaged in production. The first are under constant social control by a wide clientele, whereas the second have an anonymous market as its clientele. The first have a low level of professionalism, whereas the second a high one. The first usually do not have an institutional backing (except in childcare), whereas the second always have.[5]

It is not easy to refute the possibility that Etzioni's factors, and not the sexual difference, are decisive, because of the difficulty in finding a control group, i.e., an all-female group that does not render personal services, but works for production. Although we do not have such a branch, we do have two approximations. A department of the industrial plant—the accounting department—is an all-female group. Unfortunately, however, the head of the department, the only licensed accountant, is a salaried clerk and a nonmember, and therefore the whole system works differently. The head accountant enjoys professional supremacy over the other four women in the department; the four, in turn, enjoy the superior status of being kibbutz members. These factors, going in opposite directions, neutralize each other; therefore, no regular hierarchy emerges. Moreover the head accountant—an old woman—is looking toward retirement and does not pay much attention to the work of others.

But inasmuch as we consider the work of the four, we can detect the above-mentioned characteristics: reluctance to accept authority, strained relations, and lack of primary relations after work.

A similar, but again not a pure case, is the accounting department of the whole kibbutz. It is a mixed-sex team headed by a woman, a senior accountant, and consisting of two more women accountants and a man whose special task is cost accounting. Here, the system is hierarchical with the usual female pattern: the women accountants are very reluctant to accept the authority of the senior accountant. In fact, the senior accountant is more successful in imposing her authority on males within and outside the team (treasurer, general manager) than on females. The only male on the team, a man of superior intelligence and wisdom, serves to a great extent as a lightning-rod, not only on his own team, but even on the team of the industrial plant. In one case the whole team faced a recurrent handicap: the data processed by the computer was full of mistakes. It turned out that the cause was that one accountant wrote the cipher 9 in a manner that it could have read both as an 0 or a 6. The women in the team were unable to convince her that she had to change her writing. The man was called to help. He simply let her sit down and write a whole page of the cipher 9 in the correct form. She obeyed, and the problem disappeared.

Nevertheless, since these cases are not pure, we can accept them only with hesitation as control groups.

In the communal storeroom, things are somewhat different. First there are two completely separate storerooms: one for the adults and one for the children (*mahsan haverim, mahsan yeladim* respectively). The first is larger, employing ten women; the second is smaller, having seven women.[6] The storeroom for adults is bigger, not only because it serves a larger population, but also because it renders an additional service, namely tailoring for women. In the children's storeroom, tailoring is done only for adolescent girls (ages 12 to 18) by two old mothers of members of the kibbutz.[7] Both storerooms have the following functions: ironing; mending; sorting the washed, ironed, and mended laundry into boxes; organizing purchase of items of clothing; producing curtains, bed covers, etc.; and budget bookkeeping.

The adult storeroom manager (*mahsanait chaverim*) is formally responsible for the whole storeroom and partially also for the laundry. She, however, has practically nothing to say in the dressmaking establishment. This is not because she is a younger woman, but mainly because the dressmakers manage a completely independent establishment. The previous *mahsanait*,[8] who was older and very domineering, also could not interfere with the dressmakers' business. The *mahsanait* in fact organizes only ironing, mending, assorting, purchasing, and budgeting. The women work in three separate rooms with access between them, but the dressmakers' room is usually closed. The atmosphere in the adult storeroom is more easy going than in the kitchen mainly because there is less stress in the work.[9] The storeroom is frequently overpopulated with women who can work only there because of some limitation (pregnancy, illness, ageing), and some of them do only part-time work. Yet the atmosphere between the dressmakers themselves and between them and the others is not easy going. Although there are only three dressmakers, the first assistant is highly critical of the head dressmaker and of the second assistant, who happens to be a relative of the head dressmaker. Most of the workers are critical of the dressmakers, both because of their illegitimate independence, and because they themselves are part of the clientele.

The children's storeroom is in one large room and has mainly two functional departmentlike niches: sorting (more important here because small children receive laundry daily whereas adults receive it once a week); and ironing and mending, together. The two old mothers work in a room separate from the storeroom; there is no interference with their work, but they receive orders on what to do. The *mahsanait* here maintains hierarchical order over her workers, but in a form called "sugar coated" in the local argot. The women working here are very touchy, sensitive, and easily offended. Every step of the *mahsanait* concerning work organization, as well as every action of one of the workers considered as a deviation from work norms, is discussed at length. Long-term strained relations between the workers are frequent, and there are no primary relations outside work hours in either of the storerooms.

Both storerooms are considered in the local folklore as the center of kibbutz gossip. The source of unsubstantiated rumor is labelled as "I've heard it in the storeroom" (*shamati bemat-*

pera). This is probably because the workers usually sit together there in a big room doing manual work that does not require too much concentration and permits uninterrupted chats. In earlier times an alternative center for gossip was the communal shower, which disappeared with the building of larger apartments in the early 1950s. Women of the storeroom angrily reject the accusation that they are the main gossipers and maintain that the men do no less gossiping than they.[10]

Work in childcare is organized in a manner that prevents the emergence of a decisive hierarchical system. Children are divided into age groups (*kitah*), and every group has a nurse who is responsible and has an assistant working usually half to three-quarters of a day. Between the ages zero and four, there are three to four such units. The kindergarten group has mixed ages and includes ten to twenty children between the ages of four and seven. Here the personnel consists of the kindergarten teacher, a trained nurse, and one or two assistants. Thus, in the preschool age (*hagil harach*), eight to ten women work, five or six of them having been professionally trained, and two to five are untrained assistants.

In everyday work, the only hierarchical factor is the authority systems within the *kitah*. The trained nurse (*metapelet*) gives orders to the assistant, who usually does the nonprofessional work of cleaning, though the *metapelet* shares this work too. In the kindergarten, the system is somewhat more differentiated. Here, in questions of education, the kindergarten teacher decides, whereas in questions of nurturing, the *metapelet* makes the decisions.

In the preschool sector, one of the nurses has unchallenged authority in questions of both education and nurturing. She is 50 years old, older than all the other nurses, and much more experienced. The kindergarten teacher is of the same age and her authority is not questioned within the kindergarten, but in the preschool sector, she accepts the authority of the former. The authority of this head nurse is also formally approved: she is usually member of the Committee on Education and she has the title of head nurse of preschool age children (*merakezet hagil harach*).

The authority of the head nurse is not activated during the routine workday. In emergency situations such as serious illness of one of the children or quarrels between parents and nurses, she is called upon to decide what to do. She also intervenes in activities of parents concerning their children. But routinely, she works as every other nurse with her own *kitah*.

At school age, there is almost no system at all. Since the children of elementary school go out to a neighboring kibbutz school, the work of the *metapelet* is curtailed to one hour before the children leave for school and for two hours after their return. There are two sections in the elementary school age group, attended to by two nurses. The high school age group consists of two sections, attended to by two half-time nurses. Except for the surveillance of the Commitee on Education on the activities of these nurses, no organized activity exists between them.

In summary, we can point out that in the three work branches described above, we found hierarchical systems of different intensity and scope. In the kitchen, hierarchical relations are best developed and their range is total. In the communal storerooms, some of the workers are exempted from the hierarchical relations, and in childcare, hierarchical relations are limited to emergency situations. The structure of work organization greatly affects both the intensity and the scope of hierarchical relations. The limited possibility for comparison with all-male groups, as well as absence of all-female groups in nonservice branches, prevents us from being definitive on the question of whether the peculiar traits of these female hierarchies may be attributed solely to their femaleness.

THE POLITICAL SYSTEM

Whereas in work we can find all-female groups, and in fact most females work in such groups, in the political system we rarely find them. *De jure* there has never been an all-female committee. *De facto* it happened that in two committees (education and culture), the few males who were elected to the committees were prevented from being active in them, and only females were present at the meetings. Although elections are by secret ballot, it almost never happens that an all-female commit-tee is elected, whereas an all-male committee has been elected several times. Usually before the ballot is cast, some members of the General Assembly, mainly females, warn against electing a one-sex committee. But, whereas an all-male committee is labeled as "not nice," an all-female committee is considered an almost "non possumus." The official argument for the first warn-ing (against all-male committees) is that females have to be represented on each committee; there were recurring motions proposed by females to allocate a minimum of one or two seats in each committee for females as females. These motions have always been turned down.

The official argument against all-female committees is that since the main executive power (general manager, work assigner, treasurer, secretary) is an all-male business (*de facto,* not *de jure*), males have to be elected to the committee because only they are able to get along with the male managers and thus assure performance. This is the formal argument and it is true to a certain extent (although females are very effective some-times in extracting performance when it is concerned with their private homes). But in private talks, several active females ad-mitted that an all-female committee would not work as well as a mixed-sex committee. Males say explicitly that women are not objective and energetic enough to pursue a task of importance in any of the spheres of life of the kibbutz.

In the three cases where such *de facto* all-female committees have existed, they were not very successful; but unsuccessful committees are not exceptional in this kibbutz. Therefore, we cannot conclude that an all-female group has less chance of success than any other combination. Because of the lack of comparative material, we can only point to the fact that the general consensus is against all-female committees, whereas there is certainly no consensus against an all-male committee. In fact, the usual election of one female to the important Economic Committee is somewhat ritualistic—"lip service" to the value of equality between the sexes. This basic lack of symmetry is clearly discernible from Table 2, which summarizes the sex distribution of chairmen and members of the committees over several years.

Years/Sex — Name of Committee	1968 Men	1968 Women	1969 Men	1969 Women	1970 Men	1970 Women	1971 Men	1971 Women	1972 Men	1972 Women	1973 Men	1973 Women	6-Year Average Men	6-Year Average Women
Secretariat	7*	2	10*	—	7*	2	6*	2	6*	2	8*	1	7.33	1,5
Economy	9*	1	9*	1	8*	—	9*	—	8*	—	8*	1	8.5	0.5
Work	5*	2	7*	2	7*	2	5*	1	5*	1	5*	1	5.66	1.5
Social Affairs	4*	3	3*	4	4	3*	4	3*	4	3*	5*	3	4.0	3.16
Education	3*	5	2*	5	2	7*	2	7*	2	7*	3*	5	2.33	6.0
Housing	2	5*	4	3*	3*	3	3	3*	3	2*	1	4*	2.66	3.33
Health Care	2*	3	2*	3	1*	3	1*	3	2*	3	2	3*	1.66	3.0
Higher Education	7*	1	7*	—	7*	1	7*	1	7*	1	7*	1	7.0	0.83
Culture	6*	3	5*	4	5*	3	4	7*	4	7*	3	5*	4.50	4.83
Total	45	25	49	22	43	23	41	27	41	26	42	24	43.5	24.5
Total Chairmen	8	1	8	1	7	2	5	4	5	4	6	3	6.5	2.5

TABLE 2.   *Sex Composition of Nine Major Committees in Ofer, 1968-73 (asterisks indicate sex of chairman)*

From the data, we can see that during the last six years 54 committees have been elected in Ofer of which five have been all-male committees and none all-female. Only three committees have an average majority of females (education, housing, and health care), but only the Committee on Education has a definitive female majority (1:2.6). But even in this case, for three of the six years, the committee had a male chairman. On the health care committee, a classic example of female activity, a male presided for five years, being the only male in the committee. Whereas total membership presents a ratio of 1.7 males to females, the chairmanship ratio is 2.6.

THE FAMILY SYSTEM

As we have indicated, a female hierarchy is plausible in an extended family where more females interact in the same unit. From all we know about the family in the kibbutz, we can certainly conclude that it is a modern family in the sense that the nuclear unit is the most important and relevant factor in the orientation of both the individual and the social structure as a whole (Shepher 1969a, 1969b). Nevertheless there is a very intensive interaction between kin, both agnatic and lateral, and both consanguines and affines. The families described above maintain such an intensive interaction. Family A has 21 members of four generations between the ages of 3 and 83. In family B, the respective number is 14 and the age range of four generations is between 3 and 78; in family C the number is 15 and the age range of three generations is one to 65. Whereas general interaction is equally intensive in the three families, only in family A do we witness a special interaction between the 11 females of the group. This interaction, if it is task oriented, reveals all the characteristics of a female hierarchy.

At the head of the system is the old matron of 78, who is a very active woman and in spite of her age, is the postmaster of the kibbutz working 30 hours a week. She is very family minded and she remembers 21 birthday dates and eight wedding dates, let alone such events such as births, circumcisions (*brith mila*), bar mitzvahs, and wedding ceremonies. Since in a group of 21 this produces on the average one memorial day per month and since such events have to be celebrated, the Old Lady organizes "her girls" to prepare the festive get-together of the whole family in the old barrack of the great grandparents. The Old Lady is a master cook and conditor (pastry maker), and she activates all the female members of the family in delivering materials from the kitchen, in peeling, cooking, baking, and table-laying, and in the preparation of gifts. Although she herself does most of the work, she is also very effective in organizing the work of "her girls." All the females of the group readily accept the authority of the Old Lady, which is transmitted by the daughters-in-law to the granddaughters.

The result of the collective work of the "girls of A" (so they are called in the kibbutz with benevolent irony) is without exception very tasty and pleasurable and creates an atmosphere of a happy and delightful togetherness of the big family.

The organized work of the "girls of A" is even more accentuated in case of such a major event as a bar mitzvah or a wedding of one of the members of the family. Only, in this case, their contribution is not exclusive. In such major events almost all the kibbutz cooperates in enhancing the importance of the ceremony.

Interestingly, whereas in family A the four-generation line is patrilineal, and in family B the same line is matrilineal, no similar hierarchy developed in family B. Although the matron of family B is also a very active woman and also a very good cook and conditor, she is not as effective in organizing her four girls, and if there is some hierarchical relationship, it is usually limited to the grandmother-daughter-granddaughter line. The situation is somewhat similar in family C.

An intensive study of a larger kibbutz with several quasi-extended families would probably reveal the extent to which the hierarchy in Ofer is characteristic of the large multigenerational kibbutz family, rather than the result of idiosyncratic factors. A factor to consider would be that in older kibbutzim the first generation has member status, whereas in Ofer they have only the status of a parent.

EXTRAORDINARY SITUATIONS

All the hierarchies heretofore described exist in ordinary, recurrent situations. Sometimes however, extraordinary situations create all-female groups in which a temporary hierarchy may develop. We shall describe two such instances.

Yom Hahaveroth (*The Day of the* Haverah)

Some years ago a kibbutz form of the well-known Mothers' Day—*Yom hahaverah*—appeared in several kibbutzim. It is not of course by chance that Mothers' Day takes a different form in the kibbutz: here the mothering aspect has been somewhat put aside since it is the joint endeavor of the mother and the *metapeleth.* At the same time, the aspect of the all-embracing responsibility of the *haverot* (the female members) for all the services in the kibbutz is emphasized. Since these services are indispensable for the kibbutz as a whole, it and not the family rewards the female on this day.

Briefly, all the adult females of the kibbutz are relieved from all the responsibilities for an entire day. Males who work in the kitchen greet the festively dressed females in the dining hall with a rich breakfast. A sight-seeing bus takes them on a whole day trip with a lot of recreation and amusement.

Men care for the kitchen and for all the children (including babies, causing no little worry to the mothers). Characteristically the communal storeroom is closed; the males can do nothing in needlework. In spite of the recreational program of the trip, it has to be organized. The organization is usually in the hands of the female members of the Committee on Culture (occasionally the chairman). Though the organizer is a very active woman, she is not a domineering type, and the organization itself does not necessarily create a hierarchy. But if something is wrong, then hierarchy comes to the foreground. In one case, spirits were very low because of an incident during the trip. The *haverot* were complaining and quarrelling. Two of the dominant women took over the initiative and with quick maneuvers changed the atmosphere. From that point of the trip on, they dictated the steps to be taken. The trip is usually a success; the women enjoy themselves and entertain one another with stories about their experiences.

An Incident During the Yom Kippur War

As opposed to the recreative atmosphere of *Yom Hahaverah*, we can describe another exceptional all-female group, in which the atmosphere was far from recreative. In the first days of the last war (called the Yom Kippur War), the district in which Ofer is situated was shelled by the Syrians with Frog missiles. In all the settlements, Ofer included, the whole population had to stay in the bunkers during the night for almost two weeks. Most of the bunkers were occupied by members of both sexes, but the best bunker had been allocated to the babies and youngest toddlers with their nurses and mothers. About 25 females were together with upset and anxious children, who were, of course, very restless and nagging because of the sudden change in their routine life style. The hierarchy quickly developed: at the head was the head nurse (described above), under her the rest of the nurses; and then the mothers. The few resting places had been allotted (the babies had beds, but the adults had to sleep on the floor and even on the steps). Watches and surveillance were organized. Cooperation and discipline were extraordinary. In the words of the head nurse: "In spite of the constant worry and fear, it was a great experience. So many women together without quarrels, fully disciplined, and fully cooperative. Everybody really gave of her best."

SOME TENTATIVE HYPOTHESES

Although the cases here described are few and the research methods are far from being refined, we shall risk some tentative remarks, the purpose of which would be to suggest directions for further research rather than to draw conclusions.

The most prominent trait of the female hierarchies described here is the rather high centralization. In almost all the groups, a single female concentrated all the authority, and there is no real gradation of authority. Marrett, in a recent article (1972) has found the same in female-dominated organizations or in organizations in which most of the participants are women. She ascribes this trait to the following factors:

1) Women in general show more need for close personal relations than males. This results in reluctance to accept tasks in which authority is involved. Decision making is left to a few persons, whose position in the hierarchical system commits them to be devoted to the cause and take upon themselves the task of commanding.

2) Women are more concerned with providing personal services to individuals, and therefore they tend to have a greater commitment to a practice role than a policy making one. Decisions about policy are thus left to the woman at the top.

3) Since women have higher turnover rates than men, the rare stable element is invested with almost monopolistic power.

4) Almost all female or female-dominated organizations are semi-professional (teachers, nurses, etc.) and in such organizations professionalism is not enough to counteract centralization.

All four points fit the situation in the kibbutz, although no direct evidence can be presented here except on point three. All the really dominant females at present are near or past menopause and thus have more stability at work than younger females of childbearing age. If we compare the present situation with the past when the dominant females were in childbearing age, we certainly may state that the hierarchical system then was less developed and more females were involved in decision making tasks.

A second characteristic trait is strained personal relations and reluctance to accept authority of females. We have already indicated that we cannot risk an explanation at this stage of research because we do not have an all-male service branch for control. We can, however, state that reluctance to accept authority from males does not exist. In all mixed branches authority is in male hands, and there seem to be no problems of discipline. The same has been found by Simpson and Simpson (1969). They, however, do not seem to detect any differences in deference by females to authority, whether it is directed toward males or toward females.

A third characteristic trait, which was not discussed previously, is the personality type of dominant females. These are women around their fifties, all of them mothers of two to four children. They are respected, not only by the females but also by the males. As compared with nondominant females they are austere, and tend to be serious and somewhat moralistic. On the other hand, dominant males are usually very active sexually. Whereas the dominant males are the sexual sociometric centers of the kibbutz, having a rather high extramarital record, the dominant females usually are of the faithful wife type. This is true in spite of the fact that females as a whole have had more extramarital affairs than males as a whole. True, half of the dominant females are wives of dominant males, but another half are not. The usual extramarital dyad is a dominant male with a younger nondominant female, but there are cases of extramarital affairs of nondominant females, who are in the age cohort of the dominant females.

A very tentative summary of all these characteristic traits is to be formulated as follows:

1) Female hierarchies in the kibbutz originate in the polar sexual division of labor, which creates all-female work branches.

2) The female hierarchies are problematic structures that have problems of discipline, reluctance to accept authority, and rather strained relations among the workers. Exceptions to this generalization are extraordinary emergency situations.

3) Authority is concentrated in a few dominant females of a special personality type who are near or past menopause and who are not and have not been very active sexually (as measured by extramarital relations).

4) There is no indication of an overall female hierarchy in the kibbutz. Dominant females are usually respected by both males and females, but their authority and influence is rather specific, more so than in several cases of dominant males.

Much more research has to be done, both at the microcosmic level as well as at the macrocosmic, in order to substantiate these tentative conclusions. Participant observation has to be checked against sociologically measured variables—attitudes toward authority, motivations to accept it, diffuseness of authority vs. its specificity—in order to assure reliability of the findings reported here. Last, but not least, efforts have to be made to find suitable all-male or mixed sex control groups in order to validate the conclusions.

NOTES

[1] Etzioni (1969:v-xviii) emphasizes the same lack of validation in studies of semiprofessional organizations that are usually all-female or predominantly female.

[2] The *ekonomith* has a special assistant, a female who helps her make sandwiches for outside workers and works in the preparation room. Also under the command of the *ekonomith* is the "male of the kitchen."

[3] This is expressed by both males and females in the kibbutz and sometimes by females within the kitchen. Examples of other kibbutzim in which there is a male *ekonom* are frequently quoted in Committees of Nomination, which prepare annual elections, and during the elections themselves.

[4] If a female has to abandon her permanent work around the menopause, the possibilities for new work are very limited. There may be many causes, which will not be described here in detail, for a female to change her work around the time of the menopause. However, what may be relevant here is the fact that the problem of reintegration into work is more severe with females than with males.

[5] The Economic Committee is the main institutional backing of all the branches of production, whereas branches of service do not have a special committee to back them (except in childcare). In some kibbutzim, service committees or committees on consumption have been established in order to diminish this important difference between branches of production and branches of service.

[6] The discrepancy between this number and the one in Table 1 is due to the fact that here we included nonmembers.

[7] Members' parents have a special status in the kibbutz: they have all the rights except political ones (voting in the general assembly

and eligibility for offices and committees), but no duties. They may work if they want, but do not have to. They may keep income coming to them from external sources, without thereby curtailing their right to full economic and social maintenance.

[8] The branch managers of the kitchen and of the two storerooms are elective offices, unlike the managers of the branches of production, who are appointed by the Economic Committee. This is explained by the distributive functions of the former, which in the eyes of the kibbutz system, needs a wide social support.

[9] Food production is a daily business. Meals have to be served at exact times under any condition. The service rendered by the store-rooms is on a weekly basis with the possible exception of babies' clothing.

[10] This might be so, but most of the males do not have comparable conditions and circumstances to do much gossiping.

REFERENCES CITED

BOTT, ELIZABETH
  1957—*Family and Social Network*. London:Tavistock.
ETZIONI, A.
  1957—Solidaric Work-Groups in Collective Settlements. *Human Organization* 16.
ETZIONI, A., ed.
  1969—*The Semi-Professions and Their Organization: Teachers, Nurses, Social Workers*. New York:The Free Press.
KOMAROVSKY, MIRRA
  1962—*Blue-Collar Marriage*. New York:Random House.
MARRETT, CORA BAGLEY
  1972—Centralization in Female Organizations: Reassessing the Evidence. *Social Problems* 19(3).
SHEPHER, JOSEPH
  1969a-The Child and the Parent-Child Relationship in Kibbutz Communities in Israel. In *Assignment Children* 10. Paris: UNESCO.
  1969b-Familism and Social Structure: The Case of the Kibbutz. *Journal of Marriage and the Family* 31:567-573.
SIMPSON, R. and I.H. SIMPSON
  1969—Women and Bureaucracy in the Semi-Professions. In *The Semi-Professions and Their Organization: Teachers, Nurses, Social Workers*, A. Etzioni, ed. New York:The Free Press.
YOUNG, MICHAEL and PETER WILLMOTT
  1957—*Family and Kinship in East London*. London:Routledge and Kegan Paul.

For Product Safety Concerns and Information please contact our EU
representative GPSR@taylorandfrancis.com
Taylor & Francis Verlag GmbH, Kaufingerstraße 24, 80331 München, Germany